The Transdisciplinary
Play-Based Curriculum
from Toni Linder

TPBA | *Play-Based* | TPBI
TPBC ™

Storybook Activities
for Young Children

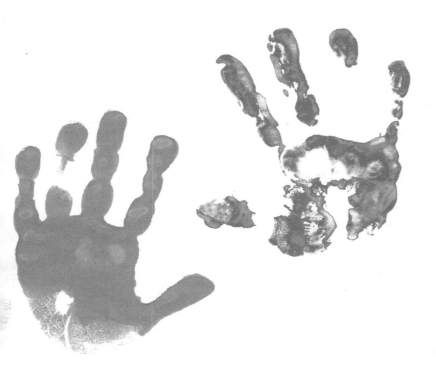

Toni W. Linder, Ed.D.

Read, Play, and Learn!®

·P·A·U·L·H·
BROOKES
PUBLISHING CO® Baltimore • London • Sydney

Paul H. Brookes Publishing Co.
Post Office Box 10624
Baltimore, Maryland 21285-0624

www.brookespublishing.com

Typeset by A.W. Bennett, Inc., Hartland, Vermont.
Manufactured in the United States of America by
Versa Press, East Peoria, Illinois.

Second printing, June 2005.

This curriculum contains activities and suggestions that should be used in the classroom or other environments only when children are receiving proper supervision. It is the teacher's or the caregiver's responsibility to provide a safe, secure environment for all children and to know each child's individual circumstances (e.g., allergies to food or other substances, medical needs). The authors and publisher disclaim any liability arising directly or indirectly from the use of this book.

Every effort has been made to ascertain proper ownership of copyrighted materials and obtain permission for their use. Any omission is unintentional and will be corrected in future printings upon proper notification.

Library of Congress Cataloging-in-Publication Data

Linder, Toni W., 1946–
    Teacher's guide for Read, play, and learn! : storybook activities
for young children / Toni W. Linder.
        p.   cm.
    Includes bibliographical references and index.
    ISBN-13:978-1-55766-400-6
    ISBN-10:1-55766-400-5
    1. Reading (Preschool)—Curricula.   2. Reading (Kindergarten)—Curricula.   3. Transdisciplinary Play-Based Assessment.   4. Transdisciplinary Play-Based Intervention.   I. Linder, Toni W., 1946–   Read, play, and learn!   II. Title.
LB1140.5.R4L56   1999
372.41'2—dc21
                                                                                    99-31608
                                                                                    CIP

British Library Cataloguing in Publication data are available from the British Library.

CONTENTS

The Author v

Foreword: Teacher to Teacher: A Personal View of *Read, Play, and Learn!*®
    Regina "Patsy" Boughan vii

Acknowledgments xiii

An Overview of the Research Base for *Read, Play, and Learn!*® xv

Making Learning Fun: A Glimpse at the *Read, Play, and Learn!*® Curriculum 1

Chapter 1:   What Is *Read, Play, and Learn!*®? 5

Chapter 2:   Read + Play = Learn 17

Chapter 3:   Getting Your Classroom Ready 29

Chapter 4:   Levels of Learning and Domains of Development 49

Chapter 5:   When a Child in Your Classroom Has a Hearing Loss . . .
    Ann D. Bruce 75

Chapter 6:   When a Child in Your Classroom Has a Visual Impairment . . .
    Tanni L. Anthony 97

Chapter 7:   The Emergence of Literacy
    Malinda Etzler Jones and Karen Crabtree 117

Chapter 8:   Encouraging Family Involvement with *Read, Play, and Learn!*®
    Susan M. Moore and Toni W. Linder 161

Appendix 205

Index 227

THE AUTHOR

Toni W. Linder, Ed.D., consults and presents on the role of play in assessment, intervention, and curriculum throughout the United States of America and abroad. Dr. Linder is Professor and Graduate Coordinator for the College of Education at the University of Denver, Colorado. She also directs the Child and Family Studies master's and doctoral programs at the university and works with infant and preschool programs in Denver. Other products by Toni W. Linder, all available from Brookes Publishing, include *Transdisciplinary Play-Based Assessment: A Functional Approach to Working with Young Children, Revised Edition; Transdisciplinary Play-Based Intervention: Guidelines for Developing Meaningful Curricula for Young Children; And You Thought They Were Just Playing: Transdisciplinary Play-Based Assessment* (videotape); and *Observing Kassandra: A Transdisciplinary Play-Based Assessment of a Child with Severe Disabilities* (videotape).

Contributors to the *Teacher's Guide*

Tanni L. Anthony, Ed.S.
Senior Consultant on Visual Disabilities
Project Director of the Colorado Services to
   Children with Deafblindness Project
Colorado Department of Education
Denver, Colorado

Regina "Patsy" Boughan, M.Ed.
Early Intervention Specialist
Science Applications International Corporation
Early Intervention Division
Ansbach, Germany

**Ann D. Bruce, BS.Ed., M.E., Ph.D.
   candidate**
Child Development Specialist
Boulder, Colorado

Karen Crabtree, Ed.D.
Professor of Literacy Education
Coordinator of Reading Program
Director of Center for Excellence in Literacy
   Education
University of Northern Colorado
Greeley, Colorado

Malinda Etzler Jones, Ed.D.
Literacy Consultant
Denver, Colorado

Susan M. Moore, J.D., M.A.-CCC
Professor
Director, Child Learning Center
University of Colorado at Boulder
Boulder, Colorado

Contributors to the Modules

Myriam L. Baker, M.A.
Senior Research and Policy Analyst
Colorado Foundation for Families and
   Children
Denver, Colorado

Teri Berkgren, M.S., CCC-SLP
Speech-Language Pathologist/Augmentative
   Communication Consultant
Northwest Kansas Educational Service Center
Oakley, Kansas

Melissa Carrico, M.S.W.
Therapeutic Case Manager
Kaw Valley Center
Olathe, Kansas

Brenda Chilstrom, OTR-L
Occupational Therapist
James Valley Educational Cooperative
Mitchell, South Dakota

Michele E. Coates, M.A.
Early Intervention Coordinator
Denver Early Childhood Connections
Denver, Colorado

Wanda Figueroa-Rosario, M.S., OTR
Department Chair
Occupational Therapy Assistant Program
Arapahoe Community College
Littleton, Colorado

Michelle Gauthreaux, Ph.D. candidate
Postdoctoral Fellow
Neuropsychiatric Institute at University of
   California, Los Angeles
Los Angeles, California

Katie Greer, M.S.
Speech-Language Pathologist
Arvada, Colorado

Karen T. Harmon, OTR
Occupational Therapist
Sewall Child Development Center
Denver, Colorado

Richard E. Hire, M.S.W., LCSW
School Social Worker
Boulder Valley School District
Boulder, Colorado

Shelby A. Hubert, M.S., CCC-SLP/L
Speech-Language Pathologist
Northwest Kansas Educational Service Center
Oakley, Kansas

LouAnn Humphrey, M.Ed.
Child Development Specialist
Co-Project Director of ENRICH
University of Colorado Health Sciences Center
Denver, Colorado

Amy E. Johannesen, M.A.
Outpatient Therapist
South Central Alabama Mental Health
Andalusia, Alabama

Karin Rasmussen, M.S.
Assistive Technology Consultant
Northwest Kansas Educational Service Center
Oakley, Kansas

Karen Riley, Ph.D.
Child Development Specialist
Postdoctoral Fellow
Child Development Unit
The Children's Hospital
Denver, Colorado

Erica Stetson, Ed.M., Ph.D.
Adjunct Faculty Member, University of Denver
School Psychologist
Jefferson County Public Schools
Edgewater, Colorado

Susan R. Taylor, M.A.
Teacher
Denver Public Schools
Denver, Colorado

Randa Vollertsen, M.A., P.T.
Pediatric Physical Therapist
Northwest Kansas Educational Service Center
Oakley, Kansas

Mindy Wolfe, B.S.
Early Childhood Special Education Teacher
Smith Center Elementary
Smith Center, Kansas

Cynthia B. Woodman, M.S.W.
Family Advocate
Sheridan Public Schools
Englewood, Colorado

FOREWORD

Teacher to Teacher:
A Personal View of Read, Play, and Learn!®

Regina "Patsy" Boughan

IN THE BEGINNING

I was trained in England in the early 1970s, and one of my first assignments at college was to choose a well-known story and, using what I knew of Piagetian theory, develop math, reading, writing, and art activities based on the story. I remember selecting *The Enormous Turnip* (Parkinson, 1987) and having a wonderful time working with the story. The goal was to develop activities that motivated children to explore and experience in a genuine way the ideas, concepts, and themes found in the book. I had enough activities for a month!

A THEORETICAL SHIFT

As I moved from English Infant School to special education, I found the focus of classes I was taking shifting. At this point, I was trained in working on the child's areas of weakness, drill-and-skill development, and task analysis. I recall looking at tasks and breaking down the steps necessary to execute them correctly and then developing plans for students to practice these skills over and over. Gone was the broader idea of the child's learning through experiences. Although I provided many opportunities for students to work on their goals and objectives, the environments tended to be sterile and clinical. For example, I worked with children on dressing skills and had some poor little guy taking off and putting on his shoes over and over again so that I could see if he could do it four out of five times. When he could do this, I could then say that he had mastered this goal based on the criteria written in his individualized education program (IEP). The situation was manipulative and artificial. Children waited to be told what to do; there was very little room for individual preference and choice, which we now know is important in early childhood programs. Generalization to other environments was often minimal. Although I know our work benefited children, I always believed that we were too narrow in our outlook.

Likewise, my approach to assessment was quite traditional. Prior to being introduced to *Transdisciplinary Play-Based Assessment* (TPBA), I used traditional standardized and criterion-referenced tests whereby children were presented with items until they failed several items in a row. This often occurred after they had reached their peak frustration level. Both the child and his or her parents often appeared anxious and tense at the time of testing. Most of the time, I felt that I had only a small part of the total picture regarding who this child was, how he or she functioned, and the level of his or her abilities. Other therapists did separate testing, and when we met at the child's IEP meeting, we each presented our little piece. Parents would sometimes add what they actually saw at home, but for the most part, the meetings were professionally oriented and were intimidating to parents, even when committees tried to be "parent friendly." IEP goals and objectives were driven by test results, specifically by items missed on the particular instruments.

The curriculum, consequently, attempted to address these narrow, item-based goals. Although attempts were made to make activities fun and motivating, the planned activities were fragmented and tended to be domain specific. For instance, if the child missed an item on a test regarding knowing the primary colors, the objective would become, "Given a set of colored blocks, Mary will be able to label correctly 'red,' 'blue,' and 'yellow' 9 out of 10 times." The teacher would then plan activities in language time to allow Mary to practice naming these colors (usually with colored blocks). Typically, as the classroom teacher, I was responsible for developing and implementing lesson plans. I planned activities based on goals and objectives in IEPs, and the children were expected to participate. Opportunities for the children to make choices were few.

THE TRANSITION

When I moved to Denver, I became involved in the TPBA and *Transdisciplinary Play-Based Intervention* (TPBI) approaches. Once again I was using developmental approaches in a storybook framework. Now, in a transdisciplinary play-based program, I feel that I am on firm ground developmentally. I can provide age-appropriate and individualized activities and experiences for young children.

I became enthusiastic about this approach with the very first book that I used in my classroom in Denver. I saw children actively engaged in and even modifying activities on their own. I saw excitement among the children and opportunities to engage in a wide variety of levels of play within a single classroom. Children no longer took off their shoes only to be asked to put them on again. They took them off to go into the Japanese Teahouse because the sign outside said "Take shoes off" and because everyone else, including the teacher, had done so. Children with goals to improve gross motor skills did not have to leave the room for therapy. Depending on the story being read at the time, they could crawl along the tunnel that led to Mr. Groundhog's house, they could climb the ladder to pick apples, or they could pull a wagon full of pumpkins. While addressing the therapeutic goals, they were still fully engaged in the community of the classroom.

WORKING WITH A TEAM

One of the major differences in moving to a play-based assessment and intervention program has been working with a transdisciplinary team. The shift to working in tandem with parents and other therapists enabled me to expand my knowledge (both general and specific) to meet the diverse needs of all of the children in the program. I could draw on the expertise of others to develop truly meaningful interventions for children with disabilities, and education and therapy could be provided in a rich, emergent literacy, play-based program.

Prior to teaching in a classroom that uses the **Read, Play, and Learn!**® transdisciplinary play-based curriculum (TPBC), I planned alone, sometimes getting ideas from therapists on what I could do with particular children but rarely obtaining ideas for the whole class. I actually had no idea how wonderful it could be to share this task. I always believed I was creative, and I managed to come up with motivating activities and interesting ideas for various centers.

In the TPBC, the team plans together, divides up tasks, and shares responsibility for classroom preparation and program implementation. We ask parents for help in choosing books and collecting props. We brainstorm ideas and talk about how best to implement IEP goals within the newly created environments that emerge when a new book is begun. We work together to modify and adapt activities and materials so that every child can participate.

Once I began to plan with other team members in this way, I realized how much richer a program is when more than one imagination is at work. I have also been told by my team members that my input as a teacher has had a positive effect on them as therapists, enabling them to discover many new ways of incorporating therapeutic goals into naturalistic environments.

OUTCOMES FOR CHILDREN

As I watched the children in the class engage in storybook curriculum activities, I found that children seemed to play with materials in more meaningful ways. Block building became more than building a tower to knock it down. Castles and airports emerged. Children of diverse ability levels played and created together in an integrated environment. Children didn't have to leave the room for motor or speech therapy. Therapists worked with individual children in the centers chosen by the children themselves. Strategies to increase or decrease tone, increase stability, provide sensory input, encourage the use of certain sounds, model language structures, expand vocabulary, or use augmentative modes of communication were incorporated into consequential, naturalistic play situations. Because children selected where they wanted to play, there were fewer power struggles and less time spent on trying to get children to comply with requests to participate. Behavior problems were reduced.

RESPONSE OF PARENTS

Parents seemed to sense the difference in the program during the assessment process. Here, for the first time, parents heard professionals emphasizing their children's strengths and talking about all of the things their children *could* do that would serve as a basis for learning new skills. John was referred to our team in the summer. John's mother, Karen, had said that she wasn't sure that she wanted to go through with the assessment process. When she realized that she would be present throughout and would actually be part of the assessment team, however, she consented. John and his mother both thoroughly enjoyed the play-based assessment. In fact, John didn't want the session to end! After the play session, when the team had discussed all of the wonderful things that John could do, we began to write down the goals that Karen generated. At this point Karen was close to tears. She expressed that this assessment had been her first positive assessment experience with John and that for the first time she felt hopeful that John could succeed in school. This example is not unusual. We receive such feedback from parents all of the time, from the TPBA through the TPBC. Perhaps this is because goals and objectives more closely reflect the priorities of parents, and the parents delight in seeing their child do what most typical children do in a fun, learning environment.

OUTCOMES FOR ME

Faced with the responsibility of implementing programs that will address the needs of a wide variety of children, I have been able to embrace fully the play-based storybook curriculum approach. Within the parameters of the curriculum, I can provide a philosophically sound, developmentally appropriate program that addresses individual needs. I can use the interests and skills that children bring to the program to move children to higher levels of cognitive, social, motor, language, and literacy development. Using books and play as a foundation for early childhood programs makes both philosophical and practical sense to me. We all want children to grow up loving books, understanding books, and using books to expand their learning. Children in early childhood programs need to be actively exploring and experiencing their world. I can think of no better way to ensure that this occurs than by incorporating the wonderful, magical ideas and themes of storybooks into situations in which children can play interactively with meaningful props and engage in activities and games that reinforce the development of concepts, skills, and relationships.

ADAPTING TO A CONSULTATION MODEL

Since I began to use a storybook curriculum, I have had two quite different teams and environments. The first model was an outreach program of Sewall Child Development Center, housed in an elementary school. The team consisted of a speech-language pathologist, an occupational therapist, a paraprofessional, and myself, an early childhood special educator. In this environment, we truly functioned as a transdisciplinary team, planning together, working together, and taking responsibility for the success of the program as a team. We brought our individual backgrounds, perspectives, and expertise to the planning sessions and worked as a team in the classroom.

More recently, I worked in a school district early childhood environment. The team consisted of two group leaders, a paraprofessional, and myself. Therapists were spread across the district, and their time with our program was limited. An occupational therapist, a physical therapist, and a speech-language pathologist provided some direct but mostly consultative services. They had very limited time to plan with me and very little direct service time in the classroom. In a very different way, they provided ideas and support and made the lessons a team effort. Sometimes I would get telephone calls or notes about an idea for an activity that might go well with a certain book. I also received written ideas pertaining to working with individual children. All of the team members felt a buy-in to the philosophy and brought in props or games from other sites or from home. We provided opportunities for all members of the team to help select the books we used and made sure that everyone had a complete list of books for the year so that they could think about the stories and plan ahead. These efforts helped keep everyone motivated and excited about sharing ideas.

Prior to implementing the storybook curriculum in my new environment, the paraprofessionals in the program helped and supported the children with special needs in the classrooms complete the tasks for the day. They followed the plans I had developed, but there was little opportunity for them to contribute their own ideas. Therapy sessions were often unrelated to what was going on in the classroom. As we shifted to the storybook curriculum, I saw the paraprofessionals become more involved in planning and, therefore, implementing the creative ideas we generated. The therapists became more interested in working in the classroom; the resulting benefit was that other staff could observe the therapists, question them about their strategies, and begin to replicate and generalize the therapeutic strategies throughout the day.

The outcomes from this model are similar to those seen in the environment where one therapist worked with the children in the classroom on a daily basis. Although I still prefer the more integrated team, I have seen dramatic changes in the levels of play in the classrooms that use the *Read, Play, and Learn!* curriculum. Children are more intensely involved in their play, and their play has become more creative. Blocks can be castles; cardboard boxes can be trucks, trains, and boats. The House Area can be transformed into a train station one day and into a restaurant run by a knight and a dragon on another day. Children are motivated to expand their motor skills, not just because a therapist wants them to but because an enticing ladder leads up an apple tree, and if they climb up, they can pick apples to make an apple pie. Language and communication are amplified because children have something important they *want* to make known. Children love to demonstrate their memory for characters, actions, and vocabulary in the story. They look forward to the new stories and are proud of the burgeoning storybook environment that develops over the course of 2 weeks.

One aspect of *Read, Play, and Learn!* that we learned through a parent survey needs special attention is parent involvement. Informing parents about the philosophy of the storybook curriculum and providing them with specific information about how the curriculum will address emerging literacy and preacademic skills are critical. It is difficult for the casual observer to understand all of the developmental skills that are integrated into the play environment. Parents want their children to succeed in school, and they expect preschool and kindergarten to provide the foundation for that success. They need to have information about the content of the curriculum, the developmental sequences needed to promote academic learning, and the strategies that are used in the classroom to strengthen acquisition of preacademic skills as well as other developmentally appropriate outcomes. When parents understand this rationale and the tactics being used by the educational and therapeutic team, they become strong advocates for the approach. When taught about developmental sequences and natural means for building literacy, parents can become not only advocates but also collaborators in the learning process. Our study revealed, however, that the team needs to make a structured, concerted effort to involve parents actively in the curriculum approach or they may misconstrue the purpose of the play environment.

In my experience, when children with special needs are integrated with typical children, parents need to be reassured that *all* of the children will be getting their educational needs met. Parents of children with disabilities commonly recognize the positive aspects of having typically developing peers with their children. Similarly, parents of typically developing children usually understand the unique opportunities for learning that arise when their children are integrated with children with disabilities. Both, however, want to be sure that an inclusive environment does not detract from developmental goals or decrease academic learning opportunities. For this reason, educators and therapists need to make concerted efforts to ensure that all people who teach the children—professionals, paraprofessionals, and parents—are well informed about the most effective ways of enhancing learning and development. The parent component (Chapter 8) included in this curriculum is an attempt to address this issue.

SUMMARY

Many models and curricula can be successfully implemented in inclusive classrooms. A storybook curriculum is just one. ***Read, Play, and Learn!*** provides a sound framework for developing a program that meets the needs of all children. Storybooks provide a wide variety of themes that are of interest to young children. The concepts and themes in storybooks often serve as a springboard to more complex play and peer interactions. Children can delve into the concepts presented in the books in as much depth as desired, guided by their level of interest and motivation.

The key for me has been that with one lesson plan, developed with transdisciplinary input, I can easily meet the needs of all of the children in my classes. I can stretch every student (from those with disabilities to those who are above average in ability), help each to develop a love of literature, and support all in their progress along the road to academic success.

And on top of all that, *I* have fun too! What more can a teacher ask for?

• • •

Author's note: Patsy Boughan is one of many gifted teachers and team members who has assisted in the development, implementation, and evaluation of ***Read, Play, and Learn!*** She brings a wealth of knowledge and experiences as well as enthusiasm and dedication to her work.

ACKNOWLEDGMENTS

As is often the case with a major endeavor such as this curriculum, many people are responsible for the final result. The origins of *Read, Play, and Learn!*® can be traced back to many curricula for young children that rely on play or literature as a basis for learning. My personal interest in a curriculum based on storybooks began in 1977 when, as a teacher in a summer preschool for gifted children, I used Greek mythology books as a foundation for the curriculum. This approach was so successful that I began to expand this approach into classes for children with disabilities. Two people who were influential in the evolution of this process were Sue McCord, then director of a preschool for children with language impairments at the University of Denver, and Mary Calkin, then the director of Mapletree Preschool, a program that addressed the needs of children with emotional and other developmental delays. In the 1980s, both were developing a storybook approach to curriculum. They shared with my classes their experiences and expertise on preschool intervention and further supported the idea that storybooks could serve as an important tool in the development of children with special needs. I share my gratitude for their inspiration and example. I also recommend Sue McCord's book *The Storybook Journey: Pathways to Literacy Through Story and Play* (Prentice-Hall, 1995) as an excellent resource for developing additional modules.

When I began my work with Sewall Child Development Center in the 1980s, we not only used *Transdisciplinary Play-Based Assessment* (TPBA) and *Transdisciplinary Play-Based Intervention* (TPBI), we began to develop the curriculum that resulted in *Read, Play, and Learn!* Executive Director Cheryl Caldwell and Program Director Heidi Heissenbuttal supported and helped make possible the development of these projects. A special thanks to Heidi, who responded to each and every request! In a reverse mainstreaming classroom, where the majority of children had disabilities, the team field-tested numerous modules. Over the course of writing this curriculum, the people on this team changed, but the input of a teacher, occupational therapist, and speech therapist remained constant. The following professionals all played a role: teachers Mary Dodd, Patsy Boughan, Susan Taylor, Joyce King-Martin, Meg Albers, and Sue Okerson; teaching assistants Bevin Rolf, Kelly Walsh, Molly Hammerberg, Wendy Miller, and Mary Gonzales (especially Mary!); speech therapists Yoruba Bryant, Caroline Sweitzer, Katie Greer, and Amy Jones; and occupational therapists Mary Sue Johnson and Karen Harmon. I owe all of them an enormous debt of gratitude!

Over the years, as I observed teachers and students in action, it became clear to me that one problem with many traditional curricula was that no advice was given as to how to individualize for children at different developmental levels or with various disabilities. Realizing that many early childhood educators do not have a background in special education, I believed that it was important to add this component. An attempt to simplify the individualization process beyond that in

TPBI led to the addition of the three developmental levels: sensorimotor, functional, and symbolic.

Concurrently, my "dream team" came together. This team, consisting of Patsy Boughan (a fabulous teacher, who contributed the Foreword as well as a module), Katie Greer (speech-language pathologist extraordinaire), and Karen Harmon (a wonderful occupational therapist, who has labored with me the longest of any of the team members), met with me on a regular basis to review each module and give input on what did and didn't work. Their feedback and support were critical. I am indebted to them for their energy, ideas, persistence, and dedication!

The development of the curriculum also involved the efforts of many graduate students and colleagues from around the country. Teams from Kansas (their module is included in this curriculum), Oklahoma, Texas, and Colorado (several modules are included in this curriculum) have written and implemented modules using the **Read, Play, and Learn!** format. Dena Pinson has extended the training and research to Oklahoma. My students in the transdisciplinary play-based intervention course have also contributed modules to be field-tested (and several are in the curriculum). I especially thank Michele Coates, Karen Riley, and LouAnn Humphrey for their support and work. In addition to working on modules, they researched resources and edited sections. A special thanks to my colleagues, Susan Moore, Ann Bruce, Tanni Anthony, Karen Crabtree, and Malinda Jones for their hard work on their chapters for the *Teacher's Guide*. Kathy Keairns (the assistant to the dean) and Sikha Sibbanda, both in the College of Education, were invaluable in typing material and meeting deadlines. Thank you both for saving me!

I am grateful to all of the children and families who have participated in our classes that used the curriculum and, I hope, benefited from the activities. You are the reason we are here. And this is for you.

On a personal level, Buzz Yancey helped me to sustain these efforts in every way possible, from making sure I didn't forget to eat, to researching on-line, to editing chapters. I cannot thank him enough for his support! My friends Sue and Alan Cohen graciously lent me their magnificent mountain house for weekends so that I could be inspired by the beauty of the Rockies and write (when I wasn't in the hot tub). Can I still borrow the house now that the curriculum is done? To my friend Malinda, who contributed to the literacy chapter, what can I say? Everyone needs a friend like you! And thank you, Fred, who began this journey with me and continued to assist me with emotional support and care of Adam until the last punctuation mark was written.

I also thank all of the wonderful people at Paul H. Brookes Publishing Co. who have worked with me over the last 18 (can it be?) years. Paul Brookes (with this one I know you'll need a new bookshelf), Melissa Behm (who not only reads and edits my work but also listens to the saga of my life), Sheila FitzGerald (who toiled on TPBA), Kathy Boyd (who labored on the videotapes and TPBI), Joanne Galantino (who amazingly recognizes my voice when I call), Erika Page (who troubleshoots my problems), particularly Mary Olofsson (who has been mired in editing this work for what seems like forever), and all of the other supportive staff of this fine publishing company. Thank you! Thank you! And, finally, to my son, Adam, I once again give thanks for his creativity, imagination, and love of play, drama, and costumes. He is a continual inspiration to me. I love you so much, Adam. Your spirit is reflected in every page, and in that way I share you with many other children.

AN OVERVIEW OF THE RESEARCH BASE FOR *READ, PLAY, AND LEARN!*®

Several studies are underway to look at the outcomes of *Read, Play, and Learn!*

RESEARCH ON *READ, PLAY, AND LEARN!*®

In one on-going study, Coleman, Linder, and Linas (2005) and Coleman, Linder, Linas, and Meyer (2005) have found significantly higher developmental skills as measured by standard scores on the Mullen Scales of Early Learning for 50 preschool children who have been immersed in *Read, Play, and Learn!* for 1 year compared to children entered in the program for 3 months or less. Analysis using a linear regression indicated that immersion in *Read, Play, and Learn!* predicted both significantly higher overall developmental scores and receptive language sub-scales scores ($p = .01$).

Another study, done with developmentally younger children from Early Head Start (Child Development Resources, 2005), used *1-2-3 Read!*, an adapted version of *Read, Play, and Learn!* for younger children. This study looked at developmental growth in 24 children from low income and diverse backgrounds whose mean pre-test developmental quotient (DQ) on the Early Learning Accomplishment Profile prior to using the curriculum was 83. At post assessment, the mean DQ was 102. All children, including the 6 with identified disabilities, showed substantial developmental gains. Overall, children showed a 12-month gain in 9 months. This study demonstrates the effect of the *Read, Play, and Learn!* model on children who are developmentally younger, from high risk environments, and culturally diverse backgrounds. In addition, 100% of families reported, post-test, reading daily to their children. This is in sharp contrast to a study (Halfon, McLearn, & Schuster, 2002) showing less than half of parents from diverse socioeconomic backgrounds reading daily to their children under age 3.

Similar results were found with middle income families whose children used the *Read, Play, and Learn!* model. A survey of 87 families of children using *Read, Play, and Learn!* in five preschool classrooms found that as a result of using the curriculum, families read to their children more frequently, used the vocabulary being taught in the classroom, and followed through with activities done at school more frequently than they had before having their children enrolled in the program with the *Read, Play, and Learn!* curriculum (Coleman & Stokka, 2003, unpublished paper).

In a qualitative study conducted with teachers who had children with disabilities in their classes where they were using *Read, Play, and Learn!*, Coleman (submitted for publication, 2005) found that teachers were able to adapt the curriculum to meet the needs of a wide range of children. Children remained engaged and participated in the curriculum using creative modifications. The curriculum was found to assist teachers in making environmental, lesson planning, and other daily adaptations.

Read, Play, and Learn! integrates the findings from literature on development, learning, play, and literacy. With the passage of the No Child Left Behind (NCLB) Act of 2001, schools are under increasing pressure to find and use evidence-based curricula to align with the scientifically based research criteria outlined in NCLB. Unfortunately, in the aftermath of NCLB, the value of play as a foundation for learning has been diminished (Zigler, May 27, 2002, childcareexchange.com). If play is to continue to serve an important role in the education of young children, empirical research is needed to document potential developmental and academic outcomes, in addition to other developmental benefits, of play. The above studies and a growing body of research, as described in part below, are finding that a play and literature-based curriculum can have significant impact on children, families, and teachers.

COMPONENTS OF LITERACY

The *Read, Play, and Learn!* curriculum is founded on important research findings about how children learn early literacy skills. With the active support of adults, these skills should develop in an integrated manner (Ollila & Mayfield, 1992). Components of literacy (Depree & Iversen, 1994) include: 1) oral language, with the subcomponents of listening (accessing information from speech) and speaking (expressing information orally); 2) written language, with the subcomponents of reading (accessing information from print) and writing (expressing information in print); and 3) visual language, with the subcomponents of viewing (accessing information from sources other than print, e.g., pictures, maps) and presenting (expressing information in visual form other than print, e.g., art, charts).

A brief description of research support for these aspects within *Read, Play, and Learn!* follows.

RESEARCH ON ORAL LANGUAGE: Listening and Speaking

In order to have facility with oral language, children need to be exposed to an environment rich in language and interact with adults using language in a social context (Bruner, 1975; Cazden, 1992; Chomsky, 1965; Halliday, 1975; McNeill, 1970; Menyuk, 1977; Morrow, 1991). *Read, Play, and Learn!* explores new literature themes every 2 weeks, ensuring that language is constantly changing. Adults help children use new language concepts throughout the day. Language concepts are learned in meaningful contexts and generalized. Children demonstrate dramatic gains in vocabulary and language usage (Linder, in progress).

Research demonstrates that storytelling strongly attracts children to books (Morrow & Weinstein, 1986) and that children who frequently listen to stories develop more sophisticated language structures and a larger vocabulary (Lenz, 1992). Listening to stories establishes favorite storybooks and encourages children to want to read and actively pursue the necessary skills to read by themselves (Sulzby, 1985). Research shows that listening to stories 1) enhances comprehension and knowledge about books and print (Mason, 1980), 2) develops a sense of story structure (Morrow, 1985), 3) develops positive attitudes toward reading and writing, and 4) helps children develop their own stories (Morrow, 1985).

With *Read, Play, and Learn!*, children are read to at the beginning of each day and numerous times throughout the day. Repetition gives the child mastery over story sequence and vocabulary. The stories soon become favorites. As the stories are sought out by children for rereading throughout the year (Linder, in progress), children learn the conventions of reading and print.

When telling stories, children tend to mimic the intonation of adults reading stories. This "book language" takes children beyond talking into understanding the language of reading (Cazden, 1992; Snow, 1991). Children's ability to question also develops, with questions relating to the pictures and meanings of the story. With additional maturation and practice, the questions children ask relate to the letters, words, and sounds of letters in print on the storybook page (Morrow, 1985; Roser & Martinez, 1985). Parents report dramatic gains in vocabulary and discussion about books when a storybook curriculum is used (Linder, in progress). In addition, with increasing exposure to the books and interaction with the teacher, either individually or in small or large groups, the children develop an increasing repertoire of literacy-related questions, vocabulary, and concepts related to a broad range of topics.

RESEARCH ON WRITTEN LANGUAGE: Reading and Writing

When children use functional forms of literacy in their play, they begin to understand the forms' purposes. Children use a variety of functional literacy forms throughout all of the centers in the *Read, Play, and Learn!* classroom. Each child is encouraged to work at his or her own level of learning, with teachers facilitating the child's acquisition of the next stage of learning. McCormick and Mason (1981) established three developmental levels of word recognition in learning to read: 1) identifying words through context, 2) using sound–letter cues, and 3) sounding out words. Parents and teachers report gains in children's book knowledge and understanding of basic reading skills, such as letter recognition, phonological awareness, and basic sight vocabulary. Children begin to understand the meaning of print by using syntactic cues, semantic cues, and graphophonic rules (Morrow, 1991).

As a first step in reading and writing, children learn that print has functions (Mason, 1980). Children next express interest in the forms of print—including names, sounds, and configurations of letters and words—and then learn the conventions of print—including reading from left to right and the purpose of punctuation and spacing. Sulzby (1985) identified six steps in the development of children's writing behavior: 1) use of drawings for writing, 2) scribble writing, 3) use of letter-like forms, 4) use of well-learned units or letter strings, 5) use of invented spelling, and 6) writing conventionally. All forms of literacy are incorporated into *Read, Play, and Learn!*. For example, children illustrate story concepts, construct charts and maps, follow recipes, create books, make signs for dramatic play, and write notes or messages for peers and parents. Each child's attempts are accepted at his or her developmental level and scaffolded to the next level. Children show an increase in representational abilities in symbolic expression, dramatic play, art, and print.

RESEARCH ON VISUAL LANGUAGE: Viewing and Presenting

Pictures and symbols introduce children to literacy (Schickedanz, 1999). Children need opportunities to gain information through pictures, maps, charts, and symbols. In addition, dramatic representations of story concepts assist in memory development (Rowe, 1998), syntactic skills (Vedelar, 1997), book comprehension (Rowe, 1998), and phonological awareness (Sonnenschein, Baker, Serpell, & Schmidt, 2000) and build connections between oral and written modes of expression (Roskos & Christie, 2001). The *Read, Play, and Learn!* classroom uses a variety of visual representations of emerging literacy and print. Charts of daily routines, recipes and instructions, symbols for print in books, and maps of the classroom are integrated into each module. Children also learn signs and visual symbols associated with each of the stories. Dramatizations of each story are central to the curriculum, with the teacher facilitating by introducing story props and materials; modeling and encouraging functional use of literacy tools; and mediating the social interactions among children as they integrate story, props, and dramatic interactions.

Emerging literacy requires presentation of the following language and literacy components at a developmentally appropriate level for each child: phonological awareness, vocabulary, syntax, semantics, and story sequence. These concepts are introduced through multidimensional means, including pictures, dramatization, songs and fingerplays, gestures, signs, charts, symbols, and other visual methods. Opportunities for children to express their conceptual understanding through a variety of visual means, including gestural, dramatic, and artistic, enable them to connect oral and written modes of expression (Neuman & Roskos, 1990; Rowe, 1998; Schickedanz, 1999).

Presenting visual information is integral to *Read, Play, and Learn!*. A group art mural depicting story elements, sequences, and concepts is developed for each story. In addition, children create individual art projects, drawings with dictations, charts in science projects, and two- and three-dimensional representations related to the stories. Children also render dramatic representation of story characters, concepts, actions, and sequence. Children's ability to represent ideas pictorially increases.

RESEARCH ON LITERACY, PLAY, AND SCAFFOLDING

Research shows that play can support the application of literacy skills. Play provides a meaningful setting, supportive peer interactions, and functional opportunities for using skills (Morrow, 1990; Neuman & Roskos, 1990, 1992, 1997). Play can provide settings that promote literacy activities, skills, and strategies, offer language experiences that build associations between oral and written modes of expression, provide opportunities for teachers to instruct children in functional literacy skills (Neuman & Roskos, 1990), and help incorporate literacy concepts, skills, and processes (Neuman & Roskos, 1992, 1997). When appropriately facilitated by an adult, play and literacy can be integrated to increase book comprehension and memory for stories (Rowe, 1998), assist children in learning to read environmental print (Neuman & Roskos, 1993; Vukelich, 1994), and develop phonological awareness and motivation to read print (Sonnenschein et al., 2000). *Read, Play, and Learn!* integrates play and literacy throughout the day.

Adult involvement in the early childhood environment is critical to children's learning. Adult involvement and intervention infuse literacy ideas, processes, and skills into play (Neuman, 2000; Vukelich, 1994). Scaffolding for emerging literacy skills should incorporate a sequence of developmental strategies, including shared language experiences, shared reading, guided reading, and independent reading. Concurrently, scaffolding of writing needs to incorporate a corresponding sequence of developmental strategies that include language experience, writing for children, shared writing, guided writing, and independent writing (Depree & Iversen, 1994). The **Read, Play, and Learn!** modules incorporate all of these strategies. Specific strategies for literacy are addressed in Chapter 7.

REFERENCES

Bruner, J. (1975). The ontogenesis of speech acts. *Journal of Child Language, 3,* 1–19.

Cazden, C.B. (1992). Revealing and telling: The socialization of attention in learning to read and write. *Educational Psychology: An International Journal of Experimental Educational Psychology, 12,* 305–313.

Child Development Resources. (2005). *1-2-3 read! Emergent literacy in Head Start: Implementation manual.* Norge, VA: Child Development Resources.

Chomsky, C. (1965). *Aspects of a theory of syntax.* Cambridge, MA: MIT Press.

Coleman, J. (submitted for publication, 2005). *Adaptations of a play-based early childhood curriculum for children with special needs.*

Coleman, J., Linder, T., & Linas, K. (2005). *Using play to build language and literacy in inclusive preschool settings.* Presentation at National Head Start Association Annual Training Conference: Research Track, Orlando, FL, May 25, 2005.

Coleman, J., Linder, T., Linas, K., & Meyer, K. (2005). *Effects of Read, Play, and Learn! on development of children from 3–5.* Presentation at College of Education Research Symposium, University of Denver, April, 2005.

Coleman, J., & Stokka, K. (2003). *Parental perceptions of the Read, Play, and Learn! curriculum.* Unpublished paper.

Depree, H., & Iversen, S. (1994). *Early literacy in the classroom.* Bothwell, WA: Landsend Publishing.

Halfon, N., McLearn, K.T., & Schuster, M.A. (2002). *Child rearing in America: Challenges facing parents with young children.* Port Chester, NY: Cambridge University Press.

Halliday, M.A.K. (1975). *Learning how to mean: Exploration in the development of language.* London: Edward Arnold.

Lenz, L. (1992). Crossroads of literacy and orality: Reading poetry aloud. *Language Arts, 69,* 597–603.

Linder, T. (in progress). *Outcomes of using a storybook curriculum to develop emerging literacy skills.* Unpublished manuscript.

Linder, T., Coleman, J., Linas, K., & Meyer, K. (submitted for publication). *Developmental outcomes from a play and literature-based curriculum: Read, Play, and Learn!.*

Mason, J. (1980). When do children begin to read? An exploration of four-year-old children's letter and word reading competencies. *Reading Research Quarterly, 15,* 203–227.

McCormick, C., & Mason, J. (1981). What happens to kindergarten children's knowledge about reading after summer vacation? *Reading Teacher, 35,* 164–172.

McNeill, D. (1970). *The acquisition of language: The study of the developmental psycholinguistics.* New York: Harper & Row.

Menyuk, P. (1977). *Language and maturation.* Cambridge, MA: MIT Press.

Morrow, L.M. (1985). Retelling stories: A strategy for improving children's comprehension, concept of story structure and oral language complexity. *The Elementary School Journal, 85,* 647–661.

Morrow, L.M. (1990). Preparing the classroom environment to promote literacy during play. *Early Childhood Research Quarterly, 5,* 537–554.

Morrow, L.M. (1991). *Literacy development in the early years.* Needham Heights, MA: Allyn & Bacon.

Morrow, L.M., & Weinstein, C.S. (1986). Encouraging vocabulary reading: The impact of a literature program on children's use of library centers. *Reading Research Quarterly, 21,* 330–346.

Neuman, S. (2000). Social contexts for literacy development: A family literacy program. In K. Roskos & J. Christie (Eds.), *Play and literacy in early childhood: Research from multiple perspectives* (pp. 163–168). Mahwah, NJ: Lawrence Erlbaum.

Neuman, S., & Roskos, K. (Eds.). (1990). *The influence of literacy-enriched play settings on preschoolers' engagement with written language.* Chicago: National Reading Conference.

Neuman, S., & Roskos, K. (1991). Peers as literary informants: A description of young children's literacy conversations in play. *Early Childhood Research Quarterly, 6*(2), 233–248.

Neuman, S., & Roskos, K. (1992). Literary objects as cultural tools: Effects on children's literacy behaviors. *Reading Research Quarterly, 27*(3), 202–225.

Neuman, S., & Roskos, K. (1993). Access to print for children of poverty: differential effects for adult mediation and literacy-enriched play settings on environmental and functional print tasks. *American Educational Research Journal, 32,* 10–32.

Neuman, S., & Roskos, K. (1997). Knowledge in practice: Contexts of participation for young writers and readers. *Reading Research Quarterly, 32,* 10–32.

Ollila, L.O., & Mayfield, M. (Ed.). (1992). *Emerging literacy: Preschool, kindergarten, and primary grades.* Needham Heights, MA: Allyn & Bacon.

Roser, N.M., & Martinez, M.G. (1985). Roles adults play in preschool responses to literature. *Language Arts, 62*, 485–490.

Roskos, K., & Christie, J. (2000). *Literacy-enriched play settings: A broad spectrum instructional strategy.* Mahwah, NJ: Lawrence Erlbaum.

Roskos, K., & Christie, J. (2001). Examining the play–literacy interface: A critical review and future directions. *Journal of Early Childhood Literacy, 1*(1), 59–89.

Rowe, D. (1998). The literate potentials of book-related dramatic play. *Reading Research Quarterly, 33*, 10–35.

Schickedanz, J.A. (1999). *Much more than ABC's: The early stages of reading and writing.* Washington, DC: National Association for the Education of Young Children.

Snow, C.E. (1991). The theoretical basis for relationships between language and literacy in development. *Journal of Research in Childhood Education, 6*, 5–10.

Sonnenschein, S., Baker, L., Serpell, R., & Schmidt, D. (2000). Reading is a source of entertainment: The importance of the home perspective for children's literacy development. In K. Roskos & J. Christie (Eds.), *Play and literacy in early childhood: Research from multiple perspectives* (pp. 107–124). Mahwah, NJ: Lawrence Erlbaum.

Sulzby, E. (1985). Children's emergent reading of favorite stories. *Reading Research Quarterly, 20*, 458–481.

Vedelar, L. (1997). Dramatic play: A format for 'literate' language. *British Journal of Educational Psychology, 67*, 153–167.

Vukelich, C. (1994). Effects of play interventions on young children's reading of environmental print. *Early Childhood Research Quarterly, 9*, 153–170.

Zigler, E. (2002). Zigler criticizes narrow view of literacy. www.childcareexchange.com May 27, 2002.

The *Read, Play, and Learn!*® products:

Collection 1 (see page 7 for a listing of storybook modules)
Collection 2 (see pages 7 and 8 for a listing of storybook modules)
Teacher's Guide for Read, Play, and Learn! Storybook Activities for Young Children

Also available in the [TPBA | Play-Based | TPBI | TPBC]™ system:

- *Transdisciplinary Play-Based Assessment: A Functional Approach to Working with Young Children, Revised Edition*
- *Transdisciplinary Play-Based Intervention: Guidelines for Developing Meaningful Curricula for Young Children*
- *And You Thought They Were Just Playing: Transdisciplinary Play-Based Assessment* (videotape)
- *Observing Kassandra: A Transdisciplinary Play-Based Assessment of a Child with Severe Disabilities* (videotape)

See page 236 for ordering information.

Visit www.readplaylearn.com for a free information packet, "Explore a Day of RPL" tour, profiles of real classrooms using RPL, information on standards and research, and correlation to NAEYC Guidelines.

MAKING LEARNING FUN
A Glimpse at the
Read, Play, and Learn!® Curriculum

"Yesterday I got to be the pilot and fly the airplane," 3½-year-old Anna declared as her father pulled the car into the tree-lined parking lot next to the preschool.

"Where did you fly to?" Anna's father asked. "The little boy in the book flew to visit his grandmother."

Anna's father had been reading *First Flight* to her at night, just as her teacher had been reading it to the class at school. Actually, a more accurate rendering was that Anna was "reading" the book to her father. She would point to the pictures and describe in detail what was happening in the book and how they were acting out the same things at school. She embellished the story with her own dialogue as they read. Last night she had explained what the word *turbulence* meant. "It's like bouncing up and down like this," she had said, demonstrating by bouncing on her bottom in bed.

"I flew to China 'cause I wanted to visit the panda bears like the ones on the computer."

Anna's father helped her out of the seat belt and carefully placed her into her wheelchair. As they approached the broad glass doors of the center, they passed the flower and vegetable garden that was planted and maintained by the children.

"China!" he declared. "That's very far away."

"Well, I had my compass in the cockpit so I could find it. Today, I think I'll buy a ticket and be a passenger. I'll show you."

As they entered through the front door, they passed through the lobby where several parents were sitting and chatting and by Malissa, the secretary, at the front desk. Malissa was busy changing the art displayed in the entrance area.

"Hi, Malissa. Are you going to hang my picture?"

"I think one of yours is hanging in the conference room over there. Why don't you peek in and show your daddy?"

Anna pulled her father's hand toward the conference room and, after searching the art on the walls, proudly pointed to her framed picture, a colorful collage of various materials, including green tissue paper, checkered cloth, pieces of furry material, and lines drawn with blue and green markers.

"This is the tree, and this is the mother, and this is the father, and this is the baby, and this is the picnic, and this is the tablecloth, and this is the sky, and this is the grass. And this is Somebody."

"That must be for the story *Somebody and the Three Blairs*. I remember that one from weeks ago. It looks great in here. They must have chosen it because you are quite the artist."

Father and daughter proceeded down the hall, past other children's artwork toward Anna's classroom.

"Hi, Anna." The voice behind them was Anna's teacher, Felicia, who had just emerged from the large storage area and was pushing a cart loaded with plastic containers. "I'm bringing in the airport set today to add to the block area where you all built the airport yesterday."

Felicia was Anna's favorite teacher. She always let Anna sit up close when they read the story at the beginning of the day. Sometimes she would let Anna "read" a page or tell something about what was happening in the story. She also let her choose songs and fingerplays during snack. Of course, the other children got to choose, too, but Felicia always made Anna feel special.

"Why don't you show your daddy the plane you flew yesterday?"

Anna pulled once again on her father's hand, trying to hurry him up. As they entered the room, Anna spotted 5-year-old Mark up on the climber labeled as a "control tower," talking into the walkie-talkie headset to 4-year-old Meagan, who was flying the "plane." Meagan was in front of two rows of chairs, sitting in a chair inside a large box that had all kinds of knobs and dials glued onto the inside. She was holding a compass in one hand and an old computer joystick in the other.

"Tay off!" shouted Mark. Mark usually did not talk very much, or very clearly, but the children could usually figure out what he was saying if they paid close attention.

"Okay. I'm going up high," Meagan shouted.

"That's the cockpit, Daddy. And that's where the passengers sit." She pointed to a row of small chairs lined up behind the cockpit.

Anna's father looked around the large, sunny room that seemed each day to be transformed a little bit more into whatever scenario the group was dramatizing that week. The previous week, when the class started reading *First Flight*, the room contained only a few props related to flying. Now, in the second week, the room had undergone an amazing transformation as the children had created props, artwork, and charts, and taken photos of their activities. One area of the room had a large sign hanging from the ceiling proclaiming the area to be the Denver International Airport. Another area had suitcases lined up ready to be inserted into a large box on a table that was open on both ends and labeled "Security." A slide was perched on the edge of the table ready to take the suitcases that were pushed through the box down to the floor. Next to the security area was a stand that proclaimed it was the place to purchase "tickets." Old airline tickets, a cash register, pencils, and paper for writing receipts were neatly arranged on the table. A large fan and a windsock were arranged in the Science and Math Center. On the table near the center was a computer that flashed on-screen images of airplanes.

Becky, the teacher assistant, was putting the art cart over by the table near the sink. She placed a lazy Susan with several different types of art supplies in the middle of the table so that all of the children could reach what they needed.

"Are you going to finish your airplane today, Anna?" Becky asked. "Or are you going to add to our mural?"

"I don't know yet," Anna declared, rolling her wheelchair over to the art table. "Maybe I'll put my airplane *on* the mural," she laughed.

"That's a great idea!" said Yoruba, the occupational therapist, who had just entered the room. She crouched down by Anna's chair and smiled, "We'll have to figure out how to get Popsicle sticks to stay up there on the paper." Yoruba was in the classroom with the children twice a week, and Anna's father knew that she paid special attention to Anna's needs and the special needs of other children when she was there. She also consulted with the staff on appropriate sensory and motor activities and interventions for all of the children.

The team, including therapists, all had met with Anna's parents to develop her individualized program plan and to coordinate home and school activities. To keep her parents informed about the events in the classroom, they sent home a folder each week containing Anna's special projects and any communication from school. Her parents then returned the folder with any communication from home.

"Anna, I need to get to work now. Mommy will pick you up after school. Bye, sweetheart. Have a good day!"

Anna was busy studying the picture chart for making the day's snack. Her father shook his head, and as he watched her, a gentle smile crept across his face.

"Anna, your daddy is leaving. He said have a good day," Felicia commented.

"That's okay," he laughed, "I know she will!"

"Bye, Daddy," Anna replied without taking her eyes off the chart. "It looks like we're making muffins. I can tell from the muffin pan!"

Chapter 1

WHAT IS *READ, PLAY, AND LEARN!®*?

Read, Play, and Learn!® is a play-based, storybook-oriented curriculum that you and the children with whom you work are going to enjoy. Utilizing storybooks as a framework for providing highly stimulating experiences for learning, this curriculum offers a functional approach to educating young children. *Read, Play, and Learn!* allows you to incorporate skills training across all of the developmental domains while letting children select what is motivating to them and have fun while learning.

Using the charm of storybooks, you, the facilitator, with your learners' parents/caregivers and other team members, provide a theme-based approach to encouraging and supporting each child's growth and development. The curriculum consists of this *Teacher's Guide* and a series of instructional modules, each designed around a popular storybook. The modules creatively build from the concepts, ideas, actions, and events of the stories in order to make learning more relevant for children. Each module is used for 2 weeks or longer as appropriate to your needs. Each day begins with the reading of the story followed by a range of activities for the many centers of a preschool or kindergarten class or a child care program. The retelling and rereading of the storybooks each day enhance emergent literacy skills, whereas the many suggested activities help promote children's growth across the core domains of development.

The design of this curriculum not only gives you a fun way to teach children between the chronological ages of 3 and 6 years, but it also shows you, through the inclusion of specialists in the planning process, how to incorporate therapeutic interventions for children functioning at a younger age, even those as developmentally young as 1 or 2 years. Employing themes in the classroom enables children to engage in a variety of activities suited to their developmental abilities and all relating to the same concepts. Repetition of these concepts across numerous and diverse situations encourages the generalization of knowledge and skills. Vocabulary, actions, and information related to the themes contained in the storybooks are expanded into activities that enhance cognitive (problem-solving), social-emotional, communication and language, and sensorimotor skills. Emerging literacy development is also encouraged through the child's familiarity and comfort with the storybook and the activities and environment developed for the module.

Although the curriculum presents ideas for centers and activities for 2-week units related to individual stories, each story is intended to serve as a flexible foundation for team planning for children of all developmental levels. The activities may be spread out over a longer period of time or may be deleted or adapted as dictated by the length of the day and needs and interests of the children. It should also be noted that the storybooks used for the curriculum framework are not the *only* books to which the children are exposed. Throughout the day at the Literacy Center and during reading time, many other books will be available and will be explored and read. The storybook serves as the thematic core around which other books can be integrated.

WHAT ARE THE GOALS OF THE CURRICULUM?

In *Read, Play, and Learn!,* the desired educational and developmental outcomes result from play activities and experiences that all derive from and relate to the expansion of concepts and actions presented in various storybooks. Reading the story and dramatizing the story are accentuated first in the *Read, Play, and Learn!* modules as they lay the foundation for the other centers and activities within the classroom. Areas, or centers set up around the room with various activities related to the story, are designed to provide toys, materials, and experiences to address specific developmental outcomes.

Individualization of instruction takes place as a result of the adaptations provided for each child within the center and the interactions among the child, other peers, and you, the facilitator, who is encouraging learning while the children are hard at play. Not only can children become involved in the telling and dramatizing of the story, but they can also have developmental needs and literacy skills reinforced through the supplemental activities in the various play areas. Infusion of emerging literacy development into a play-based, storybook-oriented curriculum is a potent means of presenting the written word, visual symbols, concepts about print, and sequential storytelling within a meaningful context for children.

The goals of *Read, Play, and Learn!* are as follows:

1. To enable all children to actively participate through play in classroom activities that are relevant, challenging, and designed to promote independent learning and facilitate developmental progress
2. To provide a literature-based framework for learning for all children that encompasses cognitive, social-emotional, communication and language, and sensorimotor development
3. To encourage learning across the above domains (Goal 2) in a literacy-rich environment that expands children's competence and methods of expression and broadens their desire to learn to read, write, and communicate through numerous modalities, including print

Thus, *Read, Play, and Learn!* is a transdisciplinary play-based curriculum (TPBC). This term represents a very important way of thinking about planning for young children's learning because it encompasses the perspectives of the different domains of development and focuses on building your curriculum with activities that are motivating to each child. (The origins of the TPBC concept, as well as related readings on transdisciplinary play-based assessment and intervention, are described briefly later in this chapter; see page 14.)

WHAT ARE THE COMPONENTS OF THE CURRICULUM?

The *Read, Play, and Learn!* curriculum is presented in a series of individual booklets, or instructional modules. Each module features a different popular children's story and presents engaging, theme-based activities to accompany that story. (The storybooks themselves are available through local libraries or bookstores as well as on the World Wide Web; you can try such sites as www.amazon.com or www.barnesandnoble.com; complete bibliographic data appear in each module.) Suggestions for additional stories are provided at the back of each module, some of which may be appropriate substitutions if you have trouble obtaining the recommended storybook. Before using any of the modules, be sure that you are thoroughly familiar with the contents of this *Teacher's Guide*.

The Storybook Modules

The storybook modules range in topic from seasonal themes to predictable sequences, from emotional issues to culture heritages. Some are based on storybooks that are just plain fun. The storybook modules of *Read, Play, and Learn!* are offered in easy-to-use booklets that are sold in boxed sets referred to as "Collections." Collections 1 and 2 each contain eight modules, and together they span a typical fall-to-spring school year (see page 74 of each module for ordering information, and contact Brookes Publishing for information on the availability of other collections or individual modules):

Collection 1

1. *The Kissing Hand,* by Audrey Penn
2. *Somebody and the Three Blairs,* by Marilyn Tolhurst
3. *Picking Apples & Pumpkins,* by Amy and Richard Hutchings
4. *The Little Old Lady Who Was Not Afraid of Anything,* by Linda Williams
5. *The Knight and the Dragon,* by Tomie dePaola
6. *Abiyoyo,* by Pete Seeger
7. *Night Tree,* by Eve Bunting
8. *The Snowy Day,* by Ezra Jack Keats

Collection 2

9. *A Porcupine Named Fluffy,* by Helen Lester
10. *First Flight,* by David McPhail
11. *Friends,* by Helme Heine
12. *The Three Billy Goats Gruff,* by Janet Stevens
13. *The Three Little Javelinas,* by Susan Lowell

14. *A Rainbow of Friends,* by P.K. Hallinan
15. *Franklin Has a Sleepover,* by Paulette Bourgeois and Brenda Clark
16. *The Rainbow Fish,* by Marcus Pfister

Throughout the chapters of this *Teacher's Guide,* you will find illustrative examples drawn from these stories.

You can use the modules in the sequence suggested by these collections or in any other order that suits your needs, that suits the time of year or your geographic location and climate, or that suits the interests of your learners. Users are also invited to develop additional modules following the same or a similar format. New modules may be developed by brainstorming with a team around creative activities and experiences or a favorite book. Selected ideas should be organized into center-based applications and sequenced to be sure that the various play areas across the day are interrelated. Modules may also be submitted for possible inclusion in future collections; inquire with the publisher, or watch for more information at our web site at www.brookespublishing.com.

The Module Format

Each module follows the same format and has the following sections:

1. *The Story:* A brief retelling or summary of the picture book, with information on where to get the book
2. *The Planning Sheets:* Charts for at-a-glance reference to all of the suggested activities for the 2 weeks
3. *Vocabulary:* A list of the key words and concepts, including labels, action words, and descriptors, to which the children can be introduced in the module
4. *Materials:* A list of the toys and equipment, supplies, food, and other items needed for the module
5. *Areas/Centers:* A description of 10 days of different activities for each area or center in the classroom, plus suggested modifications for the children functioning at the sensorimotor, functional, and symbolic levels of learning (described in the next section)
6. *How to Involve Families:* Sample letters with recommendations to help keep family members or other caregivers informed
7. *More Suggestions:* Additional storybooks and other activities (e.g., songs, fingerplays, resources, computer games) that can be used with the module

The centers, or areas of the classroom referenced previously, include a place for reading the story at the start of each day; an area to dramatize the story; a literacy center; areas for sensory and motor play; an art area; and sites for science and math activities, floor play, table play, outdoor play, woodworking, and snack. These centers may be distinct or may overlap. For example, a miniature story scenario might be found on the table, on the floor, or on the floor combined with the block area to encourage further building of the scenario. All of the areas may be set up in the room, or the team may choose to generate only a few of the areas or centers at one time. Team members from half-day and full-day programs may use the centers differently. Full-day programs may have centers grouped for morning and afternoon or may offer children more time at the centers. The team may add to or change the areas for each storybook as is deemed necessary to maintain the children's high level of involvement (see Chapter 4). Use your imagination, and have fun with the design of your classroom or child care center.

Levels of Understanding and Learning

Activities and experiences are developed within the curriculum at three developmental levels across each of the areas. These three levels are not geared to specific ages but are somewhat flexible groupings of developmental age levels in the cognitive and language domains to simplify planning for an entire classroom of children. More information about developmental levels and specific guidelines for individualized planning for children are provided in *Transdisciplinary Play-Based Intervention: Guidelines for Developing a Meaningful Curriculum for Young Children* (Linder, 1993c), as described later in this chapter (see "Are There Related Products?" on page 14).

The first level of understanding and learning is the *sensorimotor level* (sometimes called the *exploratory level)*, when children are interested in concrete labels and meanings, social interactions, and physical manipulation of the environment. Learning takes place through various forms of sensory exploration. This level corresponds roughly to the cognitive and language levels of children functioning from early infancy to about 18 months of age.

The second level of understanding and learning is the *functional level,* when children are interested in listening and watching, imitating, relating, and beginning to sequence ideas and actions. Learning becomes more socially instigated but is still very concrete and sensory, involving functional objects and actions. This level coincides approximately with children functioning from about 18 months to 3 years of age.

The third level, approximately 3 years of age and older, is the *symbolic level,* when children become interested in learning and representing their understandings though a variety of representational and symbolic means, including fantasy play, storytelling, music, dance, art, drawing, and print.

The suggestions provided in the ***Read, Play, and Learn!*** modules at these three levels will expedite planning, as these levels will encompass the ready-to-learn, or cognitive, levels of all the children in the class. Modifications will also need to be made for the physical, social, and sensory disabilities that may compromise children's learning. Suggestions for these adaptations are in Chapters 4, 5, and 6.

WHERE AND WHEN CAN THE CURRICULUM BE USED?

Read, Play, and Learn! can be implemented in any child care, preschool, early education, Head Start, or kindergarten program that emphasizes a developmental approach to learning. It can be utilized with various schedules within programs. The activities and experiences suggested in the modules can be included in "choice" times, spread out through the day, or extended over a longer period of time than the recommended 2 weeks. Your educational and therapeutic team should meet on a regular basis to determine which of the modules' activities will motivate the children to become absorbed in the play, which need to be modified, what sequence of activities is desired, and whether additional experiences will be needed to supplement the ones suggested in the curriculum. The team plans from the modules provided, implements the activities selected, and meets to evaluate and discuss the effectiveness of activities for individual children.

WHY USE *READ, PLAY, AND LEARN!?*

As a transdisciplinary play-based curriculum, **Read, Play, and Learn!** is valuable for two reasons: It ensures success in a literacy-based culture, and it capitalizes on the children's natural inclinations.

To Ensure Success in a Literacy-Based Culture

Play is the natural mode of learning for young children. Many early education programs, however, emphasize preacademics in preparation for academic curricula for school-age children. As academics assume greater significance in the early learning environments, play is frequently deemphasized. Some curricula accentuate developmental domains, with only cursory inclusion of emerging literacy development. Other curricula are primarily focused on teaching preacademic skills and stressing memorization of letters, sounds, numbers, and words. Either approach does a disservice to children. Literacy *can* and *should* be encouraged in developmentally sound sequences using motivating methods to which young children can relate. Few pastimes are more motivating to children than play. The use of literature and play activities related to storybooks provides teachers with a natural mode for developing a literacy-rich environment that infuses into the curriculum the necessary cognitive, language and communication, motor, and social components to build literacy skills. Phonemic awareness, an important component of literacy development, can be addressed along with the listening, comprehending, and communicating skills that lay the foundation for literacy development.

To Capitalize on the Children's Natural Inclinations

The combination of literature and play builds on two interests of young children: 1) the desire to learn about and communicate to others knowledge about the people, places, things, and ideas that are having an impact on the children's world; and 2) the need to increase the number of ways that such knowledge can be acquired and shared. Edwards, Gandini, and Forman (1995) identified many "languages" that children use. In addition to verbal language, children use bodily expression to communicate in many ways, including gestures, actions, words, dramatizations, and pictures, among others. Emerging literacy development can best be fostered through means that tap into these natural forms of learning and expression, specifically through the highly stimulating venue of play. Dramatic play enables a child to represent his or her world through symbolic actions. Communication through words or signs enables a child to communicate through yet another symbolic system. Learning to read and write involves developing an understanding of a new symbol system to represent words and ideas. Once children develop an awareness of this written symbol system and learn to use symbols as a means of expression, they then can move through the cognitive, language, and fine motor developmental sequences needed to use this symbol system to both acquire and impart information.

WHO CAN BENEFIT FROM *READ, PLAY, AND LEARN!?*

The benefits of a curriculum based on literature and play are numerous. Although young children are the obvious targets of the curriculum, others profit as well. Individuals who work with children and parents/caregivers in homes with young children will acquire new knowledge and skills that will improve their abilities to enhance children's development.

Young Children

All young children whose cultures recognize the importance of self-expression in its many forms can benefit from *Read, Play, and Learn!* Children, whether typically developing, advanced, or experiencing delays or deviations in their development, need a foundation that will inspire them to learn to listen, think, communicate, and learn about their world in as many modes as possible. The use of storybooks that capture interests and imaginations provides the framework for young learners to become involved in experiences that challenge them developmentally.

People Who Work with Young Children

Because the storybook curriculum incorporates ideas from all developmental domains and modifies activities and interactions to meet the needs of a wide spectrum of children, the people who work with young children can also benefit from this curriculum. Most teacher-training programs do not prepare teachers adequately to understand the disparate learning and developmental needs of young children with a broad range of abilities. In fact, most "methods" courses for teachers of young children focus on typically developing children. The trend toward including children of all ability levels into a single learning environment, however, necessitates the expansion of teachers' knowledge and skills related to working with a group of children with diverse learning needs.

This curriculum provides teachers and other team members with strategies as well as the justification for using those strategies to facilitate the development of children with and without disabilities in all of the developmental domains. When transdisciplinary teams use the curriculum for planning purposes, team members learn from each other how best to meet the needs of individual children. Discussing what modifications will be needed for specific children, planning for the adaptation of content and strategies, and identifying the facilitation techniques appropriate for each child lead to better teaching and intervention for all children.

Parents/Caregivers

Parents of young children are viewed as key players in *Read, Play, and Learn!* After all, the "T" in TPBC stands for "transdisciplinary," and that means parents, too. Parents know their children better than anyone else, and teachers miss an important opportunity to extend learning if they do not invite family members to participate. The storybook themes provide an easy mechanism for parents to replicate school readings at home as well as a centerpiece for discussing the child's experiences at school each day. You can provide parents with guidelines for helping their children to love listening to, reading, and writing words and stories. (Chapter 8 gives you plenty of information, including handouts to photocopy and send home, that shows families how they can use the storybooks and make their homes literacy-rich environments for everyone.) In addition to the family materials in this *Teacher's Guide*, each module includes sample letters you can send to parents. The letters introduce each book, explain what is going to be happening in the classroom, and provide suggestions for how the fun at school can become fun at home. Back-and-forth communication between home and school is an important element of a successful program. Through written communication, spoken exchange, and classroom participation, parents should be integral members of your educational team.

Substantial family participation and involvement is critical for effective child assessment and education. Research has shown that children's development is enhanced across all domains and that children show an increased interest in school when their parents are involved in their education (Coleman, 1991; Powell, 1989; Rich, 1985). Indeed, parents, teachers, and schools overall benefit from effective communication, information exchange, participation in school activities, and educational planning (Wishon, Crabtree, & Jones, 1998).

WHO CAN USE *READ, PLAY, AND LEARN!*?

Most curricula for young children are designed to be used by teachers or early childhood educators. By its very label as a *transdisciplinary* play-based curriculum, however, it is clear that *Read, Play, and Learn!* can be used by professionals in many disciplines. As classrooms become larger or more children with special needs are included in general education classrooms, teacher assistants and other professionals come to play a vital role in the implementation of the curricula. Administrators, too, now play a greater role in supporting classroom environments and explaining the curriculum to parents and the community.

Teachers, Early Childhood Educators, and Reading Specialists

The curriculum can be used by child care providers, Head Start instructors, preschool and kindergarten teachers, early childhood professionals, and reading specialists in consultation with related-services professionals. The recommended model is 1) *inclusive,* integrating children with special needs into the classroom; 2) *transdisciplinary,* integrating various disciplines into assessment, planning, and direct classroom education and intervention; and 3) *developmental,* integrating hierarchical skills and developmental processes into the curriculum. Teachers will be able to use *Read, Play, and Learn!* to plan for both groups and individual children.

Therapists and Related-Services Personnel

The curriculum will assist speech-language pathologists, physical therapists, occupational therapists, mobility specialists, vision and hearing specialists, and other professionals in incorporating intervention and therapy into the functional, meaningful activities of the classroom. Professionals can also use the classroom activities as a common basis for discussion of approaches in communicating with each other about individual children's needs. Other members on your team could include a nurse, psychologist, nutritionist, or any specialist assisting the children in your classroom.

Teacher Assistants

Teacher assistants can be more meaningfully involved in the classroom program because the curriculum involves all staff in planning and implementing the daily activities as well as modifying them to meet individual children's needs. The structure of the *Read, Play, and Learn!* curriculum will enable the assistant to understand not only the activities but also the justification for modifications. The assistant should be involved in planning meetings with the rest of the staff.

Administrators

Administrators will be able to use the curriculum to define the goals, outcomes, and educational and therapeutic processes that frame education for the early years. The philosophy of *Read, Play, and Learn!* and the other transdisciplinary play-based products supports the acquisition of developmental and preacademic skills necessary for success in the elementary school years. The unification of cognitive, language, social, and motor development with emerging literacy development creates a program that is educationally and developmentally sound.

ARE THERE RELATED PRODUCTS?

Read, Play, and Learn! is an extension of the other transdisciplinary play-based work from Toni Linder. Because most classrooms and child care settings today have children of varying ability levels, you will likely want to become familiar with the other transdisciplinary play-based products as well. *Transdisciplinary Play-Based Assessment: A Functional Approach to Working with Young Children, Revised Edition* (Linder, 1993a) presents a process for assessing the functional level of children from birth to 6 years of age, across cognitive, social-emotional, communication and language, and sensorimotor development. The process enables people observing the child's play to also determine the child's learning style, interests, and most positive interactional patterns. The information gained from this assessment can then be translated into educational and/or therapeutic program plans. *Transdisciplinary Play-Based Intervention: Guidelines for Developing a Meaningful Curriculum for Young Children* (Linder, 1993c) presents strategies, materials, and learning experiences appropriate for children at varying levels of development from birth to age 6 who demonstrate differing learning and interaction styles. The strategies provided are individualized for the children depending on their developmental level and personal characteristics. These two volumes link assessment and intervention to provide a holistic approach to learning for each child.

Read, Play, and Learn! provides a means for bringing the individualized focus of transdisciplinary play-based assessment (TPBA) and transdisciplinary play-based intervention (TPBI) into use in group settings. The TPBI approach introduces the use of storybooks but does not highlight it as a key component; *Read, Play, and Learn!* ties together cognitive, language, motor, and social aspects of development. In other words, *Read, Play, and Learn!* lets you integrate developmental and cross-domain intervention and education into a classroom of children of varying ability levels. *Read, Play, and Learn!* can be used in conjunction with other assessment and intervention approaches, but the model is designed specifically to build on the same theoretical and philosophical foundations as TPBA and TPBI. The holistic appraisal of individual children's abilities and needs through observation of play is fundamental to all of the components of the play-based system. As with TPBA and TPBI, flexibility in order to better meet the needs of children is vital. All of the transdisciplinary play-based books, forms (Linder, 1993b), and training videotapes (Linder, 1995, 1996) are available from Paul H. Brookes Publishing Co.

Professionals who want to use *Read, Play, and Learn!* but are unfamiliar with the TPBA and TPBI can use the storybook curriculum as their starting point. The other volumes are not necessary but will help you when you need to write individualized family service plans (IFSPs) or individualized education programs (IEPs) for any of the children in your classroom. Observing children while engaged in various play activities within the classroom using the TPBA guidelines can help team members assess where and how children are functioning. The TPBI volume then actually gives you a "Planner" of play materials and suggested opportunities, intervention guidelines, and more to develop individualized programs for children who need extra assistance.

IS A TRANSDISCIPLINARY TEAM ESSENTIAL?

Read, Play, and Learn! is meant to be used by a transdisciplinary team, and staff who are using the curriculum are encouraged to seek professional consultation when planning for the needs of children with developmental delays or disabilities. The greater the input obtained from related-services professionals on adaptations and intervention strategies, the more effective the curriculum will be for each child. The goal of having each child participate to a maximum level in each module can best be achieved through team planning, demonstration, and support. Consequently, team members also need to be involved *in the classroom* as often as possible. It is recognized, however, that not all programs have access to specialized professionals on a regular basis. For this reason, the curriculum provides some guidance on how to modify activities for children with differing ability levels and various types of disabilities.

HAS *READ, PLAY, AND LEARN!* BEEN FIELD-TESTED?

The modules contained in the curriculum have been field-tested in two programs with differing levels of professional involvement. At one site, implementing a reverse mainstreaming model, therapists functioned as part of the classroom team, with a teacher, a teacher assistant, and one therapist (alternately a speech-language pathologist or an occupational therapist) in the classroom with the children. All of the team members were involved in planning and evaluating the program together. In another inclusive site, teacher assistants were responsible for classroom program implementation with outside consultation from representatives of various disciplines. The model was effective in both sites, with children of all levels and with all types of disabilities, as well as with children who were within the average or gifted range of abilities. In the Foreword "Teacher to Teacher: A Personal View of *Read, Play, and Learn!*," one teacher who taught in both sites provides a qualitative review of her experiences with the curriculum in both of these sites. Pages xv–xx provide an overview of the research on which *Read, Play, and Learn!* is based, and additional information is available at www.readplaylearn.com, including descriptions at other schools using the curriculum.

CONCLUSION

Whether you use *Read, Play, and Learn!* alone or in combination with other programs and models, keep in mind the importance of each word that TPBC stands for. Recognize the need for individualization and the benefit of obtaining input from others (including parents), encourage children to engage in activities that are motivating to them, and approach learning in your classroom holistically. *Read, Play, and Learn!* will be most effective when you can combine the creative ideas and individual perspectives of several colleagues from different disciplines, of family members, and/or of administrators. Ask your school or program administrators to consider program structure, staffing patterns, and time for team planning to help everyone benefit from *Read, Play, and Learn!*

REFERENCES

Coleman, J. (1991). *Planning for parent participation in schools for young children.* Bloomington, IL: ERIC Digest.

Edwards, C., Gandini, L., & Forman, G. (1995). *The hundred languages of children: The Reggio Emilia approach to early childhood education.* Greenwich, CT: Ablex Publishing Corp.

Linder, T.W. (1993a). *Transdisciplinary play-based assessment: A functional approach to working with young children* (Rev. ed.). Baltimore: Paul H. Brookes Publishing Co.

Linder, T.W. (1993b). *Transdisciplinary play-based assessment and intervention: Child and program summary forms.* Baltimore: Paul H. Brookes Publishing Co.

Linder, T.W. (1993c). *Transdisciplinary play-based intervention: Guidelines for developing a meaningful curriculum for young children.* Baltimore: Paul H. Brookes Publishing Co.

Linder, T.W. (Producer and writer), & Newman, R.S. (Director and editor). (1995). *And you thought they were just playing: Transdisciplinary play-based assessment* [Videotape]. Baltimore: Paul H. Brookes Publishing Co.

Linder, T.W. (Producer and writer), & Walker, M. (Director and editor). (1996). *Observing Kassandra: A transdisciplinary play-based assessment of a child with severe disabilities.* Baltimore: Paul H. Brookes Publishing Co.

Powell, R. (1989). *Families and early childhood programs* (Research Monographs of the National Association for the Education of Young Children, Vol. 3). Washington, DC: National Association for the Education of Young Children.

Rich, D. (1985). *The forgotten factor in school success—the family: A policymaker's guide.* Washington, DC: Home and School Institute.

Wishon, P., Crabtree, K., & Jones, M. (1998). *Curriculum for the primary years: An integrative approach.* Upper Saddle River, NJ: Prentice-Hall.

Chapter 2

READ + PLAY = LEARN

Is the adult need to facilitate the development of literacy incompatible with children's desire to play? Teaching literacy is considered structured and adult directed, whereas play is seen as unstructured and child directed. Children's literature combined with play, however, may unite the two concepts.

Children are typically motivated to play. Think about how much more motivated to read children would be if reading stories and using print materials enriched and enlivened their play. Consider the extensions that the written word could bring to a child's play. And imagine the interest children could take in writing if they could express the ideas they learned through play. For example, children can come to understand the *functions* of print as they use print in their play to make a "get well" card or to write a check at a pretend store. They can come to understand the *forms* of print through manipulating and experimenting with pencils and papers, stamps, or words and pictures cut out of magazines to make lists or tickets.

The thoughtful blending of emerging literacy and play in the preschool and kindergarten years should lead to more confident, expressive, animated children in the elementary grades. Research has led us to a burgeoning understanding of the importance of play to a child's development (Johnson, Christie, & Yawkey, 1987; Van Hoorn, Nourot, Scales, & Alward, 1993). At the same time, there is an increasing awareness of the need for a literate society and an expanding knowledge of the means for enhancing literacy skills. The time is right to look at how these two elements, which both are important to optimal development and achievement, can be combined.

Both literacy development and play involve creating, planning, shaping, sequencing, communicating, predicting, synthesizing, participating, producing, and evaluating. Both involve representations of the child's feelings, thoughts, and actions and representations of actual and imaginary worlds. Expression of self is heightened; yet, incorporation of others' perspectives is also encouraged. Literacy development and play can promote understanding and acceptance of others and provide safe boundaries to examine who one is and who one wants to be. Let's look first at play, then literacy, and next bring the two together again in ***Read, Play, and Learn!***®

PLAY

Play is known as "children's work." It provides a means of taking in new information about the world but at a pace matched to the child's level of understanding. During play, children can discover new things, process what they learn, and make adaptations to skills and understandings in a nonthreatening, motivating, and functional manner. Gradually they adjust new skills and concepts to the demands of their environment.

Children play at their individual developmental levels and within a contextual framework. Therefore, the medium of play requires those interacting with children to adjust their cognitive, language, motor, and social expectations to the level of each child and to attend to each child's need for meaningful context if learning is to take place. Children acquire new skills and concepts through a gradual adjustment or adaptation of their existing skills and concepts to meet the needs of their environment. During play, children can take in new information, process this information, and make adaptations of skills and understandings in a nonthreatening, motivating, and functional manner.

The Piagetian (1962) concept of *equilibration* underlies the reason why play supports development. As the child takes in new information, confronts problems, and encounters unique situations, modification of existing behavior and thought patterns is necessitated. Equilibration is the process by which the brain modifies existing schemes to be able to adapt to the new processes. Play allows the child to use common patterns and experiment with variations and transformations of these thoughts and behaviors to increase his or her range of functioning and conceptual understanding of the world.

Play not only enables a child to experiment individually with new schemes but, through interactions with adults and other children, play also encourages the child to use others as models for shaping additional patterns of thought and behavior. This does mean that you, as teacher or facilitator, and the other team members need to adjust cognitive, language, motor, and social expectations to the level of each child and to attend to each child's need for meaningful context if learning is to take place. As Vygotsky (1978) theorized, observations and interactions with others provide the means for learning new paradigms and problem-solving approaches. The examples provided by others and the verbal exchanges in play provide a highly motivating environment for learning.

While allowing adaptation for maturational, temperamental, sensory, and interactional differences, play also is accommodating of cultural variations. The learning of cultural mores and cultural social interaction patterns is also acquired through play. Play allows children to imitate and practice the cultural values, behaviors, and language expected of their culture of origin or of other cultures to which they are exposed. Cross-cultural research has demonstrated that distinct cultures display significant differences in parental goals, expectations, interaction patterns, developmental norms and processes, and interpretations of what encompasses quality education (New, 1994). Play is an element of all cultures, although the nature of play in cultures may vary. Play is also a principal instrument for practicing the manners, customs, behaviors, and routines that are important to the lives of children. Play is pleasurable, is valued by the participants, is spontaneous and voluntary, and requires the active involvement of the players (Bronfenbrenner, 1979; Garvey, 1977; Linder, 1993a, 1993b). Because play promotes the development of cognitive, social, language and communication, and sensorimotor skills (Linder, 1993a, 1993b), the concept of integrating play into school is not revolutionary.

LITERACY

In most cultures, written symbols are a primary mechanism for communication and transmission of information. In addition to the acquisition of spoken language, learning to read and write is necessary for success in most Western cultures. Indeed, literacy has always been a goal of Western education. It is "a lifelong developmental process" that involves learning to use oral and written language effectively to reason and to think within the context of a given culture; to accomplish personal goals; and to meet the demands experienced within home, school, workplace, community, and society (Wishon, Crabtree, & Jones, 1998, p. 153).

The inclusion of reading and writing in grade school has historically been taken for granted as a key element in the school curriculum. Focusing on literacy in preschool and kindergarten is a much newer idea, and one that is sometimes met with controversy. But what if we think of literacy as McCord does, not just as learning to read and write letters and words on a page but as something larger:

> Literacy is listening, learning, and quality of life. It is reading, writing, thinking, scribbling, drawing, and being motivated to find meaning. It is interpreting, inventing, associating, communicating, responding, sharing, and being able to set visions into action. Our challenge as educators is to make it possible for all children, regardless of ability, experience or cultural heritage, to feel successful in their attempts to be literate. (McCord, 1995, p. 125)

Now literacy learning is transformed into an important goal for preschool and kindergarten children. Children can learn to express themselves through all of their "natural languages, or modes of expression, including words, movement, drawing, painting, building, sculpture, shadow play, collage, dramatic play, and music" (Edwards, Gandini, & Forman, 1995, p. 3). The development of literacy skills parallels the development of skills in other developmental areas. Learning through reading becomes another pleasurable means of taking in others' stories and information, and sharing through writing becomes one more way of expressing one's own feelings and ideas. A critical goal of preschool and kindergarten, then, is to instill in children the *desire* to read and write and to facilitate the process of becoming literate.

The Emergence of Literacy

All children come to preschool with some exposure to spoken and written language. Oral and written languages develop simultaneously, with each lending support to the child's comprehension of the other (Schickedanz, 1994). Both join in a social context, with both adult and peer social mediation contributing to the child's acquisition of interest, motivation, understanding, and use of literacy skills. Thus, most preschool and kindergarten children have already internalized many of the rules for learning language; many have an understanding of the purpose of print and can read environmental print, such as fast-food signs or culturally relevant symbols; and many already associate books with reading and regard reading as a pleasurable activity (Schickedanz, 1994).

Research on emerging literacy has begun to shape our view of the type of experiences early education programs should include. More information on emerging literacy and a full discussion of the stages in reading development are included in Chapter 7. With careful observation as well as a knowledge of naturally occurring developmental sequences related to emerging storybook reading, language comprehension and forms of communicative expression, story sequencing, and fine motor skills necessary for drawing and writing, adults can create an environment that promotes literacy development. A literacy curriculum should include the following elements (Wishon et al., 1998):

1. Experiences to expand background knowledge and vocabulary
2. Oral/aural language opportunities
3. Reading aloud by the teacher
4. A variety of literacy contexts (themes and purposes for using literacy)
5. A variety of literacy materials
6. Teacher observation time without mediation or intrusion
7. Time for children to converse and share reading, writing, and learning with each other and with adults
8. Independent reading time
9. Independent writing time
10. Individual and small-group mediated reading (shared reading, supported reading)
11. Individual and small-group mediated writing (interactive writing)

In addition to exposure to spoken language and the written word, children need to develop *phonemic awareness,* or the understanding that language is composed of small sounds that correspond to the alphabetic system. Helping children develop phonemic awareness is an important aspect of emerging literacy (Adams, Foorman, Lundberg, & Beeler, 1998). Activities and experiences that allow children to playfully experience rhyme, rhythm, and listening to sounds will stimulate the children's interest in discrete sounds. These types of activities have been shown to help children develop phonemic awareness, which in many studies has been shown to account for as much as 50% of variance in reading proficiency at the end of first grade (Blachman, 1991; Wagner, Torgesen, & Rashotte, 1994).

Since the mid-1970s, the field of reading has been confronting the issue of the most appropriate method for teaching reading. The whole language approach has been both touted and maligned. Likewise, the phonics approach has seen the pendulum swing from approbation to condemnation and is, for many, back in favor again. The dilemmas that have confronted teachers have been comprehensively discussed in *Learning to Read and Write* (International Reading Association & National Association for the Education of Young Children, 1998), *Literacy at the Cross-roads* (Routman, 1996), and *Preventing Reading Difficulties in Young Children* (Snow, Burns, & Griffin, 1998). As with the purported literacy–play dichotomy, however, the seeming dichotomy between whole language and phonics may be a misconception. Oral language "play" to help children segment words into sounds appears to contribute importantly to reading and writing development (Adams et al., 1998). Children can learn to differentiate speech sounds, the association of those sounds to letters, letters to words, and words to meaning within the context of play and meaningful exposure to print within play. Therefore, balance is needed between 1) attention to the meaning and use of written language and 2) the components of phonemic awareness and word recognition that unite to create meaning. You will find more discussion of phonemic and phonological awareness in Chapter 7. Experts in the field are looking for a more balanced approach between whole language and phonics in the search for more effective strategies in teaching reading.

Knowledge of reading and writing development may not be acquired in many teacher preparation programs, and professionals must acquaint themselves with the issues and with strategies. Such references as *Literacy Development in the Early Years: Helping Children Read and Write* (Morrow, 1997); *Emerging Literacy: Preschool, Kindergarten, and Primary Years* (Ollila & Mayfield, 1992); *More than ABC's: The Early Stages of Reading and Writing* (Schickedanz, 1994); and *Curriculum for the Primary Years: An Integrative Approach* (Wishon et al., 1998) should be helpful.

Literacy and the Family

The growing recognition of the importance of the early years to later educational, economic, and societal outcomes reinforces the importance of examining early literacy development in the home environment as well. According to a Children's Defense Fund (1997) report, literacy skills equate with increased probability of school success and, therefore, increased opportunity for economic stability. Light and Kelford-Smith (1993) and Marvin (1994) found that families, regardless of socioeconomic level, incorporate a variety of literacy experiences into their daily routines. Yet studies have shown that children from disadvantaged backgrounds often are not only less frequently exposed to literacy materials, but they are less knowledgeable about phonemic awareness (Kaplan-Sanoff, Parker, & Zuckerman, 1991; Scarborough, Dobrich, & Hager, 1991). In addition, King-DeBaun (1990) noted that families of children with special needs also provide fewer literacy experiences for their children. Early childhood professionals can play an important role in helping families understand how their interactions with their children regarding the print in their home and community activities can contribute to learning in school.

Early exposure to positive literacy experiences in the home and in preschool and kindergarten may provide a foundation for later accomplishments related to literacy and learning. Scarborough et al. (1991) found that although parental reading levels appeared to have little influence on later child reading achievement, children with less literacy *exposure* were more likely to be defined as "poor" readers on the reading cluster of the Woodcock-Johnson Psychoeducational Battery–Revised (Woodcock & Johnson, 1989) than those children with more exposure to literacy in their backgrounds. Thus, a curriculum that imparts literacy experiences in the classroom along with involvement of families in early literacy activities may assist children in acquiring the necessary skills for academic success.

The challenges of those who facilitate the literacy learning of young children are to build on the backgrounds and experiences that the individual children bring to school; to actively engage the children in highly personal, emerging literacy experiences; and to encourage risk taking and experimentation with beginning reading and writing. A *natural literacy* model (Watkins, 1996) is one in which children are exposed to and interact with many different kinds of literacy events throughout the day. Such a model is incorporated into **Read, Play, and Learn!**

READING + PLAYING

Reading and writing requires learning a symbol system and understanding its meaning and application. Children learn this symbol system best when they are motivated to use the symbol system in a consequential form, in other words, when they can see the consequences of the written materials. Incorporating reading, writing, and phonemic awareness into the highly motivating activities of play can create an important incentive for learning the symbol system and using it functionally.

Such a curriculum should address three essential components for early literacy development: 1) *early exposure to literacy-rich environments,* 2) *use of storybooks and availability of literacy props* (e.g., paper, markers, crayons, pencils, ink stamps, message pads, cookbooks, folders, calendars, signs, tickets, menus, maps, songs, rhymes, fingerplays), and 3) *the active involvement of adults* to facilitate literacy play and skill development (Schons, 1996).

Within the first component, a literacy-rich environment, early exposure includes the use of many forms of symbolic communication and print materials. Books, magazines, signs, charts, and labels are among the possibilities.

The use of storybooks and literacy props, the second component, is recommended to allow the children opportunities to *use* the written signs and symbols in many meaningful and relevant ways. Neuman and Roskos (1991) noted that literacy props in children's play need to be items that the children choose independently (although items can be preselected and provided by the teacher), real items, and items used in the children's play and activities.

Exposure to props alone, however, does not appear to be sufficient to promote literacy development. Christie and Enz (1992) found that adult facilitation and guidance of the literacy play activities, the third necessary component, increased both the level of children's play and their emerging literacy skills. Adams et al. (1998) noted that activities that also guide children through phonological differentiation requiring listening to sameness, difference, number, and order of speech sounds can build skills that are essential for learning to read and spell.

Combining literacy and play through storybooks allows just such exposure, as the ideas and actions expressed in print come to life through the children's dramatic representations, drawings, social interactions, and playful classroom activities related to the stories. The use of storybooks and other holistic strategies in supporting literacy development is endorsed by the Early Childhood and Literacy Development Committee of the International Reading Association (1986, 1990). The committee noted that some packaged early reading programs that focus on discrete skills and emphasize the use of drill and practice do not attend to the social, emotional, and intellectual development of the child. This committee also noted the importance of building on children's existing knowledge, through meaningful experiences and meaningful language, rather than on isolated skill development; the importance of the inclusion of language and cultural aspects relevant to individual children; and the importance of helping families to understand literacy development and ways it can be enhanced. In addition, the committee recommended the development of skills within natural environments. A curriculum that combines play and storybooks can provide such a natural environment, as both are "natural" to children. They also noted that well-known stories provide children with a sense of control and confidence. In *Read, Play, and Learn!*, repetition of various forms of the story and child participation in the development of fun activities motivates children to apply concepts.

Many of the storybooks in *Read, Play, and Learn!* on which the modules are based involve predictable patterns of words or sounds that can be written on paper or on interactive charts so that the children can combine seeing and hearing the letters and sounds. This curriculum reinforces the children's opportunities to learn by exposing the children to these sound games across many contexts and at many times through the day. Phonemic awareness can be incorporated into storytime; the sensory area; dramatic play; the literacy center; motor activities involving singing, dancing, and fingerplays; and in oral-motor activities prior to snack. Children can be encouraged to listen and differentiate sounds, make rhymes, follow rhythms, and sequence sound patterns all as part of the play activities related to the storybooks. Thus, varied occasions for practice within motivating experiences are provided. Rather than sitting in a group and practicing phonemic games, you, the facilitator, can incorporate sound play and phonemic practice across all of the areas and activities in the modules. This also allows teachers to make modifications for the ability levels of individual children. The naturalistic inclusion of both functional and phonemic awareness of print provides a foundation for emerging literacy. In the modules included in *Read, Play, and Learn!*, suggestions are provided for how to incorporate each of the following strategies.

Involve the Children in Reading the Story Each Day

Each module begins with your reading and discussing the story and progresses to the children having a larger and larger role in the sharing of the story each day as the weeks progress. The children's participation involves helping "read" the story through anticipating or retelling parts of the story; identifying key characters, actions, and so forth in the pictures; remembering and restating key phrases or words; pretending to read various sections (or, for some children, actually reading sections); and discussing the vocabulary, feelings, and meaning of events in the story. This process allows you to present key concepts and relate the story ideas to the children's experiences. At the same time, it allows children to remember and use these concepts in a meaningful way each day, to practice predicting and making inferences, and to develop the ability to sequence and express ideas.

Facilitate the Children's Dramatization of the Story

Dramatization of the story enables children to understand specific vocabulary terms and express their feelings and thoughts about the story in an enjoyable way. Children who are unable to verbally express their knowledge can demonstrate their understanding through role playing. Inclusion of story-related and literacy-based props serves as a means for prompting the memory of actions and words, learning story sequences, and reinforcing print meaning and function. Dramatization also develops cooperative social skills, problem solving, and the ability to co-ordinate actions with peers. Thus, for example, when dramatizing the story of *Picking Apples & Pumpkins*, the children can be prompted to remember the story sequence by seeing the wagon and following the signs and arrows to the pumpkin patch and apple orchard. They can be motivated to play with money and write out receipts at the cash register. In addition, they will need to organize roles and determine actions and interactions related to or deriving from and expanding on the story.

Encourage Expression Through Art and Other Visual and Tactile Projects

Art and other visual and tactile projects enable children to symbolize their thoughts nonverbally. At the same time, these playful efforts can develop fine motor skills, representational abilities, and sharing. The addition of written labels and descriptions provides children with supplementary opportunities for storytelling and seeing their words in print. The children who make a collage of soft, fluffy, prickly, scratchy, or sticky objects as related to *A Porcupine Named Fluffy* are learning concepts, categorizing, practicing fine motor skills, and managing visuospatial relationships as they play.

Promote Experimentation Through Science Projects

Concepts of *one-to-one correspondence, sequencing of events, numeration, measurement, comparison,* and *classification* can be learned through science and math experimentations with concepts related to the storybooks. Thus, a book such as *The Snowy Day* can provide the impetus for measurement of ice and snow, experimentation with melting, charting of the weather, and so forth.

Encourage Assertion of Ideas
Through Song, Dance, and Movement

Verbal and nonverbal "languages" (e.g., song, dance, movement) allow children to memorize, sequence, imitate, practice balance and coordination, and express feelings and representations related to the storybook's theme. For example, the book *The Rainbow Fish* may provide the inspiration for pairing of peers in song and dance to the song "The More We Get Together." Gross motor movements, finger-plays, and modeling of actions can be incorporated.

Assist Children in Putting Their Own Ideas
on Paper or Hearing Their Ideas Read Back to Them

The storybooks in **Read, Play, and Learn!** not only provide a model of how ideas can be put on paper, but they also provide a catalyst for children to put their own pictures and ideas on paper. The children can be helped to express their ideas in many forms—through pictures, drawings, stamps, symbols, printed words, and dictations as well as many others. For example, the book *Friends* may inspire the children to want to create their own book of pictures of their friends, with names and descriptions dictated to you or printed or stamped on the page. Children can then "read" to their parents or peers, allowing them to practice the process of associating pictures with specific words and matching their oral language to print on the page.

Relate the Concepts in the Story
to Real Experiences and to Other Stories

Events in the storybooks can be related to events in the children's lives, even if the stories are based on fantasy characters. Thus, the children may assist you in reading *The Knight and the Dragon* and then act out the events in the story guided by written words (e.g., "Dragon's Cave," "Knight's Castle") and pictures to stimulate the children to remember the events of the story and relate the cave and castle to their own homes and animals' homes. They may create a restaurant like the knight and the dragon did. They may experiment with how tools can be used for more than one purpose, such as how the shield is used as a serving tray in the story. They may sing songs and make up dances about fighting and making friends. They may make up their own stories and dictate them to an adult. The opportunities for vocabulary expansion, concept development, interaction, and problem solving are innumerable if the children are excited about the adventures brought to life in the story. Your role is to ensure that the storybook, props, classroom activities, and experiences are tied to the children's experiences of fighting, making friends, cooperating, and sharing. The story provides a safe medium for exploring feelings related to these concepts.

A HOLISTIC MODEL

As can be seen from the research and discussion presented in this chapter, there is no need to dichotomize play and literacy, developmental and preacademic approaches, or whole language and phonemics. All of these words imply both content and process and may define specific approaches. By careful planning, all can be integrated into a holistic model for early education. A transdisciplinary play-based storybook curriculum, as presented in the *Read, Play, and Learn!* modules, offers just such an opportunity.

REFERENCES

Adams, M.J., Foorman, B.R., Lundberg, I., & Beeler, T.D. (1998). *Phonemic awareness in young children: A classroom curriculum.* Baltimore: Paul H. Brookes Publishing Co.

Blachman, B.A. (1991). Getting ready to learn: Learning how print maps to speech. In J.F. Kavanagh (Ed.), *The language continuum: From infancy to literacy* (pp. 41–62). Parkton, MD: York Press.

Bronfenbrenner, U. (1979). Toward an experimental ecology of human development. *American Psychologist, 32,* 513–531.

Children's Defense Fund. (1997). *The state of America's children: 1995.* Washington, DC: Author.

Christie, J.F., & Enz, B. (1992). The effects of literacy play interventions on preschoolers' play patterns and literacy development. *Early Education and Development, 3*(3), 205–220.

Early Childhood and Literacy Development Committee of the International Reading Association. (1986). Joint statement on literacy development and pre-first grade. *Reading Teacher, 39*(8), 819–821.

Edwards, C., Gandini, L., & Forman, G. (1995). *The hundred languages of children: The Reggio Emilia approach to early childhood education.* Greenwich, CT: Ablex Publishing Corp.

Garvey, C. (1977). *Play.* Cambridge, MA: Harvard University Press.

International Reading Association. (1990). *Literacy development and early childhood (Preschool through grade 3): A joint statement of concerns about practices in prefirst grade reading instruction and recommendations for improvement.* Newark, DE: Author.

International Reading Association & National Association for the Education of Young Children. (1998). Learning to read and write: Developmentally appropriate practices for young children: Joint position statement by the International Reading Association (IRA) and the National Association for the Education of Young Children (NAEYC). *Young Children, 53*(4), 30–46.

Johnson, J.E., Christie, J.F., & Yawkey, T.D. (1987). *Play and early childhood development.* New York: HarperCollins.

Kaplan-Sanoff, M., Parker, S., & Zuckerman, B. (1991). Poverty and early childhood development: What do we know, and what should we do? *Infants and Young Children, 4*(1), 68–76.

Katims, D.S. (1994). Emergence of literacy in preschool children with disabilities. *Learning Disability Quarterly, 17*(1), 58–69.

King-DeBaun, P. (1990). *Storytime: Stories, symbols and emergent literacy activities for young, special needs children.* Solana Beach, CA: Mayer and Johnson Company.

Light, J., & Kelford-Smith, A. (1993). The home literacy experiences of preschoolers who use augmentative communication systems and of their non-disabled peers. *Augmentative and Alternative Communication, 9,* 10–25.

Linder, T.W. (1993a). *Transdisciplinary play-based assessment: A functional approach to working with young children* (Rev. ed.). Baltimore: Paul H. Brookes Publishing Co.

Linder, T.W. (1993b). *Transdisciplinary play-based intervention: Guidelines for developing a meaningful curriculum for young children.* Baltimore: Paul H. Brookes Publishing Co.

Marvin, C. (1994). Home literacy experiences of preschool children with single and multiple disabilities. *Topics in Early Childhood Special Education, 14*(4), 436–454.

McCord, S. (1995). *The storybook journey: Pathways to literacy through story and play.* Englewood Cliffs, NJ: Merrill.

Morrow, L.M. (1997*). Literacy development in the early years: Helping children read and write* (3rd ed.). Needham Heights, MA: Allyn & Bacon.

Neuman, S., & Roskos, K. (1991). Peers as literacy informants: A description of young children's literacy conversations in play. *Early Childhood Research Quarterly, 6*(2), 233–248.

New, R.S. (1994). Culture, child development, and developmentally appropriate practices: Teachers as collaborative researchers. In B.L. Mallory & R.S. New (Eds.), *Diversity & developmentally appropriate practice: Challenges for early childhood education* (pp. 65–83). New York: Teachers College Press.

Ollila, L.O., & Mayfield, M.L. (1992). *Emerging literacy: Preschool, kindergarten, and primary years.* Needham Heights, MA: Allyn & Bacon.

Piaget, J. (1962). *Play, dreams, and imitation in childhood.* New York: W.W. Norton.

Routman, R. (1996). *Literacy at the crossroads.* Portsmouth, NH: Heinemann.

Scarborough, H.S., Dobrich, W., & Hager, M. (1991). Preschool literacy experience and later reading achievement. *Journal of Learning Disabilities, 24*(8), 508–511.

Schickedanz, J.A. (1994). *More than ABC's: The early stages of reading and writing.* Washington, DC: National Association for the Education of Young Children.

Schons, M.K. (1996). *Development and validation of locally derived preschool curriculum-based early literacy and math measures.* Unpublished doctoral dissertation, University of Colorado, Denver.

Snow, C.E., Burns, M.S., & Griffin, P. (Eds.). (1998). *Preventing reading difficulties in young children by the Committee on the Prevention of Reading Difficulties in Young Children.* Washington, DC: National Academy of Sciences.

Van Hoorn, J., Nourot, P., Scales, B., Alward, K. (1993). *Play at the center of the curriculum.* New York: Macmillan.

Vygotsky, L. (1978). *Mind in society.* Cambridge, MA: Harvard University Press.

Wagner, R., Torgesen, J.K., & Rashotte, C.A. (1994). Development of reading-related phonological processing abilities: New evidence of bi-directional causality from a latent variable longitudinal study. *Developmental Psychology, 30,* 73–87.

Watkins, R.V. (1996). Natural literacy: Theory and practice for preschool intervention programs. *Topics in Early Childhood Special Education, 16,* 191–212.

Wishon, P., Crabtree, K., & Jones, M. (1998). *Curriculum for the primary years: An integrative approach.* Upper Saddle River, NJ: Prentice Hall.

Woodcock, R.W., & Johnson, M.B. (1989). *Woodcock-Johnson psychoeducational battery–Revised.* Allen, TX: DLM.

Chapter 3

GETTING YOUR CLASSROOM READY

As you know by now, **Read, Play, and Learn!**® is made up of instructional modules that are based on popular children's storybooks. After you select a module, you will be using it each day for 2, or possibly 3, weeks, depending on your calendar for the year. As described in this chapter, each day will start out with a reading (and often also a dramatization) of the story, after which children are encouraged to engage in a variety of play situations and activities related to the story at different centers in the classroom. These multiple experiences are designed to foster domain-specific (cognitive, social-emotional, communication and language, and sensorimotor) skill development, while fostering emerging literacy skills. The children's acquisition and generalization of knowledge and skills are generally supported. This chapter shows you how to set up your classroom and to schedule your day. It then discusses how you and your team can get started with your first use of the **Read, Play, and Learn!** modules and facilitate participation by everyone involved.

CLASSROOM LAYOUT

The classroom for a transdisciplinary play-based curriculum (TPBC), like **Read, Play, and Learn!,** must be inviting and solicit the active participation of all children in the selection of activities and materials. When using **Read, Play, and Learn!** you will want to arrange your room in centers and areas that you modify as the weeks progress and as the stories change. Depending on the size of the room, the number of children in the class, and the individual needs of the children, the number and type of centers may vary. All of the centers will need to include the appropriate adaptive devices to enable children with disabilities to participate. Toys, games, and materials in each area will change depending on the story.

Areas/Centers

Depending on the space available, the story, and the planned play activities, you will want to vary the number, arrangement, and type of centers or areas you provide. *Centers* are usually localized to a table or specifically delineated space, whereas *areas* are usually more flexibly interpreted and designed around the classroom. The centers and areas that you could set up include the following:

Reading the Story

Your first activity every day, Reading the Story, requires a large group area in which the story can be read while all of the children are gathered around. Consider keeping in this area other books related to the current *Read, Play, and Learn!* theme, interactive word charts or storyboards, a tape recorder for listening to the story, a slide projector, and versions of the books that have been adapted for use by children with special needs. (See, for example, the description of how to make adapted books for children with visual impairments in Chapter 6.) You might want to have mats and pillows handy to make the area a comfortable and relaxing place for listening.

You will find that interactive word charts or storyboards help the children associate print with the spoken word. These word charts or storyboards can be made from flannel or felt, magnetic boards, large pieces of cardboard, and so forth. You can decide how you would like to have them available to the children. If you are using a flannel board, for example, you could attach words that make up a sentence with Velcro to the board. Some children may be able to point to or place familiar words, or you can place them as you read the story. You can also point to the words or sentences as you read them from the book. Children love interaction; therefore, any kind of interactive word chart will foster their literacy skills.

Dramatic Play: Theme Area

Most days, especially in the first week of a module, after Reading the Story, you and your class will want to reenact the story. Designate space for a Dramatic Play: Theme Area because it will be one of the most active spots in your classroom. Across the days that you use one module, the story will be reenacted in numerous ways. In the beginning, when the story is still new to the children, you and the other team members provide a model for an action sequence of three or four events, along with a short script to act out. The events should be simple, offer an opportunity to use both story and literacy props, and consist of a short series of actions. In this way, all children in the class can be involved in an action, a sequence of actions, or a sequence of events in the story. As you progress with the module, the children will begin to embellish and change the reenactment; at this point, children can choose to go to the Dramatic Play: Theme Area on a given day or to skip it in favor of another center or area.

Props and materials in the Dramatic Play: Theme Area will change frequently. Call on your team members' imaginations, and have fun. For example, you could arrange the area to look like a bridge in the module based on *The Three Billy Goats Gruff* or transform a large portion of the area into the various settings at an airport for the module based on *First Flight*. A House Area is frequently part of the Dramatic Play: Theme Area, as in the module based on *The Little Old Lady Who Was Not Afraid of Anything*, where woods, a garden, and a house are needed, or in the module on *Somebody and the Three Blairs*. Although some curricula emphasize the use of the House Area as a continuing center, in **Read, Play, and Learn!** the House Area is viewed as an area that tends to promote routine, rather limited play experiences, such as cooking, if it is not used thoughtfully. Use the House Area only as a center if it relates in some way to the story and can be modified with props that encourage creative expression and story-specific play sequences.

Advocates of "discovery learning" may balk at the demonstration of a sequence and the use of a script as a model, but the developers of the **Read, Play, and Learn!** modules have found that this process enables *all* children to 1) become more involved sooner in dramatic play; 2) remember the story sequence more easily; 3) use vocabulary and concepts relevant to the story; and 4) participate, even if they have a disability. Some of the modules have a sample script for you to use. The script is short and is typically a few phrases taken directly from the story or modified from the story. For example, in the module based on *The Kissing Hand*, the script is only seven lines long, but it encompasses the heart of the story. (Chester, the raccoon, cries and says he does not want to go to school. His mother responds that there will be things at school that will be fun and says she has a secret for him. When Chester asks, "What secret?" his mother tells him about the Kissing Hand. She kisses the palm of his hand and tells him to hold it against his cheek whenever he feels lonely. Chester kisses his mother's palm; says, "I love you"; and goes off to school.) This story simplification allows the children to reenact the key elements of the story. Within a day, children are embellishing the story and adding words, phrases, lines, and new actions to the dramatization.

Literacy Center

Children need time to explore the books repeatedly by themselves, and a Literacy Center is an ideal place for this. This center will provide children with important opportunities to study the pictures, turn the pages, notice the print on the pages, and perhaps see a recurring picture or sequence. The Literacy Center should include a table that will seat up to four children. Locate it near the area for Reading the Story. You will want a storage cart or storage space for literacy materials, including pencils, markers, a stapler, letter tiles, stamps and stamp pads, magazines with pictures and large print, paper for experience charts, storyboards, books, and frequently asked-for words or words related to the story written on large cards. The Literacy Center can overlap with the Reading the Story area so that a larger, quiet area is also available that contains pillows, puppets, and a flannel board, providing the children a comfortable area on the floor to "reread" or retell the story.

Plan on having an adult (parent or staff) make an audio recording of each book you use; place each tape and a tape recorder the children can operate in the Literacy Center. Then, children can return to the area to listen to and "read" the story again for themselves, with or without assistance. The tape will enable children to independently practice the process of reading, telling a story in sequence, and possibly matching the words to the pictures in the book.

If you can have several copies of the storybook available, more children may be encouraged to "read" the story, and some children may look at the story and discuss it together. An additional copy of the book may also be purchased, taken apart, the pages laminated, and then reassembled in a binder with pages that are easier to turn. This version can also be used in a variety of literacy games and activities. If possible, a computer should be included along with a variety of software that can be integrated with the different storybooks and themes. (Refer to the software lists in the More Suggestions section at the end of each module.)

Science and Math Center

The Science and Math Center should contain a space for measuring, writing, and concocting. It also needs storage for materials, such as math manipulatives, counters, rulers, string and fasteners, containers for sorting, and magnifying glasses, as well as space for growing plants and nurturing live animals. It is helpful to have a computer in the Science and Math Center. If necessary, the computer used in the Literacy Center can be placed between the two centers.

Art Area

Locate the Art Area near a sink to allow for quick cleanup. Both an easel and a flat table surface should be available to allow for adaptations for children's different ability levels. Besides allowing for painting on various surfaces, the Art Area can be used for various art projects with three-dimensional materials, such as clay. Provide an art cart or storage area adjoining this area. Additional areas, such as floor space, wall space, or chalkboards, can also be considered to be part of the Art Area.

Sensory Area

The Sensory Area is included to ensure that children experience a variety of sensory experiences. So, you will want it to contain a variety of sensory materials. A sand and water table can be used for exploring various tactile materials; small tubs filled with beans, rice, or other items provide sensory play with diverse textures; and numerous noisemaking devices, including a tape recorder, record or CD player, and musical instruments, give children opportunities to experiment with sounds. This area could also have containers with different scents and special materials (e.g., Lightboxes for children with visual impairments). (Lightboxes are lighted boxes on which materials can be placed so that the objects, color, shape, and size can be more clearly perceived. Other special materials for children with hearing loss or visual impairments are described in Chapters 5 and 6.)

Motor Area

Motor activities are typically integrated into the Dramatic Play: Theme Area; therefore, the Motor Area should be located nearby. For example, a climbing structure could be incorporated into the airport as a control tower for the module based on *First Flight*. It is wise to arrange the room to preclude large, open spaces that encourage running. If large spaces are needed, such as for a ramp and a belly board for "sledding" in the module on *The Snowy Day*, then the space can be adjusted as needed.

Floor Play

The Floor Play area gives children the chance to play on the floor with blocks, miniature dramatic play scenarios, manipulatives, puzzles, and other items for a particular story. Floor play, more so than table play, encourages social interaction among children. Some children will prefer to play on the floor rather than at a table, and some children may need to be positioned on the floor (e.g., in a sidelying position) to enable them to interact with toys and materials. This area needs to be at the side or in a corner of the room to minimize the traffic caused when children move from one area to another and to prevent children from tripping over toys or each other. This is the area where a miniature scenario for the selected storybook can be set up and used for story reenactment throughout the module. The children will add to the miniature scenario, which usually contains small figures, characters, toys, and other items related to the story, throughout most of the modules.

Table Play

Just as some children will interact best on the floor, others will be able to play more easily seated in a stable position with their feet on the floor so that their hands can be free to manipulate objects. Table Play can incorporate the same type of activities as the Floor Play area, with the exception of large block play, and may also include some art activities or craft projects.

Outdoor Play

Outdoor Play can include large objects, such as slides, swings, and climbing equipment. This area can be used as both an extension of the indoor Motor Area and the Dramatic Play: Theme Area so that large motor games and dramatic play activities can be done outdoors.

Woodworking Center (A Possible Additional Center)

Occasionally, the Woodworking Center is a fun addition to the room. In this center, children can plan, problem-solve, and manipulate tools to connect materials and form simple props to go with the storybooks. Of course, be sure that proper supervision is provided.

Snack

Snack is viewed not just as a time to feed the children but also as an important time for integrating thematic concepts, self-help skills, oral-motor skills, and conversation into the classroom. The area must be located near the sink and kitchen appliances for convenience in serving and cleaning up. A separate area is not needed for snack, as snack typically follows play in centers and the Table Play and Art Area tables may be cleaned for the snack.

Arrangement

Centers and areas are arranged so that related centers may merge at times and children can see their options as they make choices about the areas in which they wish to play. You may wish to set the House Area close to the Dramatic Play: Theme Area for some stories. For example, for the module based on *Somebody and the Three Blairs*, which primarily takes place in a house, much of the classroom converts to the rooms of a house. Other stories, such as *Night Tree*, take place in separate locations, so the house may be used for packing a picnic and the starting place for the "pick-up truck" to drive to the tree in the woods, which will be located in a different part of the room. Many of the other areas may be in more permanent locations. For example, you might place the blocks (if applicable) close to the area in which the miniature scenario is located or where the Floor Play area is laid out so that the blocks, miniature characters, cars, trucks, and so forth can be combined as needed. An area that is quiet and somewhat contained is suggested for the Reading the Story area. This area can be used for another purpose, such as a reading or music space, after the story is over. The idea is that all of the areas are flexible and can be modified for the purposes of the stories. The children will look forward to coming in every 2 weeks and seeing what new surprises await them. Keeping the location of some centers somewhat constant will provide the needed continuity for children, whereas the variations will add the spice! The diagram in Figure 1 illustrates one layout that you might find works well for you.

PROPS, TOYS, AND MATERIALS

Story props, such as costumes and objects related to the story, can be placed in many of the centers and areas. Literacy props, such as notepads, receipt books, and blank checks, as well as pictures and materials relating to the story, also need to be visible and accessible to the children as they enter the room. Materials in the centers can be placed to entice children to explore their usage. Care should be taken, however, that the room is not overstimulating and that quiet, unobtrusive areas are available.

The toys and materials within the centers will also be modified, not just for each module but also within the 2-week module. The room should acquire the personality of the children as the activities progress each week. The number of props as well as children's projects, murals, and artwork will grow throughout the module and will vary depending on the composition and individuality of the children. Again, it is important that some fundamental elements of the room and the props remain constant throughout the 2 weeks so that the children can comprehend the nature of the story and the centers related to the story. For example, during the module based on *The Kissing Hand*, the playground area might remain in the same spot but contain changing motor equipment (e.g., a platform swing, a Sit 'n Spin, a rocking boat, a climbing structure and slide, a trampoline, and other equipment could be added or subtracted after several days of use). This gradual shifting of materials allows children to practice and have fun repeating activities, as children love to do; but interest in new activities and practicing newly acquired skills are enhanced by the novelty of the changing toys and materials.

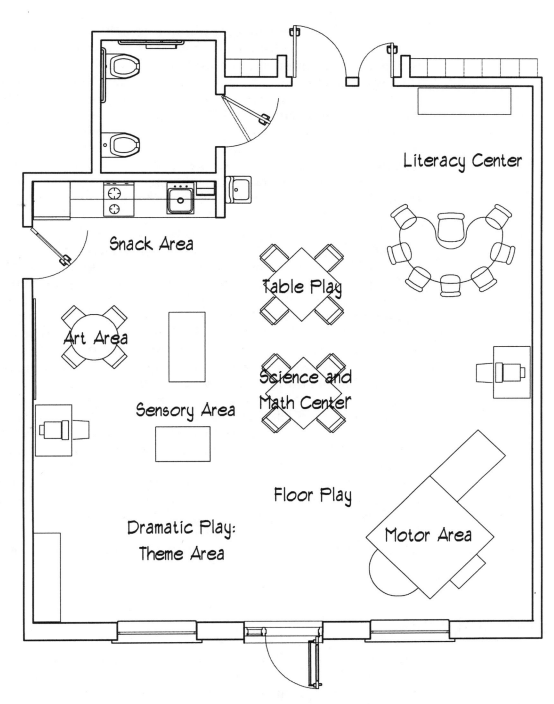

Literacy Center

Snack Area

Table Play

Art Area

Sensory Area

Science and Math Center

Floor Play

Dramatic Play: Theme Area

Motor Area

Figure 1.   A typical preschool classroom layout. (Layout courtesy of Mark Rodgers, University Architect, University of Denver and Andrews & Anderson, P.C., Golden, Colorado.)

Placement of the materials within a center is also important. A simple lazy Susan in the center of the table may encourage children to share materials and may make it easier for children with motor disabilities to have access to the items. Chairs tightly grouped can encourage communication as well as provide structure to an activity. For example, if an activity is limited to three children, placing three chairs at the table can help children monitor the availability of the center for use. If only one child is interested in a board game for two or more children, suggesting to the child that he or she place extra pieces on the board so that they are visible to peers can encourage someone to join the activity (along with a verbal invitation). The use of props that require more than one child, such as walkie-talkies for the module based on *First Flight*, will encourage social interaction and communication.

Think about changing the placement of materials from day to day, too. In the module based on *A Porcupine Named Fluffy*, the game "Hungry, Hungry Hippo" can be played both on the floor and at a table. This requires children to use different positions to play. For some children, motor issues may prohibit their playing well on the floor, so other Table Play options will enable them to participate. Adaptive equipment and modifications should always be considered to maximize the participation of all of the children. Switch toys are popular with all children, so the addition of a switch to a battery-operated animal (e.g., a pig in the module based on *Friends)* will allow children at the sensorimotor level (see page 9) or those with motor impairments to share in the activity and to cooperate with their more capable peers who also want a chance to operate the toy!

You may have determined by now that having a storage space for props, toys, and materials is important. The use of large, plastic containers with lids or large boxes for each story is recommended. The items, such as miniature castles and knights, small character figures, and other props related to each story, can be stored in these containers or boxes to be used by each classroom. Each box should have a list of the materials that it contains so that all items will be returned for future use. Some items or materials will be used for numerous stories and can be stored in more generic containers. If minimal closet or cupboard space is available, the containers can be decorated so that they form an attractive divider for a center or end wall in the room.

SCHEDULE

The schedule for the day will vary from program to program depending on your needs and those of your learners. Beginning the day by reading the storybook, however, sets the tone for the day and reminds the children of the concepts and how the activities of the day are related to the events or ideas in the story. Dramatization of the story and the center experiences logically evolve out of the story reading. Each implementation team will determine the amount of time devoted to the centers, the number of centers, and the staffing of the centers for each module. This flexibility allows each classroom to add other programmatic elements they believe are important for their children. For example, Snack and Outdoor

Play are included in the modules but are not centers. These aspects of the day can be included as appropriate for your program.

For a typical half-day program (with bathroom time fit in as needed), the schedule might look similar to the following:

8:00 A.M.–8:30 A.M.
Arrival and greetings. (Let those children who are dropped off early [those who do not come on a bus] play in the Dramatic Play: Theme Area or look at books in the Literacy Center.)

8:30 A.M.–9:00 A.M.
Reading the Story. Read the storybook as a group with the involvement of the children.

9:00 A.M.–10:30 A.M.
Centers or choice time. At the beginning of a 2-week module, before the centers begin, the team members may demonstrate acting out the story for the group for the first few days. This allows the children who choose the Dramatic Play: Theme Area to have a model and a plan with which to experiment and to modify as they become more familiar with the story. Children are free to move from center to center; but the facilitators in the room are responsible for seeing that 1) the children remain interested and actively involved at the chosen centers; 2) the children are able to make the transition from one center to another so that everyone can be involved in a variety of activities and the needed developmental experiences; 3) the concepts, skills, and processes needed across all four domains (cognitive, communication and language, sensorimotor, and social-emotional) as well as emerging literacy skills are addressed each day; and 4) individualization takes place within each center for each child. Children are also engaged in the cleanup at the end of this center time. If certain centers necessitate a limited number of children, you can allocate tickets, bracelets, or a specified number of materials or toys for the maximum number of children. For highly desirable yet space-limited centers, a timer may be used to enable all of the children to have an opportunity to participate.

10:30 A.M.–11:00 A.M.
Oral-motor play and snack. This time should involve the children in the preparation and serving of the snack. (Preparation of the snack is sometimes part of the Science and Math Center, as cooking involves measuring, classifying, observing change, and so forth.) Songs and oral-motor activities are suggested in the modules. This is also a good time for conversations about the children's morning activities and experiences, news from home, and general dialogue.

11:00 A.M.–11:30 A.M.
Outdoor play. This time will be dependent on the weather, of course; it may involve individual or small-group play and can be related to the story. If playground equipment is available, supervision is critical and adaptations should be considered for children with sensory impairments or physical disabilities.

11:30 A.M.–12:00 P.M.

Book time. This time is not included as a center in the modules, but you and other team members will want to plan for a daily book time. Children individually, in pairs, or in small groups "read" books related to the theme and interact with peers and facilitators around reading at their own level of development. Having time for children to look at many books in addition to the particular storybook on which the module is based is critical. Picture books, predictable books, simple stories, and more complex books related to the module theme may be available for the children at this time. Consider using this time to read to the children; to have the children "read" their own stories or predictable books to you, another adult, or other children; and to assist the children in enhancing and generalizing their emerging literacy skills. Team members may use this time to continue to individualize for children by providing one-to-one support, by pairing peers who are at a similar level, or by involving parents or "buddies" from higher grades who come in to read to the children. At the end of each module, a list of other books related to the storybook's theme is provided. Team members may find these lists useful sources of augmentative books for book time. (Some of these books may also serve as replacements for the module storybook if it is unavailable; these titles are noted with an asterisk.)

Of course, programs that do not meet for a full half-day would adjust this sample schedule accordingly. Likewise, programs that meet all day may include a rest period and an afternoon center time, snack, book time, and/or outdoor play time. Some of the activities may remain the same, whereas others may be modified for variety. The sequence of these events can also be changed as is determined to be most workable for each program.

PLANNING AND IMPLEMENTATION

Your planning will begin with your decisions about which *Read, Play, and Learn!* modules to use. Collections 1 and 2 provide you with 16 modules designed to extend over an academic year, beginning in early September and ending in late May. Each module provides 2 weeks of activities, although enough activities are presented to extend the modules for a longer time period than 2 weeks. Assuming, however, that a 2-week break is taken in December and a 1-week break is taken in the spring, one of the modules will need to be expanded to 3 weeks. The modules have been ordered to coincide with the seasons and holidays, but you and your team are encouraged to modify this sequence as desired. If several classrooms are using the curriculum, the modules may be sequenced differently for each to allow materials to be shared.

Let's start with one module and work through the implementation process. If you are working with others, these steps should be undertaken as a team. Plan to meet at least once each week to review the upcoming week's activities.

1. **Obtain a copy of the storybook, and read the story together.** Most of the stories offer a predictable sequence, focus on a socialization principle, or revolve around a season that can become your classroom theme. Identify

and discuss the concepts from the story that you want to emphasize for the children in your classroom.

2. **Review the module's activities, and select the ones that are appropriate for your class.** The modules may be used as they are written, but it is anticipated that teams will want to add their own creative touches and ideas to each one. These individualized alterations and additions are important as they will allow your team to acquire "ownership" of the modules by adding their own distinct "signature." Furthermore, in most cases, more activities are presented than will actually be used. This overplanning is intentional so that teams can then select activities that match the interests, abilities, and educational and developmental needs of their children. To complete this selection process, work from the Planning Sheets at the beginning of each module. The sheets provide at-a-glance reference to all the suggested activities for the story. (Detailed descriptions of each activity then follow.) First, mark the centers and areas you will be using; then, select corresponding activities for as many days as your program will use the module. If you prefer, you can select just enough for a week's use of the module until you meet the following week, or you can plan the full 2 (or even 3) weeks at one meeting.

    Blank curriculum planning sheets that you can fill out (just like the completed versions in each storybook) are available in the appendix at the end of this *Teacher's Guide*. The forms provide a planning grid, with a column of boxes down the left side for listing the events of the day and/or the centers and areas to be available. The days of the week are listed across the top. When your team meets to lay out the week's activities, you can fill out these planning sheets. Within each intersecting box corresponding to the day and the center, the team writes a brief description of the play or activity that will take place. These planning sheets serve as a guide to the sequence of events for the storybook theme you are following. The planning sheets can also be photocopied to be sent home to parents so that they are aware of the activities planned for a given story.

3. **Make a tape recording of an adult reading the story.** You will want to have this available with a tape player in the Literacy Center so that children can listen to the story again on their own. You can make the recording yourself, ask another team member or a classroom volunteer, or invite a parent to do the reading. (This is a good way to have some of the parents participate in the curriculum; see Chapter 8 for details.) Read slowly for the recording, with appropriate inflection. To assist children in following the story on the audiotape, an adult may want to point out what is happening in the picture on the page and verbally indicate when to turn the page the first time that children are listening to the tape.

4. **Select a sequence of three or four actions or events within the story to act out, and prepare a simple script that the children can follow.** As described previously, this will be used in the Dramatic Play: Theme Area during the first days after a new storybook is introduced. In some modules, a script is provided for you to follow if you would like; however, you do not need to follow the provided script.

5. **Consider each center and the needs for each.** How will they be organized in relation to each other? What do you need at each location? How will they incorporate developmental and emergent literacy objectives? The following outline gives you some of the basic questions to review:

For Reading the Story:
What props are needed to support the story reading?
What visual aids (e.g., slides, word cards, enlargements) are needed?
How will all of the children be included? Are adaptations needed?
How can the materials be modified for all developmental levels?
What picture charts or other aids need to be made prior to class?
What adaptive tools or equipment are needed for individual children?
What adaptive equipment may be needed to ensure that all children can participate?

For the Dramatic Play: Theme Area:
What props are needed?
How should the center be arranged?
Where should the center be located so that other centers that integrate with it are contiguous?
What specific literacy props will be included?
Which props or materials can the children make in the Literacy Center or other centers?
How will all of the children be included? Are adaptations needed?
How can the materials be modified for all developmental levels?
What picture charts or other aids need to be made prior to class?
What adaptive tools or equipment is needed for individual children?
Do adaptations need to be made for children who are still "mouthing" items?
What adaptive equipment may be needed to ensure that all children can participate?

For the Literacy Center:
What other related books will be made available in this center?
What computer software (if any) will be used?
What materials are needed for the literacy activities?
What literacy tools (e.g., stamps, magnetic letters, felt board) will be needed?
How can the materials be modified for all developmental levels?
How will all of the children be included? Are adaptations needed?
What picture charts or other aids need to be made prior to class?
What adaptive tools or equipment is needed for individual children?
Do adaptations need to be made for children who are still "mouthing" items?
What adaptive equipment may be needed to ensure that all children can participate?

For the Science and Math Center:
What resource books will be placed in the center?
What materials and equipment are needed?

What picture charts or other aids need to be made prior to class?

What computer software (if any) will supplement the center?

How will all of the children be included? Are adaptations needed?

How can the materials be modified for all developmental levels?

What adaptive tools or equipment is needed for individual children?

Do adaptations need to be made for children who are still "mouthing" items?

What adaptive equipment may be needed to ensure that all children can participate?

For the Art Area:

What materials are needed?

What space will be needed for murals, easels, and so forth?

How and where can artwork be displayed "professionally"?

What adaptive tools or equipment is needed for individual children?

How will all of the children be included? Are adaptations needed?

How can the materials be modified for all developmental levels?

What picture charts or other aids need to be made prior to class?

Do adaptations need to be made for children who are still "mouthing" items?

What adaptive equipment may be needed to ensure that all children can participate?

For the Sensory Area:

What equipment (e.g., sensory table) or materials are needed?

Where can the materials be placed so that all children can have access to them (e.g., on the floor, on a low tray or bench, on the table)?

Do adaptations need to be made for children who are still "mouthing" items?

How will all of the children be included? Are adaptations needed?

How can the materials be modified for all developmental levels?

What picture charts or other aids need to be made prior to class?

What adaptive tools or equipment is needed for individual children?

What adaptive equipment may be needed to ensure that all children can participate?

For the Motor Area:

Where should the Motor Area be located?

What equipment will be needed?

What adaptive equipment may be needed to ensure that all children can participate?

How will all of the children be included? Are adaptations needed?

How can the materials be modified for all developmental levels?

What picture charts or other aids need to be made prior to class?

What adaptive tools or equipment is needed for individual children?

Do adaptations need to be made for children who are still "mouthing" items?

For Floor Play:

Where will the miniature scenario be placed so that it is accessible for the whole module?

What items can be used to make a miniature scenario to re-create the story?
What games or puzzles are available or are needed?
How will all of the children be included? Are adaptations needed?
How can the materials be modified for all developmental levels?
What picture charts or other aids need to be made prior to class?
What adaptive tools or equipment is needed for individual children?
Do adaptations need to be made for children who are still "mouthing" items?
What adaptive equipment may be needed to ensure that all children can participate?

For Table Play:
What puzzles, games, or, in some cases, miniature scenario figures are needed?
What picture charts are needed?
How will all of the children be included? Are adaptations needed?
How can the materials be modified for all developmental levels?
What picture charts or other aids need to be made prior to class?
What adaptive tools or equipment is needed for individual children?
Do adaptations need to be made for children who are still "mouthing" items?
What adaptive equipment may be needed to ensure that all children can participate?

For Outdoor Play:
What materials and equipment are needed?
What alternative activities or modifications can be made in case of inclement weather?
How will children with motor disabilities be included?
How will all of the children be included? Are adaptations needed?
How can the materials be modified for all developmental levels?
What adaptive tools or equipment is needed for individual children?
Do adaptations need to be made for children who are still "mouthing" items?
What adaptive equipment may be needed to ensure that all children can participate?

For Snack:
Are any children allergic to any of the planned snacks?
What adaptive utensils will be needed for specific children?
What songs and fingerplays can be incorporated?
Do any children have nutritional restrictions?

6. **Discuss modifications or activities for individual children or small groups of children.** More information on the sensorimotor, functional, and symbolic levels of understanding and learning, introduced to you in Chapter 1, is provided in Chapter 4; and other chapters give you tips for children with physical disabilities or sensory impairments. Among the special characteristics of ***Read, Play, and Learn!*** are its flexible design and specific guidelines that help you tailor the curriculum to what each child in your classroom is ready for. Adaptations are also described in each module.

7. **Assign individual team members to be responsible for obtaining the various items.**

8. **Determine which team member(s) will be responsible for the various centers and which centers can be combined into zones.** *Zones* are a way of grouping the centers and areas according to which team member or classroom volunteer will be providing oversight for the children at those centers. Think about combining centers that do not require a lot of adult supervision with another that does need adult assistance. In this way, one team member can cover more than one center or area.

9. **Establish a schedule for your program's use of the curriculum, taking into account the number of hours in your program day and the number of days per week you see the children.** If, for example, a whole day program is offered, which centers will be available in the morning and which will be available in the afternoon? Refer to the sample schedule provided earlier in this chapter.

10. **Working from the sample letter to be sent home to parents (or primary caregiver) provided in each module, individualize the letter for your program and for the families who will receive it.** More ideas for corresponding with families are included in the next section in this chapter and in Chapter 8.

11. **Schedule your next team meeting, confirm your starting date for the module, and . . .** *Read, Play, and Learn!*

A CURRICULUM BUILT ON INTERACTIONS

The interchange among team members, the interactions between team members and children, the communication among children, and the communication between team members and family members as well as between children and their parents create the philosophical and functional foundation of the ***Read, Play, and Learn!*** storybook curriculum. The stories and activities offered in the collections of modules will not be used to their best advantage until all potential participants are interacting fully.

Interchange Among Team Members

Although the modules presented in ***Read, Play, and Learn!*** have had the input of a team, perhaps including a teacher, a speech-language pathologist, an occupational therapist, and a psychologist, as well as consultation from a reading consultant, your team needs to adapt and adjust the basic ideas presented in the curriculum to match the needs of the individual children in your classroom. Team composition will vary from program to program; and activities may be deleted, added, or modified as needed. Team members should discuss and alter the fundamental skeleton provided in each module according to the needs of the children in their classroom. The input of team members, representing disciplines relevant to the development of children in the class, is critical to effective implementation of the curriculum. As each team member discusses how modifications in the environment, communication strategies, materials, and so forth will be needed, the other team members will incorporate these ideas into their understanding of what the children need. In other words, a transdisciplinary discussion of each module as it pertains to individual classrooms and children will enable all team members to have more effective interactions with the children. All team members need to become more sensitive to and knowledgeable about children in relation to their 1) families, culture, and communities; and 2) developmental levels, skills, and challenges or special needs in order to address appropriate goals, select effective strategies, and coordinate with the relevant family or community members.

Interactions Between Team Members and Children

The nature of the interactions between team members and children is extremely important to meeting the primary goals of the ***Read, Play, and Learn!*** curriculum (see page 6). The adults in the classroom, regardless of whether they are teachers, therapists, specialists, assistants, or volunteers, play several different roles in the classroom (McCord, 1995). They are observers and assessors of development, skills, and learning style. They are facilitators, playmates, and providers of materials and experiences. They are models and motivators. They are conversationalists and extenders. They are adapters and supporters. To fulfill all of these roles, adults need to follow several basic principles of interaction (Bricker, Pretti-Frontczak, & McComas, 1998; Linder, 1993; McCollum & Bair, 1994): 1) Children need to be allowed, whenever possible, to lead their play; 2) adults need to know developmental sequences and variations and be able to "bump children up" in their play, communication, and emerging literacy skills through understanding developmental sequences, individualizing tasks, modeling, and supporting progress; 3) adults need to read the children's cues and behaviors as meaningful communication and respond to the temperament, preferences, and capabilities of the children; and 4) adults need to build on the children's initiations. Using Vygotsky's (1978) concept of the *zone of proximal development,* you should offer just as much challenge and support as will keep the child motivated and interested and provide the next learning steps. If each adult is capable of shifting roles as needed and using the basic principles of interaction, scaffolding, and structured guidance for the child only as needed, then the classroom will become a highly motivating, yet challenging, environment that will enable the goals of the curriculum to be met.

The increasingly diverse classroom necessitates the use of a wide range of interaction strategies. On a continuum that stretches from child-centered to teacher-directed strategies, teachers must try to gauge just the right amount of support so that a child is able to maximally engage with the objects, people, and events in the environment in order to achieve developmental progress. The goal should be to match the learning style and most effective interaction patterns with each child, integrating knowledge of familial, cultural, or linguistic expectations into the developmental observations of the child's needs. You and your team members need to be prepared to make critical judgments about 1) the skill level of the child; 2) the amounts of direction, modeling, prompting, and reinforcing that are effective; 3) the type of cues to which the child best responds; 4) the amount of guided assistance; and 5) the type of positioning, material, and environmental adaptations that are required to enhance learning and developmental progress (Mallory, 1994).

Communication Among Children

The classroom engaging in a transdisciplinary play-based curriculum like *Read, Play, and Learn!* will not always be quiet. One of the major goals, after all, is to maximize social learning by promoting communication. Through your environmental structuring of the play centers and areas in your classroom and by prompting, modeling, and reinforcing, you will help children interact with peers, develop prosocial behaviors, and enjoy associative and cooperative play. Try, with the other adults in the room, to shift the usually dominant adult–child communication patterns to child–child communication patterns. You want your classroom to be one of dialogue and discourse, not question and response. You will be rewarded with more positive social and emotional development as children tell their ideas to others through words and actions, through verbal and nonverbal means, and through both written and spoken symbols that can be shared and interpreted by others.

Communication Between Team Members and Family Members

An important premise of *Read, Play, and Learn!* is that what is begun at school can be supported and expanded at home. In addition, values and goals that are important to families can be supported and expanded at school. This kind of mutual appreciation of the goals of the school and the values of the home helps establish a learning partnership. Communication between families and team members is critical. The team needs to understand the family members' perspective on 1) what the child brings to the classroom in terms of literacy exposure, behavioral experiences, and understanding of the world; 2) the level and type of support they desire and believe is effective for their child's development and academic learning; 3) how they read and interpret their child's behaviors, temperament, preferences, and capabilities; and 4) what interaction patterns and supports are most effective for sustaining the child's interest and motivation for learning. Individual differences in family values and expectations will emerge. York (1991, as cited in Villarruel, Imig, & Kostelnik, 1995) noted that cultural differences influence all elements of child rearing, including age-related expectations of children; concern over children's acquiring certain skills by a particular age; sleep patterns and bedtime routines; children's roles and responsibilities within the family; toilet training; diet and mealtime behavior; discipline and child guidance techniques; how adults talk to children; how adults show affection to children; importance of gender identity and sex roles; dress and hair care; illness and approaches to cures and remedies; use of supplemental child care; acceptance of, attachment of meaning to, and response to crying; and expectation concerning children's attachment to adults and separation from adults. The more knowledge you have in these areas, the more you will be able to avoid misinterpreting behaviors and to successfully individualize the child's learning experiences.

Communication Between Children and Their Parents

Communication between children and their parents increases the family's understanding of the learning that is taking place in school and enables parents to reinforce their children's efforts. Share with families as much as possible what is happening in your classroom. To start, families can be notified ahead of time about the upcoming books you will be using. In most cases, the books on which the storybook modules are based can be purchased in paperback and/or are available in neighborhood libraries.

You will find sample letters to send to parents or caregivers in each module; they are easy to adapt to fit your program's needs and the books you have selected. Each week, plan on sending home a copy of the curriculum planning sheets (modified by the team to reflect your classroom) with a letter explaining the targeted goals and activities. Include the vocabulary words and concepts that you will be working on during the week, and encourage parents to use these words, too.

Family members can also become involved in many ways with the modules right in the classroom; from reading books onto an audiotape for the classroom to contributing materials from home or participating in the classroom, parents can be encouraged to be facilitators. Some of the play that occurs at school can then be enjoyed again at home with parents and other family members. The more the parents know about what you are doing at school, the more they have to talk about with their child.

Chapter 8 has photocopiable handouts for parents. Send them home one at a time or all at once as a booklet. Besides introducing the *Read, Play, and Learn!* curriculum, they give great tips to parents and families on how to read with their child, how to make their home "literacy rich," and how to make the reading both fun and educational.

The goals of the curriculum will be more fully recognized if participation is fun for families as well as for children and staff. Remember, *Read, Play, and Learn!* is a dynamic process that should fully involve parents and children as *integral members* of your team.

CONCLUSION

The discussion of the classroom environments, as outlined in this chapter, is based on research from many diverse arenas, including studies on typical child development, development in children with disabilities, efficacy of different types of early education programs, parent–child and teacher–child interaction, the development of literacy skills, and studies on children from backgrounds of poverty. *Read, Play, and Learn!* integrates the findings from this research into the content and processes advocated by a TPBC. The classroom environment is a visible expression of the beliefs of the program. Great care should be taken to ensure that this environment reflects your desired program philosophy.

In the next chapters, you will learn more about how the team can best facilitate the play and learning of each child within the classroom by recognizing the child's level of understanding and learning (sensorimotor, functional, or symbolic), how the modules help provide instruction across the developmental domains (cognitive, social-emotional, communication and language, and sensorimotor) and for emergent literacy, and how the team can introduce adaptations for children with hearing loss or visual impairments. To promote true transdisciplinary understanding, ask all of your team members to read these next chapters, too.

REFERENCES

Bricker, D., Pretti-Frontczak, K., & McComas, N. (1998). *An activity-based approach to early intervention* (2nd ed.). Baltimore: Paul H. Brookes Publishing Co.

Linder, T.W. (1993). *Transdisciplinary play-based intervention: Guidelines for developing a meaningful curriculum for young children.* Baltimore: Paul H. Brookes Publishing Co.

Mallory, B.L. (1994). Inclusive policy, practice, and theory for young children with developmental differences. In B.L. Mallory & R.S. New (Eds.), *Diversity & developmentally appropriate practice: Challenges for early childhood education* (pp. 44–61). New York: Teachers College Press.

McCollum, J.A., & Bair, H. (1994). Research in parent–child interaction: Guidance to developmentally appropriate practice for young children with disabilities. In B.L. Mallory & R.S. New (Eds.), *Diversity & developmentally appropriate practice: Challenges for early childhood education* (pp. 84–106). New York: Teachers College Press.

McCord, S. (1995). *The storybook journey: Pathways to literacy through story and play.* Upper Saddle River, NJ: Prentice-Hall.

Villarruel, F.A., Imig, D.R., & Kostelnik, M.J. (1995). Diverse families. In E.E. García & B. McLaughlin (Eds.), with B. Spodek & O.N. Saracho, *Meeting the challenge of linguistic and cultural diversity in early childhood education* (pp. 103–124). New York: Teachers College Press.

Vygotsky, L. (1978). *Mind in society.* Cambridge, MA: Harvard University Press.

Chapter 4

LEVELS OF LEARNING
AND DOMAINS OF DEVELOPMENT

In addition to the recommended structural arrangements and scheduling for your room described in Chapter 3, **Read, Play, and Learn!**® offers two conceptual frameworks that help you facilitate skill development and learning for all children in your classroom. Both are described in this chapter.

The first framework, briefly introduced in Chapter 1, helps you identify the *level of understanding and learning* for which each child is ready. These levels are not meant to delineate specific chronological ages, but they do help, in a more informal and practical way, to classify how a child typically is engaging the environment and employing thought processes. Let's study these three levels in more detail:

1. *Sensorimotor:* At this first level of development, children are primarily concerned with object exploration. They are creating concrete meanings through physical manipulation of the environment around them. This stage is also called the *exploratory* level. Typically, children at the sensorimotor level are 18 months of age or younger.

2. *Functional:* At this second level, children are exploring simple combinations and functional uses of objects. They are listening and watching, imitating, relating, and beginning to sequence ideas and actions. This level coincides roughly with ages 18 months to 3 years.

3. *Symbolic:* At this third level, children are gaining the ability to represent their world through diverse symbolic means. They are interested in fantasy play, storytelling, music, dance, drawing, and print. Children at the symbolic level are typically 3 years of age or older.

The second framework focuses on *developmental domains*. The domains distinguished in **Read, Play, and Learn!** are the following:

• *Cognitive:* Skills in this domain include sequential thinking, classification, one-to-one correspondence, representation through drawing and writing, and problem solving.

• *Communication and language:* These skills include not only a child's ability to express him- or herself (expressive communication) and understand what is communicated (receptive communication) but also the pragmatic ability to engage in communicative interactions. Articulation and phonemic awareness, drawing and writing, and reading are important areas of development within this domain; their discussion offers particular opportunities to consider how to infuse emerging literacy skills into the thematic centers.

- *Social-emotional:* Development in this domain tracks a child's social interactions and emotional well-being.
- *Sensorimotor:* This domain encompasses sensory (e.g., visual, auditory, tactile, olfactory) development as well as motor skill acquisition, both fine (small muscle) and gross (large muscle) motor. (*Note:* The sensorimotor domain of development should not be confused with the sensorimotor level of understanding and learning. The domain addresses development in sensory [e.g., reacting to sounds, responding to touch] and motor [e.g., jumping, standing, reaching] skills.)

The four domains are described in more detail in the other transdisciplinary play-based volumes, *Transdisciplinary Play-Based Assessment* (Linder, 1993a) and *Transdisciplinary Play-Based Intervention* (Linder, 1993b). You may want to refer to these two books, which provide detailed observation guidelines in each domain and corresponding intervention guidelines with recommendations for play materials and learning opportunities to help you assess a child's abilities and individualize instruction (see p. 236 for ordering information).

Both recognizing a child's level of functioning and associating objectives for the child with the developmental domains are critical precursors to designing appropriate instruction. The rest of this chapter explores these two major frameworks and their relationship.

LEVELS OF UNDERSTANDING AND LEARNING

Two of the activities in *Read, Play, and Learn!*—Reading the Story and participating in the Dramatic Play: Theme Area—provide some of the earliest, and perhaps best, times to identify at which level of understanding each of the children in your classroom is starting. Merely reading the story and then dramatizing it will not result in developmental "scaffolding" (a skill sequence that allows a child to master progressively more difficult skills) or the acquisition of emerging literacy skills. Your team needs to ensure that goals for these two components of the day are articulated and carefully addressed. What you and the children do within these areas of your classroom is pivotal to the thematic play that takes place in all of the other centers or areas. In the subsections that follow, we use Reading the Story and the Dramatic Play: Theme Area to more clearly demonstrate how to adapt your instruction to children at all three levels of understanding and learning. As you look at these general teaching strategies, remember that specific ideas for instruction with each storybook, as well as accommodations and modifications for children with special needs, are offered throughout the individual *Read, Play, and Learn!* modules.

READING THE STORY

You will begin each day by reading the story, mindful during each of these readings of the classroom goals you and your team have identified for the module. The rereadings—by you, another team member, or perhaps a visiting caregiver or parent—allow all of the children repeated exposure to the story. Certainly, repetition is important to emerging literacy (see Chapter 7), and how the story is read and discussed will have an impact on what the children understand, remember, and are then able to link to the activities planned for a particular storybook. You may need a variety of techniques to hold their attention.

During Reading the Story, you should do the following:

1. Observe the children's understanding of vocabulary, concepts, story sequence, and meaning. Adjust the way the story is read or told to meet the level of understanding of the various children in the group.
2. Consider story relevance for individual children. Depending on cultural background and/or previous experiences with being read to at home (Sulzby, 1985, 1989), you may notice differences across children.
3. Determine how individual children best construct new understandings through different types of mediation or scaffolding.
4. Model conventional reading (e.g., directionality, tracking, voice modulation, intonation).
5. Build concepts about print in relation to word meaning.
6. Demonstrate strategies for understanding the story (e.g., identifying pictures, defining words and concepts, thinking about sequence and story structure, discussing cause and effect, hypothesizing next events).
7. Respond to the children's attempts to relate to the story, describe pictures, share knowledge, compare, predict, make inferences, evaluate, and "read" or tell the story.
8. Extend the vocabulary, language patterns, and knowledge base of the children.
9. Involve children in story reading in different ways, depending on their communicative ability. Some may point to their own picture cards, some may point out pictures on a page, some may tell what is going to happen next, and so forth.

Young children's emergent reading behaviors tend to follow a predictable sequence. We can look at this development across the three levels of understanding and learning.

Sensorimotor Level

Children at the sensorimotor level are not yet aware that print in the book represents words. They are more interested in the sound of the words being read, the pictures in the book, and the concrete associations of the words that are meaningful to them. Some children may not even be very interested in pictures. The use of concrete objects or meaningful words and phrases needs to be incorporated. The key words and concepts in the book (each module provides a list) can be emphasized and, if needed, signed for these children.

The goals for children at this level are to be able to listen to the story, acquire new concepts and words, begin to associate concrete objects with an illustration and a spoken word, and begin to enjoy listening to and looking at books. These children may benefit from seeing actual items shown in the pictures, such as using real apples and pumpkins as props while reading *Picking Apples & Pumpkins* or using puppets while reading *The Rainbow Fish*. Books with clear, uncomplicated illustrations are best for children at this level. Using slides can also capture the child's interest and enable him or her to participate by pushing the advance button.

Functional Level

At the functional level, children are interested in listening to the story, but they are still engaged more in talking about the pictures than in discussing the story. They will benefit from all of the previous sensorimotor, concrete means of sharing the story and emphasizing the concepts. Children at the more mature end of this level will begin to connect the actions across pictures; they will understand and benefit from the illustrations in the book.

The goals for children at this level are to be able to listen to and understand the basic story; link ideas and concepts together in a short, remembered sequence; and name characters, objects, actions, or events of the story. Each day that the story is told, you can ask the children to remember aspects of the story (e.g., "What happened to [the main character] next?"). After several days of reading the story, you may leave out a key word or phrase while showing the illustration in the book for the children to fill in. By the second week, many of the children at this level will be able to help read the story by pointing out and labeling or describing pictures or actions in the story.

Symbolic Level

It is at the symbolic level that children become interested in the print, story sequence, and telling of the story. The children at this level are beginning to understand that words tell the story, and they are beginning to "read" the book to their classmates from the clues given by the illustrations.

The goals for children at this level are to be able to listen to and comprehend the story sequence; relate the story to actual events; make comparisons, make predictions, and draw inferences; and participate in the telling of the story. You need to allow these children opportunities to share their understandings of the story. In addition, you can begin to model how books are read by pointing to words as they are said, demonstrating how the words are written across and down the page, and so forth. Observation of understanding can also be incorporated as you ask higher level, problem-solving questions as part of the storytelling. Questions relating to what caused something to happen; questions starting with "What if . . . "; and questions requiring the child to make inferences, evaluations, and judgments are all appropriate for these children. You may also relate incidents or "truths" in the story to other related happenings in the children's lives.

Children at this level can benefit from *bibliotherapy* or the use of literature to help them explore emotional conflicts, fears, or troubling events in their lives. They will be able to see the relationship between characters in the story and themselves. Stories such as *The Kissing Hand* and *Friends* are examples of books that may help children cope with difficult issues, such as leaving home and going to school for the first time or working out friendships.

For children who need the emotional support offered by the themes of a particular book, further reading and discussion of individually relevant books in the Literacy Center on a one-to-one basis is warranted and may be extremely beneficial. Having family members take turns making an audiotape of the books to be replayed in class allows children an opportunity to hear different people reading the books and gives children the chance to proudly "share" their family members with the rest of the class.

It is very important that all teachers be aware of the developmental sequence for reading and that they individualize their activities for children. Although teachers may be accustomed to planning for children at the symbolic level, they also need to be able to meet the needs of children at the sensorimotor and functional levels. With the increase in the number of children with special needs in general preschool and kindergarten programs, teachers need a greater understanding of how children can be included in the classroom in such a way that their individual needs are met.

Teachers who are unfamiliar with children with disabilities should pay particular attention to the recommendations in each module made for the sensorimotor and functional levels. In addition, later in this chapter and in Chapters 5 and 6, ideas for children with physical disabilities, hearing loss, and visual impairments are provided. Children with physical disabilities may be able to more easily operate a button (or an adapted switch) than to turn the thin pages of a book. Books can also be taken apart, laminated, and reconfigured in a three-ring binder. Lamination strengthens the pages so that they can withstand multiple turnings by little hands, and the three-ring binder allows the book to lie flat so that it is easier to control. Positioning a child directly in front of the reader of the story and signing key words will help the child with a hearing loss. Slides, by adding size and lighting, will benefit children with certain types of visual impairments.

DRAMATIC PLAY: THEME AREA

Especially during the first week you are working in a new module, you will want all of the children to participate in the story reenactments that take place in the Dramatic Play: Theme Area. The simple script you have prepared or use from the module booklet provides a beginning point for all children, a common thread to assist those who have limited vocabulary to use story-related language, those with limited comprehension to have a model for action, and those who are more able to have a means to incorporate their peers in the dramatization. Having a simple script also helps the children to learn new vocabulary and language structures, to practice remembering a simple line, and to sequence ideas.

As the children become familiar with the story and language, story props, and literacy props, less guidance is needed. The intent is for the facilitators to become less and less involved and for creative experimentation to take over, building on the themes in the stories. Children at lower developmental levels can imitate their peers. Children at higher levels of understanding and learning can become involved in the play in a variety of roles. You will need to ensure that each child is challenged at his or her own level to meet individual learning objectives. Examples are given in each module for introducing dramatic play at each of the three levels of understanding and learning, but some general guidelines are also provided here.

Sensorimotor Level

Children who are developmentally at the sensorimotor level will be interested in manipulating objects to explore their characteristics and perhaps the cause-and-effect properties of objects as well. Children at this level will need you to provide basic labels for objects and actions. These children may not be directly involved in the acting out of the story, but they may enjoy exploring the props in the theme area or imitating the actions of their peers.

The goals for children at this level are to be socially involved, even as observers or at a parallel play level, and to use the sounds, words, signs, or actions related to the story in a meaningful way. Manipulating the props will provide an opportunity for exploring, problem solving, and labeling of new materials.

Functional Level

At the functional level, children understand one role, manipulate objects functionally, use objects in a concrete way, and can act out a sequence of actions in one event. Children at this level are interested in the props and objects within the story and enjoy performing the actions involved. They may be able to do the actions in one or more of the events but may not be able to link events. Focus on increasing the number of actions the children can link together in a sequence to create a story "event." They may or may not be able to use a word or phrase with the actions; thus, an appropriate goal for these children is the labeling of objects, descriptors, actions, and feelings (see the section "Communication and Language Development" later in this chapter). These children should also begin to understand and explore the functional use of many of the literacy props, such as a pad and pencil, picture charts, and so forth.

You will need to ensure that a sufficient number of props are available so that these children remain interested in the dramatic play sequences. Without the key objects, they may easily lose interest and wander off to another area. These children will also benefit from the modeling of actions provided by the children at the symbolic level. You may need to prompt associative interactions with peers at the symbolic level, as children at the symbolic level may not automatically include peers at a lower cognitive or language level.

Symbolic Level

Symbolic is the level at which children can imagine and act out roles and sequences of events, use props in creative and imaginative ways, think in terms of one thing representing another, and think conceptually and represent objects or ideas symbolically. They will be able to fully act out sequences within the stories, elaborate on the concepts presented in the stories, and come up with alternative approaches or solutions. Their memory and conceptual skills can be expanded through reenactment, elaboration, and problem solving. These children can help to prepare the Dramatic Play: Theme Area by planning and making story and literacy props and setting up the area. This involvement will help them to relate the props to the story and will prompt them to take a leadership role in assisting other children in the dramatization of the story.

The goals for children at this level are to expand their representational abilities, to increase their abilities to understand character and dialogue, to elaborate on sequences of events, to promote conceptualization and problem-solving abilities, and to increase cooperation and positive social interactions. Literacy can be promoted through the use of scripted lines from the book, enactment of the story, and insertion of written labels on objects or cue cards with written prompts. Adding writing materials and other literacy props as well as a reason to use them in the script will also prompt these children in pretending to write and read. For example, in *Somebody and the Three Blairs,* the Blairs eat breakfast. Setting out actual cereal boxes and milk cartons with writing on them will prompt the children to "read." A recipe for pancakes can be placed with other props for cooking. Later in the story, Mrs. Blair calls the police. A telephone book, note pad, and pencil for writing down the number of the police can be made available for the children to use.

Children at this level can also begin to understand the various roles of the characters within the story so that the opportunity for cooperative play is increased. They can assign roles and direct the action. Often, a whole sequence can be acted out and embellished by the children in the class with the highest level of symbolic representation skills. Some children may be interested in dictating action and dialogue to you to write down. You will need to ensure that children at this level have an opportunity to work together. This can be done by creating props together, by assisting or "directing" those who do not understand the sequence of events, and by discussing how certain actions make one feel. Social problem-solving situations may frequently arise as children vie for roles, props, and attention.

Teaching Children at a Mix of Levels

Typically, children do not automatically include children with special needs in their play, especially those with lower cognitive and language abilities and those with unusual behaviors. But following your modeling and the use of the simple script, the peer leaders in the group will begin to extemporize and build their own expansions of the story and will be more likely to involve their peers with special needs. For example, in a reenactment of *The Kissing Hand,* a deaf child could sign I LOVE YOU, and in a reenactment of *The Snowy Day,* a child with a visual impairment could feel the coldness and texture of snow.

Children will use objects in more exploratory ways, in simple functional uses, or in more representational and symbolic means, depending on their developmental level. In the vignette in "Making Learning Fun: A Glimpse at the ***Read, Play, and Learn!*** Curriculum" (pages 1–3), Anna, although physically limited and in a wheelchair, is functioning at the symbolic level. She understands and can retell the sequence of a story and discerns the symbolic meaning of the props. In addition, she is able to recognize the meaning of pictures on a chart in relation to the events of the day, such as baking muffins. Marco is at a functional level, moving into the symbolic level. He is able to use the props functionally in a one- or two-step action sequence, but he is not yet able to reenact the story. In addition, his language is limited to approximately two-word phrases that are familiar to him as a result of repeated story play. Meagan, who is "flying" the plane, is at the symbolic level. She demonstrates her understanding of the use of the compass and joystick props in pretend play and uses her imagination when she anticipates the action of the plane "going up high." In this brief vignette, there was not a child at the sensorimotor level represented. A child at this level might have been seen at the water table playing with the float planes or just dumping and filling the water.

DEVELOPMENTAL DOMAINS

After Reading the Story and Dramatic Play: Theme Area, the various other centers or areas in your classroom will support diverse aspects of development, whether the children you are working with are at the sensorimotor, functional, or symbolic level of understanding and learning. Activities planned within each module reinforce specific concepts and skills that the children need. Shifting to the second organizational framework, the developmental domains, provides an excellent way to review general guidelines for how to infuse skill development into all thematic centers in your classroom.

Cognitive Development

Cognitive skills, such as sequential thinking, classification, one-to-one correspondence, representation through drawing and writing, and problem solving, can be incorporated at the three levels of sensorimotor, functional, and symbolic understanding and learning across all of the centers. Each of the storybook modules in the curriculum presents specific suggestions for each center and highlights specific recommendations for children functioning at each level, but general principles are presented here.

Sensorimotor Level

At the sensorimotor level, children learn through exploration. Each of the centers should have materials that the children can manipulate (even mouth), bang, shake, and investigate with simple actions. Both the Sensory Area and Floor Play, and the materials that they contain, will be of more interest to children at this level than the Dramatic Play: Theme Area, Science and Math Center, or Literacy Center. A variety of materials should be available so that the children can make choices. For example, the area for Floor Play may have switch toys, a Lightbox, containers for dropping things into and taking them out of, and simple cause-and-effect toys. The goals for children at the sensorimotor level are to expand their repertoire of actions on objects, to increase their motivation to cause an effect on their environment, to increase the number of actions that they can sequence, and to increase their social interactions or turn taking in play. Specific skills, such as using a pincer grasp or poking with an index finger, can also be integrated into selected activities to increase children's repertoire of play schemes.

For children at this level, each of the centers will need to be modified to include appropriate materials; but even more important, those adults facilitating each center will need to alter their interaction patterns to address the developmental needs of each child. It makes no sense to have a child at the sensorimotor level sit at a table at which peers are cutting and pasting and have the adult cut out a piece and then glue it on paper and label it with the child's name. The child does not benefit from this process. The child at the sensorimotor level could scribble, tear paper, and put the pieces into a hole in the top of a container instead. Other children may be making clay animals, whereas the child at this level might enjoy squeezing the clay or pulling it apart. The goal for the child at this level is not to be able to create a representational figure. The goal is to expand the child's ability to combine objects (putting objects together or putting something "in"), to increase fine motor control (ability to hold and manipulate a small object), and to expand sound production or vocabulary. For some children, even these objectives may be too advanced and will need to be altered to match developmental functioning.

Functional Level

All of the centers should be cognitively motivating to children at the functional level. They will enjoy the sensory aspects of the materials but will be ready to engage in higher level manipulation. Various utensils may be added to the Sensory Area and various tools may be added to the Woodworking Center to provide opportunities for these children to try new manipulative skills beyond simple exploration.

With prompting, children at this level may make something (probably recognizable only to the child) at the Table Play area or Art Area and give it a name. This marks a big shift into representational thinking! You should reinforce this effort by labeling the child's work with the child's words. This will allow the child to see print associated with his or her words and will enable family members to relate to the picture and discuss it with the child. One-to-one correspondence may be incorporated through counting whenever appropriate. Art activities, such as painting on easels or on a mural, offer the chance to share the concepts presented every day in the story and in dramatic play and a means for beginning to represent ideas in a symbolic form. Although children at the functional level will not yet be able to clearly represent their ideas in this form, they can be encouraged to make that shift by using real pictures from magazines, by coloring their own primitive renderings, or by just adding concrete elements, such as cotton for clouds in the module based on *A Porcupine Named Fluffy*.

Although building an actual structure may be beyond their abilities, children at this level can stack blocks in parallel play next to their peers who are building more complicated representations. You can "bump them up" by relating their efforts to elements in the story, such as a wall in the town in the module based on *Abiyoyo*, and adding other props from the story, such as a magic wand to make objects "disappear" behind the wall. The children may even come in the next day, build the same structure, and add the props without any suggestion from you.

The children at this level will primarily combine objects when they are in the Science and Math Center. They may be able to follow through on simple sequences with their peers, but they will not be able to explore the reasons behind their classifications. The goal is to begin to move these children into experimentation with "likeness" and "difference" and cause and effect for discrimination and problem solving and to nudge them into forms of representational thought. For example, the children at this level may want to match toy animals from *Night Tree* to their pictures, using one-to-one correspondence. You can then assist them in counting the animals. Discrimination and classification skills are important foundations for emerging literacy as well as for thought processing and language production.

Symbolic Level

Children at the symbolic level can be encouraged to do higher level comparisons, discussing how and why various outcomes are occurring. You can encourage questioning (e.g., "I wonder why [there are no penguins in the forest]?" "I wonder what would happen if [the big, bad coyote in *The Three Little Javelinas* decided to pour water down the chimney]?"). You will want to encourage these children to ask questions, provide information, discover how things work, and ponder why things work the way they do. In the Science and Math Center, these children can also be encouraged to explore, compare, measure, write down their findings, and share their knowledge with their peers. They can draw, chart, label, and "read" picture charts and recipes.

The Art Area will enable children at this level to expand their means of representational expression. You should encourage the expansion of art into expression of not just characters but also actions, feelings, and modifications of the story. These children can decide on new characters or actions, and then they can draw or paint these new characters or actions into the story of the week or create stories to go with new characters. Their ideas can be represented through various media: drawing; painting; cutting and pasting with paper, cotton, and other materials; using clay, Styrofoam, or fabric to create models or puppets; and so forth. The products from the Art Area are a natural to combine with the Literacy Center. The children can write or dictate stories about their artwork or make books using their illustrations. Pictures can be labeled or described by the children and the words written down on the paper by you. Depending on the child's level of emerging literacy, you can address the child's individual readiness level. (See Chapter 7 for information on developmental literacy progression.)

Communication and Language Development

Traditionally, speech-language pathologists and child development specialists think of communication and language as encompassing *expressive communication,* which allows the child to impart meaning to others, and *receptive communication,* which allows the child to understand what is communicated by others. Expressive communication can be either verbal, using words, symbols, or signs, or nonverbal, using eye gaze, gesture, body language, or physical manipulation. Once the child begins to use sounds and oral words to communicate, the child's phonological, or sound, system and articulation become important to comprehensibility. The development of emerging literacy skills parallels both the expressive and receptive language systems as well as the development of cognitive and motor skills. For the purposes of this section, principles for strengthening language and communication development across centers are presented along with suggestions for articulation enhancement. The development of emerging literacy is briefly discussed in this chapter but is more completely addressed in Chapter 7.

Expressive Communication Skills

For the purposes of this book, expressive communication is expanded to include communication through vocal and nonvocal means and through oral and written means. Articulation is considered important to oral communication, and drawing serves as a foundation for communication through written representation. Let's look at the general guidelines for each of the three levels of understanding and learning first and then more specifically at articulation and phonology, drawing and writing, and reading.

Sensorimotor Level

Depending on the classroom composition, you may have children who are prelinguistic. Children who are not yet using words or signs to communicate can be encouraged to increase their repertoire and use of sounds and gestures. With children at this level, your utterances should be shortened and simplified to increase the children's comprehension and attention to key sounds and words. With each storybook selected, look for key concepts that can be presented at a very basic level, such as word labels, actions, and simple prepositions and descriptors. These words or signs can then be matched with a variety of concrete experiences. For example, in *Abiyoyo,* the father plays a ukulele. You can demonstrate the sign for MUSIC and use this sign when the musical refrain occurs in the story, when the children are listening to recorded music, and when the children sing songs at snack. You can then reinforce the child's communicative attempts using gestures, sign approximations, signs, or sounds or word approximations to indicate the word "music" by making comments to the children (e.g., "Music. . . . Yes! Let's sing!").

The team should agree on which words a particular child is ready for and incorporate those into the interactions with the child. You will want to encourage the child to use verbal and/or nonverbal means to communicate. If the child does not use words, the team may interpret the child's facial expressions, gestures, or movements as having meaning. For example, as the child reaches for an object, which can be interpreted as a request for an object, you might say, "You want . . . [object]"; or, as the child moves, which can be interpreted as a request for an action, you might say, "[Child's name] wants to . . . [action]." Other pragmatic intentions should be encouraged and labeled as the child plays in the environment. Pragmatic intentions, such as a comment on objects or actions (e.g., "You are petting . . . "), a protest (e.g., "You want to stop . . . "), a greeting (e.g., "Hi . . . "), or sounds that acknowledge another person's speech, should be endorsed by a verbal interpretation or response from the adult. In this way, the children will learn that sounds, movements, gestures, and words result in a reciprocal action or communication on the part of the adult.

Functional Level

Children at the functional level are associating words (or signs) with objects, actions, and pictures. Your emphasis is on increasing the vocabulary and length of phrases and sentences that the children are using as well as the range of pragmatic meanings and the functions or reasons the children use language. With guidance, the children will be able to follow a short sequence of verbal instructions accompanying a series of pictures of objects and actions. A series of two or three objects and actions is usually enough of a challenge. You may use pictures and words together to assist the children through a series of actions (e.g., through the actions needed in a cooking activity). The combination of pictures and words supports the children's movement toward a more symbolic level. For example, a sequence of pictures illustrating a child putting on winter outerwear could be placed in the House Area or in the Floor Play or Table Play areas for the module based on *The Snowy Day*. The combination of pictures, actual clothing props, and your spoken words will increase the children's comprehension as well as stimulate word production. The children at this level are also probably ready to combine words (or signs) into a minimum of two- to three-word combinations (e.g., a noun + a verb, an adjective + a noun, a verb + an object). For example, you might prompt a child (e.g., "She's wearing a hat") in the House Area, and the child might imitate "wear hat." The speech-language pathologist can suggest appropriate phrases that can be encouraged for specific children at this level for each of the storybook modules.

Symbolic Level

Children at the symbolic level will usually communicate in complete sentences. The goals for the children at this level are to increase their abilities to use language to interact with others, to express opinions, to engage in imaginative play, to gain information, to provide information, and to engage in cognitive and social problem solving. Dramatization of the story allows children at this level the opportunity to use language to engage in fantasy, to try different roles, and to direct the actions and interactions of their peers. To encourage information finding, the team can use books, real materials, computer programs, field trips, videotapes, and so forth. The team needs to prompt children at this level to ask questions, to figure out where to find the answers, and to share the information with their peers.

Children at the symbolic level can also be encouraged to use more complex language structures (e.g., an "if . . . , then . . . " structure) and problem-solving skills. For example, they may be able to use verbal mediation to help them solve science and math problems; figure out how to create structures, props, art activities, and recipes; and solve social conflicts. The team needs to use each story as a new opportunity to expand the level of communicative ability of each child by building on the vocabulary, themes, and problem-solving situations presented in each story.

Articulation and Phonology

Sound production is obviously essential to expressive language development. Normal sound production follows a developmental sequence (see *Transdisciplinary Play-Based Assessment* [Linder, 1993a] and *Transdisciplinary Play-Based Intervention* [Linder, 1993b]). It is important that the members of your team familiarize themselves with normal sequences so that children who are functioning at varying developmental levels can be advanced appropriately.

Addressing articulation disorders requires the input of a skilled speech-language pathologist who can assist the team in determining the phonological errors a particular child is making (e.g., Are the beginnings or endings of words being omitted? Are certain sounds being omitted or substituted for others? Are the errors developmentally appropriate?). Once the pattern of sound production has been analyzed, the speech-language pathologist can assist the rest of the team in determining how best to support the child's acquisition of modified sound patterns.

Your team might want to try to incorporate certain sounds into a module in a purposeful way. For example, a child who is having trouble making sounds that require the lips to come together, such as /b/ or /p/, may have these sounds targeted through specific vocabulary, songs, and oral-motor play at snack. In this scenario, you could reinforce the /b/ and /p/ sounds with this child throughout the module on *A Porcupine Named Fluffy* with the use of the words, such as "porcupine," "prickly," "pretty," "poke," "pillow," "pop," "big," "bounce," "bubble," and so forth. At snack, the oral-motor activities can include making sounds, such as popcorn popping, and singing songs or doing fingerplays that require the smacking and popping of lips. Attention to sound production, oral-motor skills, and articulation are important so that children can communicate effectively with peers and adults. The inability to make oneself intelligible to others can decrease social initiations, increase behavior problems, and even reduce a child's desire to engage in cognitive tasks requiring word production.

Games, activities, and sound play are also important for the children's development of phonemic awareness. As the children listen carefully and are able to differentiate and make sounds, they are building an understanding of how sounds are alike or different. Later in development, these different sounds will become associated with a specific letter, building a foundation for phonemic awareness.

Drawing and Writing

Literacy is related to all areas of development (particularly language and cognition) and encompasses many forms of expression. Although drawing and writing are merely two forms of literate expression, they are emphasized here with a level-by-level look at sensorimotor, functional, and symbolic learning because written expression is so important in elementary school curricula. (See Chapter 7 for a detailed discussion of the developmental approach to emerging literacy and general principles for conceptually promoting written expression.) Development of fine motor skills to enable competent writing and drawing skills is also an essential component to be considered by the team for each child.

- *Sensorimotor level and drawing and writing:* The conceptual goal related to drawing and writing for the children in your class at the sensorimotor level is to understand the relationship between the marking tool (e.g., crayon, marker, pencil) and the paper. In other words, the children learn that they can cause a mark to appear, that they are the agents who control the actions of the marker. Experiences with different types of marking tools is important. Even fingerpaints on paper, which do not require fine motor control, can help the children at this level want to make something happen on the paper.

- *Functional level and drawing and writing:* Children at the functional level know how to use different media to make marks on paper. They may be able to make some rudimentary shapes. These children will need opportunities to experiment with gaining better fine motor control over the marker. They may make a scribble and describe it as being a porcupine or a bear. They will enjoy painting and drawing with all sorts of media. Although not at the level of making letters, they may be able to recognize the configuration of letters that make up their name when you write their names on their papers. You should take the time to label and write on the children's pictures or on pieces of paper attached to the pictures their descriptions of what they have drawn. This allows them to see their words in print and allows those who view the picture to know what the children drew so that they can discuss their artwork. Thus, spoken language will be encouraged along with the recognition that words can be written down.

  The recognition that print conveys a story is encouraged not only by labeling the child's artwork but also by allowing the child to use stamp pads or cut-out words to experiment with symbols or letters that he or she is not yet able to conceptualize or form. This will encourage the child to take an interest in the printed words that tell a story as well as the pictures that tell a story.

- *Symbolic level and drawing and writing:* For children at the symbolic level who understand that letters correspond to sounds and have meaning when combined on paper, ***Read, Play, and Learn!*** presents many opportunities for emerging literacy experiences. The Literacy Center can include catalogs and magazines with pictures of characters, actions, or feelings related to the story being read. These pictures can be labeled by the children or by you. The children can also dictate stories to you, and you can write the stories on several pages to make a book. The children can then illustrate their books by cutting out pictures or by drawing pictures. Some children might enjoy "reading" their stories to a small group of children. Each of the stories will have different objects that can be labeled. The children can make or dictate the words to be printed on pieces of paper and taped up around the room. Language experience charts, based on field trips or special activities, and interactive reading charts that allow children to insert known words into familiar stories are excellent means of encouraging emerging reading skills. The goal is to give the children at this level as much exposure to the printed word as possible and to help them to see that they can write down their ideas for others to read.

Including writing in the other centers is also important. For example, in the module on *First Flight,* the "ticket agent" can write out airline tickets and stamp passports (made on the computer) in the Dramatic Play: Theme Area. Similarly, the "salesperson" in the module on *Picking Apples & Pumpkins* can write out a receipt for payment in the Dramatic Play: Theme Area, and the recipes for pumpkin and apple pies can be used in the House Area or the Science and Math Center. In *The Knight and the Dragon,* the knight and the dragon both read books about how to fight, so the children could read books on pillows near the Literacy Center about knights and dragons. In the Science and Math Center, children could draw size relationship charts for *Somebody and The Three Blairs* and *The Three Billy Goats Gruff.* The opportunities for inclusion of the written symbol are limited only by the creativity of the team. To meet the goal of increasing the children's levels of understanding of the forms and functions of print, your team needs to identify every possible occasion for the children to be exposed to and use functional written symbols and words.

Receptive Communication Skills

Receptive communication skills, that is, language comprehension, can be exhibited through behavioral, oral, and written means. Your goal is to increase, or "bump up," each child's ability to understand meaning through each of these modalities and to be able to share his or her understanding with others in increasingly more sophisticated ways. In schools, the predominant means of determining whether children *comprehend* or *understand* a concept is asking them questions. This puts the adults in the position of directing the child's thoughts and actions and makes the child a responder instead of an initiator. Alternatively, you can determine what the child comprehends through observation of behaviors that indicate understanding, through discussion and conversation on a topic, and by eliciting questions from the *child.* This implies that the adult–child interaction is more equal and parallel and that you engage the children in many different forms of communication to determine their understanding. Joint action and dialogue, shared exploration and investigation, and mutual involvement in activities replace questioning. This does not mean that every activity in which the children engage must involve an adult. It does imply, however, that in order for the team to understand what the children comprehend about concepts, actions, and problems, they must, at a minimum, carefully observe the children's actions and interactions. Furthermore, they must *interpret the meaning* of what the children are trying to do and communicate through their actions. For example, when one facilitator was reading *The Three Billy Goats Gruff,* she read that the Big Billy Goat was wearing a leather jacket. One of the children, Mark (who is nonverbal), jumped up, ran to his coat hook, grabbed his leather jacket, and brought it back to the group. Clearly, Mark's actions communicated that he understood what a leather jacket is and that he wanted the group to know that he had a leather jacket, too. (See the section "Communication Between Team Members and Children" in Chapter 3 and the previous discussion about communication in this chapter.)

Improvement of comprehension takes place through discussing, modeling, experimenting, and verifying experiences in relation to the language heard. A child might come to comprehend the concept of temperature, for example, through your explanation and labeling of things that are hot, cold, warm, and so forth; through your and their peers' modeling what to wear when it is cold or hot; through cooking and eating experiences; and through playful experimentation with materials of different temperatures.

Reading

Learning to read is a form of language comprehension wherein the children have learned that symbols and print carry meaning in the same way that the spoken word carries meaning. As discussed in Chapter 7, the development of written language decoding and comprehension can be taught in developmental progressions in tandem with oral language, using the functional activities related to storybooks. Some general guidelines for each of the three levels are also included here:

- *Sensorimotor level and reading:* For children at the sensorimotor level, recognition and identification of familiar objects, people, and actions will lead to picture identification, which is a first step toward more complex symbol recognition. Experiences with labeling of real objects and pictures of these objects will lead to the later understanding of the meaning of more complex pictures in storybooks. The children at this level need support in *identifying* the objects, characters, and actions in the books.

- *Functional level and reading:* For children at the functional level, the goal is to assist them in 1) seeing the relationships among objects, characters, and actions in the pictures; 2) listening and associating these words and pictures to actual experiences; 3) understanding that a sequence of ideas (pictures) makes up a story; and 4) knowing that print is another way of saying a word. Children at this level need very concrete experiences to enable them to make these connections.

- *Symbolic level and reading:* Children at the symbolic level are beginning to understand the nature of the form and functions of reading. The goal for children at this level is to begin to understand and enter into the beginning reading process. For this reason, they need experiences with 1) observing and listening to reading, 2) telling and dramatizing stories, 3) understanding that print rather than pictures carries the message, 4) "reading" and "rereading" stories, 5) practicing the process of reading (e.g., directionality, following print, following story sequence), 6) experimenting with sound and symbol differentiation, and 7) wanting to communicate through print.

Social-Emotional Development

Most of the activities described in the modules can be arranged to encourage social interaction among children. Social opportunities are essential for advancement of language and communication skills. You can influence the children to carry on conversations by placing them in situations in which they *need* to talk to one another.

During the reading of the story, you can prompt the child who is helping to tell the story to involve his or her friends. The child could, for example, ask his or her friends, "What part did you like in the story?"; have a friend point to the pictures as the child tells the story; or take turns with another child, with each "reading" a page during his or her turn. When given the opportunity to play "teacher," many children will imitate the actions and words they have heard from the adults who have previously read the story.

In the Dramatic Play: Theme Area, during the dramatization of the story, children naturally need to interact to role-play the story. Some additional ways in which social interactions can be promoted include having a director (who wears a director's hat and directs the dramatization) and a prop director (who helps dress the cast and arrange the props) to help with the role play and pairing peers so that a child at the symbolic level helps a child at the functional level move through the sequences. Your inclination may be to be the director and prompt the actors' words and action, but having peers assume this role teaches cooperative effort. Instead, you can prompt the director to cue the actions and words in the script. The prop director can help put on the costumes and set up the special props. By changing who plays what roles, including the directors, the children will get to interact with each other as leaders, followers, and co-players.

Social interactions are inherent in many of the stories and can be integrated into the centers. For example, in the module based on *A Porcupine Named Fluffy,* the designated sensorimotor area includes the path to Hippo. Fluffy and Hippo engage in numerous friendly activities together, including rolling in a barrel, a blanket, and bubble wrap. These situations require social interactions. The story has the two characters laughing and slapping their knees and becoming friends. This is an opportunity to build into the script friendly initiations (e.g., "I like you. Will you be my friend?") and problem-solving discussions about how friends act with one another. The story *Friends* was specifically selected because it is based on friendly play among peers and requires continual interaction. All of the centers can be arranged so that "friends" need to work or play together. Games that require more than one person to play, activities that require the help of a friend to accomplish, and limited materials being set out so that friends will need to share are just a few of the ideas that can encourage social interactions and emotional development in the centers.

Although sensory exploration, table, and art projects can be pursued alone, you can urge the children to assist each other (e.g., "Sammy needs the tongs, Jeremiah"; "Sammy, you could ask Jeremiah to pass you the tongs"), to comment on each other's experience (e.g., "Oh, look, Cissy's shaving cream is turning green"), and to carry on a conversation (e.g., "I love green. How about you, Kayla? You do, too? I like green grass. I wonder what Brennan likes that's green?"). You serve as an interactor within, a model for, and an instigator of social interaction.

The Literacy Center is an excellent area for children to share their work by reading to each other and talking about the pictures they have found or drawn. You need to be careful that all social interaction at this area is not between the adult and the child, as is sometimes the case at more "academic" centers.

Floor Play with blocks and puzzles can involve more than one child working on a cooperative effort. You can point out opportunities for children to assist each other (e.g., "John has a lot of blocks; you can ask him if he will share some"). Many of the children at the sensorimotor or functional level may choose activities at the Floor Play area or the Sensory Area. You can look for occasions that will compel the children at the symbolic level to interact with these children (e.g., "Juan is trying to get the sled on the slide. I'll bet you could show him how it works"). Often, all of the children are attracted to the switch toys, but they may need support to use them together (e.g., "It was nice of you to show Ben how to make that go. Let's watch how he does with his turn").

Children at the symbolic level are more likely to choose activities at the Science and Math Center and the Woodworking Center, as these areas challenge their developing problem-solving skills. As these children are also more likely to have higher level language, you can focus on setting up the projects so that two children need to work together. The experiments in the Science and Math Center are more fun when peers experiment together.

Music and books provide a natural opportunity for social interactions. The children can sing with each other, dance together, and read to each other. You can ensure that these activities are not done in isolation but rather in pairs or small groups.

Snack is not just for the purpose of appeasing a growling tummy. Snack offers many opportunities for social interaction. During oral-motor exercises, children can take turns being a leader and choosing an activity to model for the others. They can have a role in preparing the snacks in a cooperative effort, and they can serve each other. Conversation can be instigated about the day's activities or other topics that the children want to discuss. You can encourage children to observe and comment on the actions of the others (e.g., "You could see if Paul needs help cutting his carrot") and ask for others' opinions (e.g., "I like crackers. Mary, I wonder if Samantha likes crackers").

The development of social skills should be consciously integrated throughout the activities related to each story. At some level, each story is about social interactions, and the team needs to ensure that every opportunity for interaction and communication is maximized.

Sensorimotor Development

For the preceding discussions in the cognitive, communication and language, and social-emotional domains, guidelines for children have been organized along the levels of sensorimotor, functional, and symbolic learning. For the sensorimotor domain, it is probably more useful to think of intervention in terms of the types of issues that have an impact on the child's developmental level of functioning.

For this reason, factors relating to motor abilities rather than to levels of understanding and learning are addressed in this section. Many of the factors are interrelated and should be discussed by the team with regard to individual children. You may find it helpful to refer to the chapter "Facilitating Sensorimotor Development," by Bundy and O'Brien, in *Transdisciplinary Play-Based Intervention* (Linder, 1993b), for more intervention strategies related to specific disabilities and developmental levels and to *Positioning for Play: Home Activities for Parents of Young Children* (Diamant, 1992) for principles relating to optimal positioning for children. The latter reference is intended to assist intervention professionals and parents in understanding ways to hold and play with their children while also providing opportunities for developing motor and other developmental skills.

Muscle Tone

Addressing the issues of children who have abnormal muscle tone requires the expertise of professionals trained to work with children with atypical motor development. The occupational or physical therapist will provide essential input regarding the amount and type of stimulation needed by individual children. The team members can plan how to incorporate activities that will decrease the tone of children whose muscle tone is high (hypertonicity), which interferes with adaptive movements. Similarly, they will need to plan activities that will increase the tone of children who have low tone (hypotonicity), which prohibits normal movement patterns. Many of the activities planned to promote social, cognitive, and language or literacy development also provide opportunities to address the needs of children with increased or decreased tone. Techniques to normalize tone can and should be embodied in meaningful play activities, as effective intervention involves not only inhibition of abnormal muscle tone but also simultaneous facilitation of desired movements (Bundy & O'Brien, 1993). It is important to normalize tone in order for the child to function more adaptively in the play environment. The ideas that follow illustrate how activities that enhance tone can be consolidated into the activities for several of the storybooks.

Activities that increase tone involve rapid, repetitive movements (Bundy & O'Brien, 1993). In the module based on *A Porcupine Named Fluffy*, the children can bounce on and hit pillows in the House Area; they can slap their hands on their thighs and roll around like Hippo and Fluffy on the mats at the end of the path; and the path can be made of bubble wrap, which requires that the children jump or bounce down the path in order to pop them.

Activities that provide increased resistance also increase tone (Bundy & O'Brien, 1993). The use of heavy objects (e.g., having the little old lady in *The Little Old Lady Who Was Not Afraid of Anything* carry a weighted basket on her search for herbs) or objects that require more effort (e.g., pounding on blocks as a town wall is built during the module on *Abiyoyo*) can help build muscle tone. Stomping across the bridge during the module based on *The Three Billy Goats Gruff* gives strong, proprioceptive stimulation (input to the joints), which builds awareness of body in space.

In the sensory tubs, using heavy spoons and containers offers more resistance. You may want to encourage the child with low tone to start out using the heavier materials first, because beans and water offer more resistance than torn paper or shaving cream. At the writing table, using inked stamps of the alphabet or of fish for the module on *The Rainbow Fish* requires the use of pressure to make a mark on the paper. Squeezing clay or using cookie cutters to make fish provides resistance and may be done before the children try to draw or write. The use of a weighted cart or wagon (using real suitcases in the module on *First Flight)* can also provide resistance. Using heavier objects with children whose tone at times seems high and at other times seems low (fluctuating tone) is also generally advised, although this needs to be determined on an individual basis.

Activities that decrease tone include experiences involving slow, repetitive, linear movements (Bundy & O'Brien, 1993). For example, rocking *very* slowly in a chair in the House Area in the module based on *Somebody and the Three Blairs* before doing other activities may be effective. Neutral warmth may also facilitate decreasing tone. Placing warm water in the sensory tubs may help decrease tone in the hands. Having the child with hypertonia play at the sensory tubs before he or she engages in a task requiring fine motor skills is advised, as the child will be able to perform better if the muscle tone is more normalized. Whereas heavier objects facilitate increasing tone, lighter objects are preferred for children with increased tone. In the module based on *A Porcupine Named Fluffy,* the sensory tubs for children with low tone might have food coloring to mix in with shaving cream or cotton balls, saw dust, or lightweight balsa wood strips or Styrofoam triangles to sort and fill containers. Correct table seating and positioning is also important to normalize tone.

Stability and Weight Bearing, Balance, and Motor Planning

In order to sit, crawl, stand, walk, or move from one position to another, children need to be stable in space, to bear weight on their joints, to resist the force of gravity, and to know where their bodies are in space. They need activities that will allow them to be challenged yet safe. Facilitation of the development of the components of movement can assist children in developing a sense of trust and confidence in their abilities to make their bodies do what they want them to do.

Placing children in positions that require them to bear weight on key sets of muscles and joints helps develop hip and shoulder stability and assists in hand development needed for fine tool (pencil) use. Such practice may be necessary for children with physical disabilities before they are ready to accomplish higher level developmental milestones. Facilitation may be needed to assist the children in their movements into position, maintenance of those positions, and making the transition out of various positions. An occupational or physical therapist should be consulted to demonstrate the best facilitation techniques.

Play in prone (lying on stomach) works on the development of shoulder stability. Children may work on the floor on their tummies when creating artwork, writing, or building with blocks. For children who need it the most, this is a difficult position to maintain, so frequent shifting of positions may be necessary. Creeping on hands and knees is another good activity, requiring the stability of both shoulders and hips. If the sensory tubs are placed on the floor, then the children will be more likely to creep between them. You can then encourage the use of a hands-and-knees or a side-sit position. Children can also be encouraged to crawl into a village hut during the module based on *Abiyoyo*. This will be especially inviting if the doorway is lined with bubble wrap as they can push on the bubbles to pop them (this is also a good resistance activity). Placing small stairs in front of the door increases the challenge of crawling into the tent.

Standing requires weight bearing on the hips and legs. Standing should be incorporated into the activities for all children, even for those who cannot walk. Use of facilitated support or standers may be needed. Appropriate places for standing include the mural; the table activities; the sensory table; the table in the House Area or Dramatic Play: Theme Area; and while reading the story (with support, if necessary) to see the pictures, even for a few minutes. The occupational or physical therapist should provide ongoing consultation around various positioning techniques, adaptive equipment, and other environmental modifications needed by children with physical disabilities.

Activities that give children experiences walking and running and that require them to start and stop, change directions, and maneuver their bodies challenge the children's balance and equilibrium systems. For example, children can be motivated to chase the little javelinas during the module based on *The Three Little Javelinas* in different ways, depending on their motor skills: crawling, walking, tiptoeing, skipping, hopping, running, or other creative movements. A path that is straight, that is curvy, or that has angled corners can be made for the module on *A Porcupine Named Fluffy*. In addition, the composition of the path can be changed frequently so that the children have to make body adjustments requiring balance. As mentioned previously, maneuvering over bubble wrap and pillows is great. Climbing equipment, such as ladders for the module on *Picking Apples & Pumpkins*, a barrel for a chimney for the module on *The Three Little Javelinas*, or a slide for sledding for the module on *A Snowy Day*, can be included so that motor planning skills are required.

Differentiated Gross Motor Movements

In order to move smoothly and to make a transition from one position to another, a person must be able to move distinct body parts separately. The arms, legs, and hands need to function independently. The upper body and lower body need to be able to rotate in both directions. Activities that require children to use distinct body parts in rotational movements are helpful to all children, including those with physical disabilities or delays. The activities planned for each module offer numerous situations in which differential movements and body rotation can be emphasized.

At the sensory tubs (placed at table height for this purpose) or at the table activities, chairs can be placed sideways or at an angle to the table to encourage children to face their lower bodies away from the table and rotate their upper bodies toward the activity. For the floor activity involving the plastic animals or floor puzzles, such as during the modules on *The Kissing Hand, Night Tree,* or *The Rainbow Fish*, children who need more practice with rotation can be encouraged to side-sit, placing their weight on one arm (also good for children who need increased weight bearing) and using their opposite arm for manipulation of blocks or figures.

In the Art Area, the paints and water (or other media) may be placed on the floor next to the mural on the side of the child's nondominant hand. This will encourage the child to cross over midline and rotate the body as he or she reaches across and down. Similarly, any of the table art activities can encourage body rotation by the placement of materials. For example, during the module on *A Porcupine Named Fluffy,* when making porcupines from clay and toothpicks, the clay and toothpicks can be placed so that a child has to rotate and extend the dominant arm across the body.

Differentiated Fine Motor Movements

Many of the dramatic, sensory, art, science and math, woodworking, and literacy activities require the use of individual finger movements. Particular attention should be paid to the development of a pincer grasp (the end of the pads of the thumb and forefinger are combined to pick up and manipulate objects). The ability to use a tripod grasp (the thumb and first two fingers support a tool, such as a pencil) can also be practiced in many centers. The team members can determine means for encouraging children to develop tool and toy use with the thumb and first two fingers, with fingers three and four being used for support.

Muscle tone is also important for writing and drawing. Both neck and trunk stability are needed for writing, but muscle tone in fingers and hands must also be considered. Children with low tone may benefit from warm-up activities, such as squeezing a ball or hard clay, to normalize tone. Alternatively, increased tone may be decreased by a preactivity, such as slow massaging with warm lotion. These types of considerations should be incorporated into planning for individual children as the team members brainstorm appropriate activities for each module.

Using sign language during the module on *A Rainbow of Friends* and signing words for other stories requires specific finger movements. Such finger movements help children to develop finger differentiation skills and finger flexibility. Making guitars to act out *Abiyoyo* requires punching holes in a shoe box (necessitates squeezing and pressure against resistance), threading string through the holes (necessitates pincer grasp and eye–hand coordination), tying the string (necessitates imitation of a motor-planning sequence), and using fingers to "play" the instrument (necessitates individual finger movements). You can prompt the use of finger and thumb or a fisted grasp by using a variety of art media (e.g., small stick-on stars for the module on *Night Tree,* small sponges for painting colorful fish during the module on *The Rainbow Fish).* Computer games, which can require finger dexterity or can be modified to utilize pads or joysticks for those who need them, can be incorporated into all of the modules. Playing instruments, such as a flute, to accompany singing songs with the stories also encourages children to use their fingers separately. Attention on the part of team members to the development of such skills is important for the later development of writing and computer skills.

Environmental Adaptations for Children with Physical Challenges

Children with physical challenges, in addition to restricted movements, may also have communication limitations due to oral-motor complications, cognitive delays, and social interactions that may be negatively affected by their difficulties. Such children have been shown to receive fewer literacy experiences and reduced exposure to reading (Light & Kelford-Smith, 1993; Marvin, 1994). Special efforts, therefore, must be made to ensure that these children can participate in all of the classroom activities to the best of their abilities. Adaptations, such as symbolized stories, adapted slide projectors, adapted story notebooks, and big books, should be available (King-DeBaun, 1990), along with augmentative communication devices, switches, and other tools, to enable the children to initiate play and interaction. Environmental modifications can ensure participation, and appropriate facilitation on your part or another team member's can encourage active, independent play.

The use of augmentative communication devices enables children with severe physical and communicative challenges to use pictures, icons, or outlines to participate in classroom activities and storytelling. Lahey and Bloom (1977) suggested emphasizing words that indicate recurrence (e.g., "more"), actions on objects (e.g., "feed"), actions involved in location of objects or self (e.g., "on," "in"), attributes or descriptors of objects (e.g., "pretty"), and objects associated with people (e.g., "nice"). The emphasis on these symbols will enable children with challenges to participate in the story activities along with their typically developing peers. Language boards can be made for each story with symbols relating to key concepts. "Low-tech" assistive tools, such as individualized symbol boards worn by the teacher or positioned in front of the child, or more technology-based systems, such as the WOLF vocal output communication device (available from ADAMLAB, 33500 Van Born Road, Post Office Box 807, Wayne, Michigan 48184), allow vocabulary to be programmed into the device for retrieval by the child, parent, or other adult. Some vocal programs can be modified to model different syntactic levels. The symbols can then be used throughout the play activities to reinforce and generalize the use of these concepts.

King-DeBaun (1990, 1993) in her *Storytime* books suggested the following adaptations for storytelling and participation in literacy events for children who have physical challenges:

1. Photograph the pictures in the storybook, and show the story on slides with an adapted slide projector so that children can advance the story.
2. Place each story in a 1" thick, 8½" x 11", three-ring notebook by placing each page between a clear plastic sleeve with oak tagboard cut to fit between the pages for added reinforcement. These heavier books allow children to manipulate the pages more easily. If several copies are made, more children can look at the books.
3. Make "page fluffers" out of foam pieces that can be attached to pages of the book to enable children with fine motor difficulties to manipulate and turn the pages of the book.
4. Use published "big books."
5. Use expanded computer keyboards and tools, such as Power Pad and Talking Power Pad (Unicorn Engineering, Dunamis), to create custom activities for the classroom storybooks along with commercial programs.
6. Adapt props for use by children with physical challenges. For example, a child who wears a Velcro strap fastened around his or her hand may be able to manipulate a puppet on a stick.

7. Adapt print materials so that these children can manipulate the print and symbols (e.g., a magnetic board with magnetic shapes and forms; a Velcro board with symbols, letters, or words; stamps with adapted handles so that the children can more easily apply pressure to the stamp).

8. Use a tape recorder with a battery adapter (AbleNet, 1081 10th Avenue, SE, Minneapolis, Minnesota 55414; Don Johnston, Inc., Post Office Box 639, Wauconda, Illinois 60084), a single tactile switch that can be easily manipulated, and a loop feedback tape of 10–15 seconds (available at Radio Shack).

Children with physical challenges can be meaningfully involved in all of the *Read, Play, and Learn!* storybook modules. With careful planning and the assistance of parents, student volunteers, and community agencies, many of the modifications listed here can be purchased, designed and made, or adapted to meet the individual needs of the children in your class. The extra planning and effort will be well worth the results: seeing the active, joyful, independent participation and learning of children who might otherwise be uninvolved or require physical manipulation.

SERVING ALL CHILDREN

As this chapter has shown, each of the activity areas in the modules can be adapted to meet the needs of children with varying ability levels, and the activities provide a wealth of opportunity for skill acquisition across domains. Many children with disabilities have skeletal or musculoskeletal abnormalities or other health-related problems that preclude involvement in certain types of motor activities. The team should be fully aware of all medical records for each child and modify experiences as necessary. Children with motor and sensory disabilities should have, at a minimum, ongoing consultation from a sensory specialist, an occupational therapist, and/or a physical therapist. Likewise, children with speech-language disorders should have, at a minimum, ongoing consultation from a speech-language pathologist. Children with identified emotional disorders need, at a minimum, ongoing consultation from a psychologist.

As stated previously, both recognizing a child's level of functioning and associating objectives for the child with the developmental domains are critical precursors to designing appropriate instruction. Each child is individual, and it is up to you and your team to meet the needs of all of the children in your classroom.

REFERENCES

Bundy, A.C., & O'Brien, J.C. (1993). Facilitating sensorimotor development. In T.W. Linder, *Transdisciplinary play-based intervention: Guidelines for developing a meaningful curriculum for young children* (pp. 397–469). Baltimore: Paul H. Brookes Publishing Co.

Diamant, R.B. (1992). *Positioning for play: Home activities for parents of young children.* San Antonio, TX: Therapy Skill Builders.

King-DeBaun, P. (1990). *Storytime: Stories, symbols and emergent literacy activities for young, special needs children.* Solana Beach, CA: Mayer and Johnson Company.

King-DeBaun, P. (1993). Storytime: Just for fun! Park City, UT: Creative Communicating.

Lahey, M., & Bloom, L. (1977). Planning a first lexicon: Which words to teach first. *Journal of Speech and Hearing Disorders, 42,* 340–350.

Light, J., & Kelford-Smith, A. (1993). The home literacy experiences of preschoolers who use augmentative communication systems and of their non-disabled peers. *Augmentative and Alternative Communication, 9,* 10–25.

Linder, T.W. (1993a). *Transdisciplinary play-based assessment: A functional approach to working with young children* (Rev. ed.). Baltimore: Paul H. Brookes Publishing Co.

Linder, T.W. (1993b). *Transdisciplinary play-based intervention: Guidelines for developing a meaningful curriculum for young children.* Baltimore: Paul H. Brookes Publishing Co.

Marvin, C. (1994). Home literacy experiences of preschool children with single and multiple disabilities. *Topics in Early Childhood Special Education, 14*(4), 436–454.

Sulzby, E. (1985, Summer). Children's emergent reading of favorite storybooks: A developmental study. *Reading Research Quarterly, 20,* 458–481.

Sulzby, E. (1989). Assessment of writing and children's language during writing. In L.M. Morrow & J.K. Smith (Eds.), *Assessment for instruction in early literacy* (pp. 83–109). Upper Saddle River, NJ: Prentice-Hall.

Chapter 5

WHEN A CHILD IN YOUR
CLASSROOM HAS A HEARING LOSS...
Ann D. Bruce

Without communication skills, children miss out on the exchange of feelings, ideas, and information with others. Children with a hearing loss need special help developing these skills. The combination of storybooks and play in *Read, Play, and Learn!*® offers a framework for helping children within many modes of communication, and its variety of activities embedded in a literacy-rich environment challenges children with hearing loss to work on communicating successfully.

The children in your classroom can communicate through many vehicles, including

- Facial expressions and body language
- Gestures
- Oral language or speech
- Reading and writing
- Sign language (Nelson, 1990)

In consultation with a child's parents, you will want to encourage a child who has a hearing impairment to use as many of these forms as appropriate. The activities described in this chapter will aid in communication skill building; will encourage social interactions; will help children appreciate the similarities and differences among their peers; and, of course, will help children enjoy *Read, Play, and Learn!* Some of the strategies may already be in place in your classroom, whereas others may not have been tried but could enhance learning for all children.

SOME BASICS ABOUT HEARING LOSS

A child in your classroom might have a hearing loss that is only slight or one that is profound. Children with a hearing loss of less than 70 dB HL are considered "hard of hearing," and children with a loss of more than 70 dB HL are considered "deaf" (Steinberg & Knightly, 1997). The dB stands for "decibels," and the HL stands for "hearing level." A decibel is the unit used to measure sound intensity;

the softest sound heard by a typical person is said to be 0 dB (Chen, 1997). Loud conversation measures about 70 dB, whereas a whisper might only be 25–30 dB and a jet at takeoff would be about 120 dB. When a child is acquiring language skills, even a slight hearing loss can be a problem. There are many types of hearing loss, and other sources can give you additional information (e.g., Flexer, 1994; Northern & Downs, 1991). You will want to be sure to have a professional with training in speech-language pathology and/or audiology on your team when you have a child with a hearing loss in your class or program.

Although it is likely that a hearing loss will have been identified in a child before he or she is in your care, it is a good idea to watch for indicators of potential hearing loss. There will often be physical or behavioral signs. Children who have been sick with middle-ear infections might have temporary hearing losses. A few of the behaviors to watch for include the following:

- Pulling on the ears or putting hands over the ears
- Not responding when familiar adults call the child's name
- Seeming not to listen
- Responding very little or inconsistently to sound
- Using very limited vocalizations (Chen, 1997)

Be sure to take note of any concerns that parents have about their child's hearing, and if you observe these behaviors or others that could point to a hearing loss, you should refer the child to an audiologist (Gatty, 1996).

CAPITALIZE ON RESIDUAL HEARING

Most children, even those with a profound hearing loss, do have some available hearing. The importance of maximizing use of any available hearing cannot be overemphasized. The use of residual hearing is vital to all children with a hearing loss, either as a primary means of communication or as a supplement to a signing system. There are two primary things you and the other team members can do: 1) If the child uses an amplification system, be sure it is consistently monitored; and 2) provide consistent auditory input during meaningful and interesting daily activities (Clarke & Watkins, 1985).

Find Out About and Consistently Monitor the Child's Amplification System

Most children with a hearing loss can benefit from some sort of amplification. Some will only be able to hear noises and the sound of the voice, but even this is helpful in making them more alert and improving their voice quality and speech rhythm. Other children will be able to recognize vowel sounds, whereas still others will be able to understand words and sentences. Not all children respond in the same way to the same sound. How much the child benefits from a hearing aid and/or an assistive listening device (e.g., an FM system) depends on the type of hearing loss, the environment, and the child. It is important to note that hearing aids do not correct hearing loss the way that glasses correct vision. Indeed, a hearing aid can only make sounds louder; it does not improve clarity for the child or selectively amplify speech and decrease background noise (Steinberg & Knightly, 1997). An audiologist can tell you more about the types of hearing aids available. Basically, a hearing aid includes a microphone (to change acoustic signals into electrical energy), an amplifier, and a receiver (to convert the electrical signal back to an amplified acoustical signal). An FM system includes a microphone and a wireless transmitter worn by the speaker and a transmitter worn by the listener. Because FM systems help to reduce the background noise heard by the child, they are commonly used in difficult listening situations such as the classroom, often with a hearing aid or as an all-in-one combination (Steinberg & Knightly, 1997). A child can be fitted as soon as a permanent hearing loss is identified. Hearing aids can often help the child to feel more a part of his or her environment.

Consistent monitoring of the child's amplification system involves a *daily* listening check, troubleshooting for feedback, and caring for the system and the batteries. This monitoring is best done by a specialist in the field, such as a teacher of the deaf, an audiologist, or a speech-language pathologist. Other sources can give you more information on the use of amplification and daily listening checks (Flexer, 1994; Northern & Downs, 1991).

It is possible that a child in your class or program might have a cochlear implant. This surgically implanted prosthetic device, which electrically stimulates the cochlea (a structure in the inner ear containing the organ of hearing), was approved in 1990 by the U.S. Food and Drug Administration for use in children who are deaf and do not benefit from amplification. The electrical information perceived by the child does not imitate typical hearing but can help improve detection of environmental and speech sounds and also help with speech production. There are some controversies around the use of cochlear implants, and families considering the procedure should have counseling regarding benefits and limitations of implants (Steinberg & Knightly, 1997).

Enhance Auditory Input

Whereas the introduction of an amplification system or the monitoring of a cochlear implant will require the input of a specialist on your team, the provision of consistent, meaningful auditory input is something that you, as the classroom teacher, can do.

Fundamental to fulfilling this need is recognizing that listening is a skill that must be learned. The child with a hearing loss must be taught to be aware of sound, to discriminate among a variety of sounds, to attach meaning to sound, and then to tell from which direction sound is coming. These skills are all developed simultaneously, not separately (Bailey & Wolery, 1992). Expose the children to a wide variety of sounds, including environmental sounds, music, and speech. The strategies described in this chapter will help you get started, but first a caution about temporary hearing loss.

BE ALERT TO TEMPORARY HEARING LOSS

Middle-ear infections, known as *otitis media,* are one of the most common illnesses in preschool children. Indeed, otitis media was the most commonly diagnosed disease among children in the United States in 1990 (Roberts, Wallace, & Henderson, 1997); according to another source, 76%–95% of all children have one middle-ear infection before the age of 2 (Steinberg & Knightly, 1997). These infections, which cause an inflammation of the middle ear, interfere with hearing. A preschool child with frequent ear infections experiences a temporary loss of hearing. Even a mild, temporary loss can delay the development of language skills. The loss may continue for up to 6 weeks after the infection has healed and can be a major cause of speech and language delays. Consequently, many of the following guidelines should be incorporated into general classroom teaching strategies (Watts, Roberts, & Zeisel, 1993). Much of the information, with some modification, will be helpful for those children who are experiencing a temporary hearing loss as a result of recurrent ear infections.

HELP CHILDREN LEARN TO LISTEN

Whereas a child who is born with normal hearing may listen to surrounding talk for more than a year and understand many words before even attempting to talk, children who have hearing impairments require more listening experience as they go through the same stages of language development. Listening games are an ideal technique for helping children learn the meaning of sounds and words, and the **Read, Play, and Learn!** modules give you lots of opportunities.

When working on the module based on *Abiyoyo,* for example, assemble several different musical instruments, such as bells, a drum, and a guitar. Make a noise with an instrument, point to your ears, imitate the noise, and say, "I hear a _____." Soon the child will point to the object to show that he or she heard the sound, too. The child may even name the instrument that made the noise. Once the child becomes aware of different sounds, ask him or her to listen and identify them without looking. Play a game during which you put two or three instruments on the table and make a sound with one while the child is not looking. Ask the child to turn around and point to the toy that made the sound. Let the child do the same for you or other children.

Take advantage of the howling coyote in *The Three Little Javelinas.* Introduce other animals and their sounds. Match them to pictures or stuffed animals. This is a fun activity that several children will enjoy doing together. You can also model the activity and then encourage the child to make a game of it by inviting other children to play and take turns being "teacher." This creates a wonderful opportunity for social interactions and communicative growth.

The Little Old Lady Who Was Not Afraid of Anything presents another good opportunity to help children become aware of sound. During the dramatization of the story, encourage the child with a hearing loss to take the part of the shoes or the gloves and emphasize the accompanying sounds (e.g., "The gloves go CLAP, CLAP"). In addition, encourage the child to imitate sounds as they are heard.

The module on *The Snowy Day* also presents many opportunities to become aware of sound. During the dramatization, you could add the following script: "Crunch, crunch goes the snow—then it's very quiet. Shhhh. Plop, the snow fell on Peter's head." Introduce other crunch sounds (e.g., dried leaves, eating popcorn). Think of objects that make a plop sound.

The module based on *A Porcupine Named Fluffy* creates a chance for children to jump or bounce down a path of bubble wrap. Describe the sounds for the children as they are produced, and also draw their attention to the silence afterward. If a visual communication system is being used, incorporate signs for the sounds being made.

Listening instruction should go on throughout the child's day. Besides using the sounds of the stories, call attention to various environmental sounds, speech sounds, and music as they occur naturally during the day. For example, if a fire engine races by as the children are involved in an activity, you might sign or say, "Wow, listen to the siren. I can hear the fire truck. It's loud." These comments need not interrupt the flow of the activity in which the children are engaged but simply draw attention to an obvious sound. And, all of the children in your class are likely to be curious anyway!

The following general principles should assist you in creating an environment in which the child with a hearing loss is able to make maximum use of the hearing and/or other cues available to him or her:

- *Talk directly to the child*—Get down to the child's eye level, or bring the child up to yours.
- *Keep it simple*—Use short, simple phrases and sentences.
- *Use lots of facial and body expressions*—Use the child's eyes to alert the ears that something important is about to happen.
- *Use a natural tone of voice*—You do not need to speak more loudly, but do speak clearly and not too fast.
- *Talk about the things that are important to the child*—When the child points, gazes, or attempts to verbalize, try to understand what the child is trying to communicate and put that message into words. Say or sign, for example, OH, YOU WANT THE BLUE CRAYON. HERE IT IS, RIGHT NEXT TO THE YELLOW ONE.

STRUCTURE THE ENVIRONMENT

The design of your classroom or center is important to the success of the child who has a hearing loss. There are at least three important points to consider.

First, the child must be able to clearly see the face of the person who is talking. Speechreading and obtaining clues from facial expressions and body language are vital components of understanding language. Encourage the child to move to positions or areas of the classroom where he or she can see comfortably. This is an important step toward helping the child become independent and proactive in creating an environment in which the child can learn optimally. Lighting is also important. The light source should be on the face of the speaker and not in the eyes of the child. A common error is to stand in front of a light source (e.g., a window) while speaking or signing to the child. This creates a silhouette effect that makes it difficult to see facial expressions, lip movements, or signs.

Second, be sure the child is near the person who is talking. If the child is using a hearing aid, distance from the speaker is an important issue unless an FM system is available. It is likely that the aid will not effectively amplify sounds that have to travel around corners. The child may not respond if the speaker is across the room. If sign language is used, the child needs to be in a position that allows clear visibility.

Third, avoid background noises whenever possible. Noise of any type interferes with the ability to understand speech. This is especially true for children with certain types of hearing losses and those wearing hearing aids. Mechanical equipment such as fans and heaters, background music, buzzing lights, and the movement of chairs will interfere with understanding speech. Whenever possible, classroom surfaces, such as walls, ceilings, floors, and windows, should be covered with materials that absorb unnecessary noise. Draperies, upholstery, carpeting, and acoustical tile will all be helpful in decreasing background noise (Kampfe, 1984).

BUILD SKILLS EXPERIENTIALLY

You already know that teaching simply through structured activities, such as sitting at a table and identifying pictures, is not likely to be effective with young children. The child with a hearing loss—as with any child, and perhaps more so—needs to be able to move around, touch, feel, and manipulate the real objects.

Select objects that are meaningful, motivating, and interesting to the child, and talk about what the child is doing as he or she is doing it. In the Woodworking Center, for example, talk about and imitate the sounds that are made with the various tools (e.g., "Pound, pound, goes the hammer"). Make up sounds to accompany any other tools that are available, and vocalize these sounds as the child is using the tool. Continue activities that require the child to discriminate among several sounds. Encourage the child to imitate you and to feel the vibrations the hammer makes on the woodworking bench. Can the child feel these vibrations all the way to the floor? During the dramatization in the module based on *The Three Billy Goats Gruff*, have the child feel the vibrations as children stomp across the bridge.

At the Literacy Center, inked stamps of pictures and letters are frequently used. Model for the child using different pressure intensities paired with matching loud and soft sounds. For example, with a stamp of a picture of a bear during the module based on *Somebody and the Three Blairs*, have the children say "bear" or "grrr" loudly or softly to match the heavy or light pressure exerted on the stamp. Draw the children's attention to these differences.

Help the child to label important objects, actions, and feelings as he or she is being exposed to them. Initially, selecting one or two target words for each activity is sufficient. You can add more words gradually, as the child masters the words first introduced. During the module based on *First Flight*, talk about, imitate, and sign (when appropriate) common highway sounds: car horns, sirens, and general traffic noises. Discuss with the children the wide variety of sounds found in an airport: security alarms, loudspeakers to announce flight changes, and the sounds produced by aircraft taking off and landing. Discuss the differences between loud and soft and high and low noises.

First Flight also presents an ideal opportunity to label different emotions, such as fear and excitement. Labeling emotions is a concept that is often difficult for the child with a hearing loss. This concept should be emphasized in all of the storybooks (e.g., fear and bravery in *The Little Old Lady Who Was Not Afraid of Anything* and *The Three Billy Goats Gruff*, sadness and happiness in *The Kissing Hand*).

Another important skill-building technique is to describe what the child sees. During the dramatization of *A Porcupine Named Fluffy*, sign or talk to the child about what is happening (e.g., "The porcupine is giggling, tee hee hee. Now he is roaring with laughter, HA HA HA"). Imitate verbally any sounds that are being made as the story is reenacted; the process in making the child with a hearing loss aware of the presence of sound needs to be continual. This story also provides an excellent opportunity to talk about loud and quiet sounds. *The Three Billy Goats Gruff* is another opportunity to introduce different sound intensities (e.g., "Here's the baby billy goat. Trip, trap softly across the bridge [whisper]. Here comes the middle-sized billy goat. Trip, trap across the bridge [slightly louder]. Here's the BIG billy goat. TRIP, TRAP across the bridge [much louder]").

We cannot expect the child with a hearing loss to learn language incidentally by hearing, or overhearing, the conversations of other people as do hearing children. Expanding on the child's comments consistently in a natural and realistic manner will continue the process of building the child's communication skills. During the module based on *Picking Apples & Pumpkins*, when the child says or signs PUMPKIN, respond with "Pumpkin, that's a big orange pumpkin."

Retelling a story is a wonderful opportunity to help build children's narrative skills. Encourage story retelling using pictures from the storybooks if necessary, and have the children take turns retelling the story as a group. Write the story on large sheets of paper as they talk. They may want to add drawings to their versions. These large sheets of paper can then be hung in the hallway or on a classroom wall. For example, in the module based on *The Kissing Hand*, you can write down the child's words of what they like about their school and homes. By engaging in print-related activities such as this, young children with a hearing loss can develop oral, sign-based, and written language abilities (Katims, 1991).

WORK AS A TEAM

When you are working with a child identified as having a hearing loss, a transdisciplinary approach is ideal. The team members should plan together how to incorporate activities to enhance listening skills, adjust the classroom environment, and introduce guidelines for improving skills in language and other developmental domains. A special education teacher who has been trained in the area of deafness, an audiologist, or a speech-language pathologist should bring to the team the knowledge and understanding of hearing loss. Such a specialist is vital for input regarding the type of hearing loss and what its effects might be, the choice of communication modality, and the decisions surrounding any amplification equipment such as hearing aids and cochlear implants. If the child is communicating through the use of a visual communication system, such as American Sign Language (ASL), then a full-time interpreter is also an essential member of the team. Ideally, teachers, aides, or volunteers who are deaf should be members of the team to serve as role models and aid in communication through the use of sign language.

IDENTIFY THE CHILD'S PREFERRED COMMUNICATION MODALITY

Professionals in the field of hearing impairment are divided on the value of different approaches for helping children learn speech and language. Some of the communication choices available include the following:

- *Auditory-oral*—This approach trains the child to make the most of his or her speech and hearing abilities.
- *Total communication*—This approach uses a combination of speech, hearing, vision, speechreading, signing, fingerspelling, reading, and writing.
- *American Sign Language (ASL)*—This approach teaches the child an alternative to spoken English; it is a formal visual communication system with a structure very different from English (Kiser, 1990).

A variety of options are available across these communication modalities, and more than one can be used. Many factors must be considered before a decision is made. No one approach is best for all children. Each approach has strengths for different children and different families. It is not uncommon for parents to change approaches several times before deciding which method is best. Often, the child will help make this decision. Teachers should be aware of the child's mode of communication, be it oral, sign language, or a combination, and communicate with the child using the appropriate system. For the child with a moderate hearing loss who does not communicate with sign language, the team may need to make only minor modifications to classroom activities. An ASL interpreter or a translator, however, is a vital team member for a child whose family signs in English or uses ASL.

When working with children who have a significant hearing loss, you want to think particularly in terms of the issues that have an impact on the child's understanding of speech and language, and the child and family's preferred communication modality. With the help of your fellow team members, the following activities should be incorporated as much as possible into the classroom (Solit, Taylor, & Bednarczyk, 1992):

1. Teach basic sign on a regular basis, give each child a name sign, incorporate signing into routines, and sign songs. For example, expose all children to basic sign vocabulary for each of the storybooks as they are being presented. Hearing children will learn many of these signs incidentally and may require little explicit instruction. Research in schools that have used ASL in inclusive classrooms has shown that this approach enriches the literacy skills of all students. In fact, the children enjoy learning a second language (Andrews, Ferguson, Roberts, & Hodges, 1997; Andrews, Winograd, & DeVille, 1996).

2. Make available children's books on communication, assistive devices, and Deaf culture (see the appendix at the end of this chapter for a list of recom-

mended literature selections). (*Deaf* is usually capitalized when referring to the community of Deaf citizens who choose ASL as their primary language.)

3. Incorporate into daily activities opportunities when sign (without speech) is used. Call attention to manual communication, and encourage children and adults to acquire a basic signing vocabulary.

4. Make sure that children who are deaf or hard of hearing are given opportunities to gain an awareness and respect for Deaf culture. Make use of opportunities in the storybooks and in classroom activities to include topics on deafness, communication, and equipment needs. Include posters with the manual alphabet, videotapes with stories (see the appendix at the end of this chapter), cartoons, and fairy tales in ASL as well as sign language CD-ROMs and dictionaries.

5. During storytime, read stories as a team. Try several of these methods: a) one adult reading, and one adult signing; b) one adult reading and signing simultaneously and the other holding the book; c) telling the story without a book to ease signing; d) telling the story by both speaking and signing but using only sign to tell some of the more redundant lines; and e) using a flannel board or other visual support for the story.

Remember that the communication modalities of the students who are deaf or hard of hearing in your classroom may be dramatically different from those of their hearing peers. Some of the children with a hearing loss may speechread. Some children will communicate using signed linguistic models that approximate English meaning and form. Finally, some children may be communicating in two languages: ASL (the sign language that is typically used by Deaf adults in the United States) and English and/or different modalities of the same language (e.g., spoken, cued, signed, or written English). Most school programs use a manually coded English, not ASL (Woodward, 1990). One specific form of manually coded English is known as Signing Exact English, or SEE-2. With approximately 4,000 signs and 70 word ending, tense, and "affix" signs (e.g., *-est, -ed, un-*) (Beukelman & Mirenda, 1998), it involves signing English word order, word meaning, and English morphology. In addition, signing and voicing are simultaneous. In contrast, the linguistic structure of ASL is quite different from English. For those students exposed primarily to ASL, English is a second language (Luetke-Stahlman, 1994).

REINFORCE READING STRATEGIES

The storytelling in ***Read, Play, and Learn!*** is an excellent way for children to develop language. For children with hearing loss, storytelling is especially important because research suggests that children who are deaf or hard of hearing have not been as successful at learning to read as their hearing peers (Schiek & Gale, 1995). Reading to deaf and hard-of-hearing students will motivate them to read, promote growth in reading, and expose them to social opportunities inherent in shared reading (Marshark, 1993). The following outline of essential strategies will help students with hearing loss acquire literacy in an enjoyable manner (Luetke-Stahlman, Hayes, & Nielsen, 1996):

1. Focus on the purpose and enjoyment of reading. Parents and teachers should be seen enjoying the process of reading. Praise and encourage children to question, listen to rhythmical language patterns, use expression, and examine print.

2. Use the child's dominant language in an interactive dialogue. Provide opportunities for the child to make predictions and to answer open-ended questions. Help children construct events from the story in terms that they understand.

3. Introduce the book by showing the cover to the children, and discuss what is known and unknown. Encourage children to use the background knowledge they possess and make predictions.

4. Relate the children's lives to the book and the book to the children's lives through interactive discussion. Make attempts to connect the story to personal experiences. For example, in the module on *The Knight and the Dragon*, discuss with the children their experiences with eating out (e.g., "What's your favorite restaurant?" "Let's design menus of our favorite foods").

5. Model concepts of print. This includes stopping at periods, deliberately showing that you are reading from left to right, and pointing out differences between letters and words. Children who rely on sign language will need the correct sign for the elements of print.

6. Discuss the structure of the story and its elements. Talk about the setting, characters, problems, and solutions. This is especially important for children who are deaf and hard of hearing as this structure provides a mental framework for understanding and comprehending the story. Encourage the children to retell, rewrite, and reenact the story.

7. Discuss the meaning of specific words and phrases. Introduce new vocabulary by calling attention to picture cues, provide synonyms and antonyms, and talk about multiple meanings. Shortened versions of the story or a copy of a book can be sent home for additional experience. Signed versions can also be sent home on videotape. Encourage parents to watch the videotape with their child and read or look at the pictures in the storybook.

Reading Strategies to Suggest to Deaf Parents or Deaf Volunteers in Your Classroom

Several studies have documented strategies that deaf readers use while reading to young children with hearing impairments (Lartz, 1993; Lartz & McCollum, 1990). The data reveal a variety of strategies that help promote understanding of and participation in the storybook reading. The following strategies were used successfully by profoundly deaf mothers in several studies. These techniques may be modified for classroom use and can be presented to parents as useful strategies to employ at home.

1. *Sign placement*—The reader signs certain words or phrases, making the sign in front of the picture. This allows the child to see the picture in the book and the reader's signing at the same time.

2. *Story paired with signed demonstration*—The reader clarifies the text by demonstrating the action pictured. For example, in the story *Abiyoyo*, when signing the scene in which the villagers are frightened of the monster, after signing the text, demonstrate the sign elaborately by gesturing hair rising on the back of the reader's own neck.

3. *Real-world connections between the story and the child's experience*—Sign an example of an event in the child's life that is similar to a picture in the book. For example, during the module based on *First Flight*, remind the child of a flight taken and refer to where the child went, who was visited, and so forth. During the module based on *The Kissing Hand*, talk about what it is like to come to school on the bus or in a car.

4. *Attention maintenance*—This may involve physically securing the child's attention to the signing or to a picture in the book. These prompts might include tapping the child on the shoulder or the lap, nudging the child with an elbow, or moving the book up and down. Deaf cultural norms do not include touching a child's face or neck at any time.

5. *Physical demonstrations of character changes*—Use facial expressions and body posture to signal different characters in the book.

6. *Nonmanual signs as questions*—Use facial expressions to ask questions about a picture in the book. These might include twitching the nose, lowering and raising eyebrows, and making mouth movements.

USE THE CURRICULUM'S DEVELOPMENTAL LEVELS

The importance of including children of many developmental levels and abilities in the classroom has already been emphasized in previous chapters. Children gain invaluable skills from observing and interacting with higher-functioning peers. Children of differing developmental levels will be more motivated to engage in a variety of activities when peers are available as role models and play companions. This may involve some challenges for you and your team members, but ongoing communication, support, encouragement, and joint problem solving among team members will help ensure successful outcomes for all children. Following is a discussion of strategies that may be employed for children at different ability levels to promote communication and their awareness of sound. Use of these strategies will assist in encouraging thinking skills, increasing social interactions, promoting more sophisticated communication skills, and improving quality of movement.

Sensorimotor Level

Children at the sensorimotor level need to learn that signals have meaning and that signals can be made for communication. These signals can be sounds, facial expressions, gestures, and signs. Combining hand, facial, and vocal communication with meaningful events helps the child realize which sounds are important. For example, during the module on *The Rainbow Fish*, make a water table available, and through facial expression and vocal inflection talk about how the water feels as you and the child immerse your hands. Present two tubs or buckets of water, one cold (add ice cubes) and one warm. Capitalize on facial expression and body movement while describing the water to express the differences in water temperature (e.g., "Cold. This bucket has cold water. Brrrrrrr"; "Oooooh, I like this one. It's warm. Warm water. This feels good"). Encourage turn taking by imitating and expanding on any utterance or sign the child may make. Reward any communication attempts by smiling, praising, looking at, or touching the child after each attempt.

Many of the storybooks present wonderful opportunities to make use of music. Move to the music with the child who has a hearing loss, gently and rhythmically. Hum or sing along with the music, and allow the child to feel the vibrations your body makes.

Help the child begin to associate certain sounds with different objects. For example, hide a toy in a bag and then shake the bag and make comments on the noise. First, show the child the toy as you put it in the bag. Assist the child in finding it. Encourage the child to shake the bag, and continue commenting on the sound as it is being shaken. Comment also on the silence when the bag is not being shaken.

As with many of the activities discussed, the goal is to be less teacher directed, so provide opportunities for higher-functioning peers to engage in activities by modeling these for them and making a game of the activity.

Functional Level

Children at the functional level will enjoy the experiences described for children at the sensorimotor level as well as any expansions you can make on the activities. Encourage children at this level to label and describe various aspects of the stories. Use and expect the child to increase his or her use of functional words. For example, during the module on *The Knight and the Dragon*, as the child builds armor and prepares for battle with the dragon, emphasize everyday words such as *stop, pour, run, open,* and *wait*. Use these words in as many contexts as possible as they occur in the natural course of the project.

In the module on *The Kissing Hand*, the concept of a *secret* should be presented in many ways and in different contexts. A special treat may be made available at snack that is a "secret" between the teacher and several assigned children who will be setting out the snack. Perhaps the class could be told a "secret" about a surprise party for one of the teachers, a special event at school, or an upcoming field trip.

The module on *The Three Billy Goats Gruff* presents a wonderful opportunity to talk about sizes and the chance to expand this concept to a variety of objects. Encourage the children to compare shoe sizes, differences in height and hair length, and chair and table sizes. At snacktime, cut vegetables and fruits into different sizes and discuss these differences with the children. At the woodworking table, be certain to have available a variety of sizes of wood blocks, hammers, and nails. Encourage the children to use size descriptors when they talk about what they are doing (e.g., "I'm going to use this small wood block and nail it to this long branch. I'm making a little birdhouse").

Symbolic Level

Children at the symbolic level can be given many opportunities to make choices and plan activities to suit their own interests. They should be encouraged to problem-solve situations presented in the stories and to modify the story endings and characters. For example, in the module on *The Rainbow Fish*, ask the children how the story would be different if this were a story about a parrot. Encourage them to modify the stories in other ways: Swap the roles of the three javelinas and the coyote in *The Three Little Javelinas*, or change the characters in *The Knight and the Dragon* to a princess and a kangaroo. Continue to emphasize concepts and events from these stories in a variety of settings as the repetition helps the child to generalize these concepts to diverse situations.

Record some favorite songs and nursery rhymes that include a variety of music—fast, slow, loud, and soft. Dance, march, hop, and jump to the rhythm of the music. Comment, when appropriate, on the music (e.g., "This is fast music; it makes me want to skip"; "This music is slow. It makes me think of floating"). You could also involve the children in drawing or painting with the music. Encourage the children to paint in response to the rhythm of the music. Tape large pieces of paper underneath low tables, and allow the children to lie on their backs and paint to the beat of the music. Encourage the children to feel the vibrations on the floor and paint in response to these. Continue the process of discrimination and comprehension of environmental sounds at each child's developmental level. Children at the symbolic level should be encouraged to identify sounds they hear in the environment, such as school bells, fire drill sirens, lawn mowers, and any other sounds that may be presented. Reinforce and expand on their comments. For example, if the child comments on the noise of an airplane flying overhead, respond with, "You're right. I can hear that airplane, too. Where do you think it might be flying? Have you ever been on an airplane?"

Try to design some of the daily sound activities (e.g., those that focus on transition sounds) in such a way that the child at this level initiates the sound and can exercise some amount of control over the amount of sound he or she receives. It is important for these children to have an interaction of this sort with sound and not always be a passive recipient of sound.

NOW YOU'RE READY

Children with a hearing loss can both contribute to and learn from the many experiences available in the storybook modules presented in this curriculum. Communication among team members and inclusion of parents in the activities will help make the entire process of learning an exciting and enjoyable one. By consciously incorporating modifications for children who are deaf or who have hearing impairments, you can maximize the benefit of each module for all children in the class. For each activity, from reading the story through snack, incorporate attention to sound, maximize comprehension through a variety of visual and auditory cues, and encourage expansion of expression of ideas through a variety of means. For children with a hearing loss, the team needs to not only modify activities to match cognitive level, they must also modify interaction and communication strategies to match modalities of communication of the child. Although this may sound complicated, the team efforts will result in more learning—and more fun— for all of the children.

REFERENCES

Andrews, J., Ferguson, C., Roberts, S., & Hodges, P. (1997). What's up, Billy Jo? Deaf children and bilingual-bicultural instruction in east-central Texas. *American Annals of the Deaf, 142*(1), 16–25.

Andrews, J., Winograd, P., & DeVille, G. (1996). Using sign language summaries during prereading lessons. *The Council for Exceptional Children, 62,* 31–34.

Bailey, D.B., & Wolery, M. (1992). *Teaching infants and preschoolers with disabilities.* New York: Macmillan.

Beukelman, D.R., & Mirenda, P. (1998). *Augmentative and alternative communication: Management of severe communication disorders in children and adults* (2nd ed.). Baltimore: Paul H. Brookes Publishing Co.

Chen, D. (1997). *What can baby hear?: Auditory tests and interventions for infants with multiple disabilities. Viewer's Guide.* Baltimore: Paul H. Brookes Publishing Co.

Clarke, T.C., & Watkins, S. (1985). *SKI*HI Home Visit Curriculum: Program for hearing impaired infants.* Logan: Utah State University.

Dobo, P.J. (1982). Using literature to change attitudes towards the handicapped. *The Reading Teacher, 36,* 290–292.

Flexer, C. (1994). *Facilitating hearing and listening in young children.* San Diego: Singular Publishing Group.

Gatty, C.G. (1996). Early intervention and management of hearing in infants and toddlers. *Infants and Young Children, 9*(1), 1–13.

Kampfe, C.M. (1984). Mainstreaming: Some practical suggestions for teachers and administrators. In A.H. Hull & K.L. Dilka (Eds.), *The hearing-impaired child in school* (pp. 99–106). New York: Grune & Stratton.

Katims, D.S. (1991). Emergent literacy in early childhood special education: Curriculum and instruction. *Topics in Early Childhood Special Education, 11*(1), 69–84.

Kiser, J.M. (1990). *Teaching language to your hearing-impaired child.* San Antonio, TX: Communication Skill Builders.

Lartz, M.N. (1993). A description of mothers' questions to their young deaf children during storybook reading. *American Annals of the Deaf, 138,* 322–330.

Lartz, M.N., & McCollum, J.A. (1990). Maternal questions while reading to deaf and hearing twins: A case study. *American Annals of the Deaf, 135,* 235–240.

Luetke-Stahlman, B. (1994). Procedures for socially integrating preschoolers who are hearing, deaf, and hard-of-hearing. *Topics in Early Childhood Special Education, 14,* 472–487.

Luetke-Stahlman, B., Hayes, P.L., & Nielsen, D.C. (1996). Essential practices as adults read to meet the needs of deaf or hard of hearing students. *American Annals of the Deaf, 141,* 309–320.

Marshark, M. (1993). *Psychological development of deaf children.* New York: Oxford University Press.

Nelson, G. (1990). *Communicating with the hearing-impaired child: The aural-oral approach.* San Antonio, TX: Communication Skill Builders.

Northern, J.L., & Downs, M.P. (1991). *Hearing in children.* Baltimore: Williams & Wilkins.

Roberts, J.E., Wallace, I.F., & Henderson, F.W. (Eds.). (1997). *Otitis media in young children: Medical, developmental, and educational considerations.* Baltimore: Paul H. Brookes Publishing Co.

Schiek, B., & Gale, E. (1995). Preschool deaf and hard of hearing students' interactions during ASL and English storytelling. *American Annals of the Deaf, 140,* 353–370.

Solit, G., Taylor, M., & Bednarczyk, A. (1992). *Access for all: Integrating deaf, hard of hearing, and hearing students.* Washington, DC: Gallaudet University Press.

Steinberg, A.G., & Knightly, C.A. (1997). Hearing: Sounds and silences. In M.L. Batshaw (Ed.), *Children with disabilities* (4th ed., pp. 241–274). Baltimore: Paul H. Brookes Publishing Co.

Turner, N.D., & Traxler, M. (1997). Children's literature for the primary inclusive classroom: Increasing understanding of children with hearing impairments. *American Annals of the Deaf, 142*(5), 350–355.

Watts, M.R., Roberts, J.E., & Zeisel, S.A. (1993). Ear infections in young children: The role of the early childhood educator. *Young Children, 49*, 65–72.

Woodward, J. (1990). Communication in classrooms for deaf students: Student, teacher, and program characteristics. In H. Bornstein (Ed.), *Manual communication: Implications for education* (pp. 45–66). Washington, DC: Gallaudet University Press.

Appendix

LITERATURE AND RESOURCES PERTAINING TO CHILDREN WITH A HEARING LOSS

Assisting children with disabilities to become important and contributing members of the general classroom is an important goal for the transdisciplinary team. Equally as important, however, is increasing awareness and understanding among those students without disabilities. An excellent method of promoting this understanding is through the use of children's literature featuring children with disabilities. Experiences with stories such as the ones that follow provide chances for children to view the world from different perspectives and to grow and develop in many ways. Children who experience books about disabilities show positive growth in compassion and understanding of those with disabilities (Dobo, 1982). Turner and Traxler (1997) have studied numerous children's books featuring children with a hearing loss. A listing of several of these books along with a summary and related classroom activities to enhance experiences with the books follows:

LITERATURE SELECTIONS

Bergman, T. (1989). *Finding a common language.* Milwaukee, WI: Gareth Stevens Publications.

This is a story about 6-year-old Lina, who uses a hearing aid because she is almost completely deaf. Both the story and the amazing pictures show her life at home and at her preschool for the Deaf. She faces many daily challenges and frustrations, and the reader is shown how she copes with these. Just like any child, Lina has hopes, joys, and sorrows. Her hearing loss does not make her different in those aspects.

The content in the "Literature Selections" section of the Appendix has been directly quoted and adapted from Turner, N.D., & Traxler, M. (1997). Children's literature for the primary inclusive classroom: Increasing understanding of children with hearing impairments. *American Annals of the Deaf, 142*(5), 350–355; reprinted and adapted by permission.

- Encourage the children to talk about a time when they had a hearing test. If possible, obtain a portable audiometer and allow the children to experience a hearing test.
- Talk to the children about what is meant by the term *universal language*.
- Invite someone to come into the classroom to talk about adaptive equipment.

Booth, B.D. (1991). *Mandy.* New York: Lothrop, Lee, and Shepard Books.

This book relates the story of Mandy, who is deaf, and her Grandma, who live together in the country and are very close. Pictures show them baking cookies, dancing, looking at a photo album, and going for a walk. Mandy becomes a hero when she goes back to the woods during a storm to find her Grandma's special silver pin. Beautiful paintings show this story about a very special little girl who is deaf.

- Discuss with the children what sounds they would miss most if they could not hear.
- Mandy's grandma is very special to her. Talk with the children about a special person in their lives.
- Mandy and Grandma enjoy dancing. Play some music, and move to it. Talk about fast and slow and quiet and loud music. Have the children pick partners when dancing.
- Have the children choose a sound that is familiar to them, and have them describe that sound for Mandy as well as draw a picture.
- Discuss with the children how Mandy and Grandma communicate. Do they need a lot of words to communicate?

Charlip, R., Beth, M., & Ancona, G. (1974). *Handtalk: An ABC of fingerspelling and sign language.* New York: Four Winds Press.

This picture book communicates in full-color photographs two different languages—fingerspelling and sign. For each letter of the alphabet, there is a word that is being signed by a person in the photograph as well as fingerspelled by means of small pictures at the bottom of the page. Children will learn many of the signs and positions for spelling because they are encouraged to decode the words on their own.

- Have the children make up a secret code with a friend. Practice "talking" to each other.
- The children can learn some of the signs in the book. Have them teach what they have learned to a friend.
- People who communicate for those who are deaf are called *interpreters*. Ask the children to discuss where they have seen an interpreter at work.
- Have the children compose a sentence using sign language.

- With a partner, the children can make up new signs or expressions for words or ideas. Encourage them to try to communicate with each other.
- Choose a simple song or nursery rhyme. Sign it to the class.

Greenberg, J.E. (1985). *What is the sign for friend?* New York: Franklin Watts.

Shane loves pizza, swimming, and playing, just like any boy his age. However, he is almost completely deaf and uses a hearing aid. The story and pictures in this book tell of Shane's experiences at home, with his friends, and in his classroom with hearing children. Signs for special words are included throughout the book.

- Shane enjoys having a special treat with his family, sometimes pizza. Ask the children what their favorite treat to share with their families is.
- Shane works with a speech-language therapist, who helps him improve his speech. Invite a speech-language therapist to the classroom to talk about his or her job.
- Shane and his friend Mitchell enjoy playing on a soccer team. Have the children draw a picture of something they enjoy doing with a friend.
- Invite someone from a television station to explain how closed-captioning devices work for people with a hearing loss.
- Shane's dad wakes him up in the morning. Ask the children who wakes them up and to tell what happens in their home in the morning.

Levine, E.S. (1974). *Lisa and her soundless world.* New York: Human Sciences Press.

Lisa is a little girl who plays and works like most little girls. When Lisa does not respond to her parents' questions, however, they discover that she has a hearing loss. The story shows how Lisa learns to communicate using a hearing aid, speech-reading, and fingerspelling.

- Have the children watch a television program with the sound turned off. Ask the children to describe how it feels. Do things seem mixed up?
- Have the children try to understand what a friend is saying by speechreading. Is it easy to understand what they are saying?
- Lisa feels the vibrations that people make when they say a word out loud. Have the children find a partner and feel the vibrations that they make when they say a word.
- Lisa is left out sometimes. Have the children draw a picture or write about a time when they were left out.
- Invite someone from a hearing-aid company to demonstrate hearing aids to the children.

Litchfield, A.B. (1976). *A button in her ear.* Chicago: Albert Whitman.

This delightful book tells the story of Angela and how she came to wear a hearing aid, or "button," in her ear. In different situations, Angela misunderstands what people are saying to her until her parents take her to a doctor to be checked. After she is fitted with the aid, she shows it to her class. Her demonstration will help the reader understand the purposes of hearing aids.

- Invite an audiologist to the classroom to explain and demonstrate hearing testing to the children.
- Angela and Buzzie are friends, but they are not always nice to each other. Talk with the children about a time when they and a friend had trouble being together.
- Angela's pediatrician examines her ears. Look at a picture book that shows the parts of the ear. The children can learn the name, location, and job of each part.
- Ask the children about what they would want to ask Angela if they were in her class when she explained her hearing aid.

Pearson, J.W. (1977). *I have a sister, my sister is deaf.* New York: HarperCollins.

A young girl tells about her sister, who is deaf. She writes about how her sister is like other little girls and how she is different. Her sister can play the piano but will never be able to sing because she cannot hear the tune. Her sister does not hear wind chimes or thunder. The girl explains how her sister communicates and how she seems to feel about being deaf.

- Have the children discuss how the two sisters "talk" to each other without using words.
- Have the children wear sound-blocking headphones for a short time in class. Talk about how it feels not to be able to hear.
- Take a walk outside. Have the children identify all of the sounds they can hear. Discuss what it would be like not to hear them.

Peter, D. (1976). *Claire and Emma.* New York: John Day.

This book depicts the life of two sisters—Claire, who is 4 years old, and Emma, who is 2 years old. Both girls were born deaf. They both wear hearing aids and take lessons to help them speak well. The story tells of their lives with their mother and brother and their frustrations and joys. A better understanding of deafness and its implications can be obtained from this book.

- The book talks about several things you can do to make it easier for people who are deaf to understand what you are saying. Talk about some of these things.
- Have the children practice speechreading with a friend. Do they think it is easy?
- Claire and Emma are sisters who enjoy doing many things together. Have the children draw a picture of someone with whom they enjoy doing things.

Sullivan, M.B., Bourke, L., & Regan, S. (1980). *A show of hands: Say it in sign language.* Philadelphia: Lippincott.

Mostly in cartoon format, this book is about sign language and how it can be modified through the use of body language. It features a wonderful section on "celebrity signs," such as Hercules signing the word STRONG. This book also explains the history of fingerspelling and displays the manual alphabet. Children can learn a great deal from this book, as more than 150 signs are shown.

- Have the children draw a cartoon story similar to the book.
- Teach the children some of the signs in the book. Have them teach the signs to their parents.
- Have the children use facial expressions to show a feeling. Have their friends guess the feeling. Discuss what kinds of things make them feel that way.

Wolf, B. (1977). *Anna's silent world.* Philadelphia: Lippincott.

Anna was born deaf, but she has learned to speak and to understand people around her. She is included in a general education first-grade classroom and goes to a ballet class every week. The book and photographs tell the story of a wonderful little girl and also provide information about hearing loss.

- Anna received a special gift for Christmas. Have the children tell about a special gift they have received.
- Anna's family enjoys music and dancing. Have the children discuss some of the things their families enjoy doing.
- Anna likes to swing at recess. Have the children discuss some of their favorite recess activities.

WHERE TO FIND HELP

For deaf children who use a visual-spatial language, such as American Sign Language, a list of books that have proven successful for listening through the air (i.e., visually) is available. A team at the Kansas School for the Deaf have developed criteria for selecting books for visual storyreading that include suggestions on how to read those books to deaf children. In addition, they have many inexpensive storybook videotapes for sale. For more information, contact

Mona Huggins, Head Librarian
Visual Storyreading Program
Kansas School for the Deaf
450 East Park Street
Olathe, Kansas 66061
Voice/TTY: (913) 791-0573
FAX: (913) 791-0577   www.ksdeaf.org

Federal law requires every state to set up a comprehensive system to identify and help children and their families with hearing problems and other special needs. Every state department of education has a Child Find system. The following are some other sources of support.

National Resources

Alexander Graham Bell Association for the Deaf and Hard of Hearing
3417 Volta Place, NW
Washington, DC 20007
Voice/TTY: (202) 337-5220
FAX: (202) 337-8314   www.AGBell.org

American Speech-Language-Hearing Association (ASHA)
10801 Rockville Pike
Rockville, Maryland 20852
Voice/TTY: (301) 897-5700
FAX: (301) 571-0457   www.ASHA.org

John Tracy Clinic
806 West Adams Boulevard
Los Angeles, California 90007
Voice: (213) 748-5481
TTY: (213) 747-2924
FAX: (213) 749-1651   www.jtc.org

National Information Center on Deafness
Gallaudet University
800 Florida Avenue, NE
Washington, DC 20002
Voice: (202) 651-5051
TTY: (202) 651-5052   www.clerccenter.gallaudet.edu

National Technical Institute for the Deaf
1 Lomb Memorial Drive
Rochester, New York 14623
Voice: (585) 475-6350
TTY: (585) 475-6242   www.Ntid.RIT.edu

BOOKS AND CATALOGS FOR PARENTS

Angus, A. (1974). *Watch my words.* Cincinnati, OH: Forward Movement Publications.

Bake, C., & Battison, R. (1980). *Sign language and the Deaf community.* Washington, DC: National Association for the Deaf.

Ferris, C. (1980). *A hug just isn't enough.* Washington, DC: Gallaudet University Press.

Schick, B., & Moeller, M.P. (1998). Communicating with your young deaf child [Series of five videotapes]. Boy's Town, NE: Boy's Town Press. (1-800-282-6657)

Sign language materials catalog. (Available from Gallaudet University, Post Office Box 400, Kendall Green, Washington, DC 20002)

Simmons-Martin, A. (1975). *Chats with Johnny's parents.* Washington, DC: Alexander Graham Bell Association for the Deaf.

Chapter 6

WHEN A CHILD IN YOUR CLASSROOM HAS A VISUAL IMPAIRMENT . . .

Tanni L. Anthony

All children benefit from an experience-enriched curriculum. This is an especially important model for children with visual impairments primarily because congenital or early-onset vision loss has a significant impact on the amount of incidental learning available to the young child. Children with visual impairments are at risk for missed or fragmented information about their environment and the activities around them. As one of the two distance senses, vision provides a child with immediate information about spatial dimensions of the environment, the details and the total picture of its contents, and the nonverbal communication of others. Thus, care must be taken to address the learning styles of children who have limited or no sight. Because the avenue of visual learning is reduced or not available for these children, you will need enhanced or different teaching methodologies to meet individual learning needs. These methodologies should not be viewed as compromised means of instruction but rather as important ways to offer the child with a visual impairment equal access to the experiences given to other children within the classroom.

Children with visual impairments do not need a separate curriculum from other children in the classroom, but there will be times when you will want to make adaptations or use unique equipment to make the learning experiences fully accessible. Good advice is contained in the following guiding philosophy: "Experiences should be similar in the purposes that are achieved, rather than in the materials that are used" (Rex, Koenig, Wormsley, & Baker, 1995, p. 41).

A program like *Read, Play, and Learn!*® is rich in developmentally appropriate practices, such as early attention to language development, exposure to oral stories and books, hands-on experiences with real-life objects, and opportunities to "read," all of which fuel the process of becoming literate while enhancing growth across developmental domains. This chapter offers a number of guidelines that will help you keep your classroom accessible to children with visual impairments while benefiting the other children in your classroom as well. These guidelines include the following:

- Whenever possible, offer the child firsthand experience with the concepts and materials of the *Read, Play, and Learn!* storybook modules. Hands-on experience with real objects will provide a solid foundation for learning.

- Pay close attention to the child's learning style and literacy mode(s) so that all available sensory avenues can be fully addressed.

- Use everyday, predictable routines to assist the child in anticipating and ultimately participating in the storybook activities. Learning that occurs within a natural context helps avoid fragmented learning.

- Structure the environment and introduce adaptations to enhance sensory information throughout the curriculum and daily activities.

- When working on reading skills with a child who will be a braille reader, present braille as a literacy mode equal in acceptability to traditional print. When possible, items with print should have a braille counterpart. A braillewriter and a slate and stylus should accompany other writing equipment in the classroom. In addition, you can use tactile adaptations to promote early literacy.

- When working on writing activities, such as making a list or recapping a story, produce the item in braille, too. Use these opportunities to illustrate the purpose and process of writing in braille.

- Use a team approach to determine how best to meet the needs of the child with a visual impairment. The child's parents and a teacher certified in the area of visual impairment will be especially important members of the team.

- Take into account the child's learning needs, and identify at which of the curriculum's three developmental levels the child is functioning so that information is presented at an appropriate cognitive level.

Before elaborating on these guidelines, let's look at what is meant when we say that a child has a visual impairment.

SOME BASICS ABOUT VISUAL IMPAIRMENTS

Normal vision is defined as 20/20. This is a clinical measurement of visual acuity or the clarity of the visual image, which is one aspect of visual functioning. A person with normal vision can see a symbol (picture, number, or letter) on the 20/20 line of the eye exam chart from a specified distance. As a person's visual acuity decreases, the second number increases. For example, the smallest symbol that someone with 20/200 vision can identify on the eye exam chart at 20 feet can be seen by a person with normal vision from 200 feet away. For children between the ages of 3 and 6 years, a variety of picture acuity charts can be used such as the Lea Symbol Test (available from Precision Vision, Chicago) or the Lighthouse Visual Acuity Pictures (available from Lighthouse Enterprises, New York; produced by Precision Vision). The typical eye chart used for testing adults (the Snellen chart) can also be used for young children if the letters are replaced with capital letter Es that point in different directions (the child is asked to say which way the "legs" of the E are pointing).

Another aspect of visual performance involves something called visual field. *Visual field* refers to the entire area that can be seen without moving one's eyes or head (Levack, 1991). A normal visual field is about a 180° arc. You can find the dimensions of your visual field by looking straight ahead with your arms stretched out to either side of your body. Slowly bring your hands in toward the center of your body. Note when you can first see them; this is the beginning of your visual field. You can further experiment with different angles (e.g., on the top of your head, underneath your chin).

There are different types of visual field loss. A *scotoma* is a blind spot in one's visual field. This may occur at any location in your visual field. *Hemanopsia* is a condition in which half of the visual field is absent from one or both eyes. *Tunnel vision* is just what it sounds like: The visual field is constricted to one's central vision. A person may have normal visual acuity and reduced visual fields or deficits in both areas depending on his or her medical condition.

Legal blindness is defined as visual acuity of 20/200 or worse in the better eye with correction or a visual field that is no greater than 20° (Menacker & Batshaw, 1997; Sacks & Silberman, 1998). *Low vision* or *partial sight* is defined as visual acuity better than 20/200 but worse than 20/70 with correction (Menacker & Batshaw, 1997). Both of these categories are recognized as visual impairments by the Individuals with Disabilities Education Act Amendments of 1997 (PL 105-17).

There are a number of visual problems that can occur in the early years. Some can be medically corrected, and others cannot. For example, children who are farsighted or nearsighted can typically be corrected to normal vision with prescription glasses. Muscle imbalances, such as esotropia (crossed eyes), may respond well to early medical treatment by an eye care specialist. Sometimes a child may be patched or have surgery to correct an eye misalignment.

Conditions that frequently result in visual impairment include retinopathy of prematurity (ROP) in which the retina of a premature infant may scar or even fully detach (Stiles & Knox, 1996). Two thirds of infants born weighing less than 3 pounds will develop ROP, predisposing them to severe myopia (nearsightedness), strabismus (an inability of both eyes to look directly at an object at the same time), retinal scarring, and possible glaucoma (Menacker & Batshaw, 1997; Sacks & Silberman, 1998).

Optic nerve hypoplasia, another leading cause of pediatric visual impairment, occurs when the optic nerve does not fully develop during the gestational period. Children with this condition may be totally blind or have severely restricted vision. Another common cause of visual impairment in the early years is cortical visual impairment (CVI). In this condition, there is damage to the visual cortex, and, as such, the brain cannot fully interpret visual information (Groenveld, Jan, & Leader, 1990). Traumatic births, high fevers, or anoxic episodes are all causes of CVI.

Children who have medical diagnoses such as cerebral palsy, postnatal infections (e.g., meningitis), or syndromes (e.g., Down, Goldenhar, Turner) have an increased risk of visual problems such as refractive errors or muscle imbalances. Many of these children may also have a permanent visual loss due to an associative eye condition. For example, children who have been prenatally exposed to alcohol are at risk for optic nerve hypoplasia.

Depending on the diagnosis, an individual may be totally blind or have a range of visual functioning. Those with usable vision may experience one or more of the following: loss of visual acuity, loss of visual field, glare or lighting problems, color deficiency, poor contrast sensitivity, eye movement coordination problems, and/or visual processing difficulties (Morgan, 1994). The last is an example of a challenge imposed by CVI. It is important to understand that every child will see differently, no matter the diagnosis or acuity measurement. It takes time to learn about what helps or hinders a child's visual awareness.

There are too many types and causes of visual impairment to elaborate further, but it is important to understand that the earliest detection possible is crucial to help optimize treatment options and early development. You can play an important role in identifying a vision problem or impairment.

In general, it is wise to employ the "ABC" rule when observing whether there is a concern with a child's vision. The letter A stands for *appearance* of the child's eyes and area around the eyes. Any eye irritation, such as unusual redness, tearing, or excessive mattering, may be indicative of a visual problem. It is of concern if an eye(s) is turning in or out. Both eyes should be symmetrical in size and shape and have equal control in movement. There should be no cloudiness of the cornea, which is the front clear cover of the eye, or the pupil, which is the black center that dilates and constricts as the lighting changes.

The B stands for *behavior.* Behavioral indicators of a visual problem may include the following: squinting, excessively rubbing of eyes, covering up one eye or turning one's head while looking at an item, leaning closer to an object, bringing an object right up close to the eyes, consistently bumping into objects, pausing or stumbling over ground surface changes (pavement to grass), or over-/underreaching for an object.

The final letter, C, represents *complaints.* This is not going to be a common situation with very young children as most will not have the awareness of seeing any differently from their peers, and some will not have the language skills to talk about their visual experience. This is where you will have to be astute to other types of "complaint communication." Rather than tell you that he or she has a headache from eye strain, a young child might become irritable or disengage from an activity.

For example, one 4-year-old boy with motor nystagmus (a condition in which the eyes involuntarily oscillate back and forth) would put his head down on his arms to rest after tasks that required intense visual concentration, such as matching color strips. His teacher would then offer him a verbal explanation of what he was experiencing: "You are tired, it is time to rest." This was an important self-advocacy tool for this child, even at his young age. When he made the transition into kindergarten at age 5, he was prepared to let his teachers know when he needed to take a break from a visually demanding task.

If you think a child in your classroom might have an undetected visual problem or impairment, discuss your concerns with team members and the child's parents. An eye exam by an ophthalmologist will be needed for proper diagnosis. Quality health care is important to ensure that vision *and* hearing are maintained at an optimal level. Children should be seen by an eye care specialist on a regular basis; some eye conditions will need to be more closely monitored than others.

Annual audiological care is critical for children with a vision loss as hearing will be a critical avenue of learning. Otitis media must be carefully monitored. Even a mild hearing loss, which occurs with an ear infection, can compromise a young child's language development, balance, and awareness of the environment. For children who have concomitant hearing loss, hearing aids or FM systems (see Chapter 5) may be appropriate.

BUILD SKILLS EXPERIENTIALLY

With absent or limited vision, the child must have alternative ways of acquiring the same rich information that is readily provided to the sighted child. One key strategy for you and the others working in your classroom is to provide a wealth of meaningful hands-on experience. What cannot be seen must, as much as possible, be touched, tasted, smelled, and acted on. An apple must be felt as a whole, as a part, in a bowl as applesauce, in the produce section of a grocery store, on the tree where it grows, and so forth. Without full-bodied learning experiences, the child is at risk for compromised conceptual development that may later influence literacy skills.

The foundation of learning, language development, and, ultimately, literacy is tied to real objects. There is an interactive relationship between language and concept development, and both are promoted by meaningful experience (Rex et al., 1995). You want to be sure that a child with a visual impairment is not held accountable for understanding a concept if it has not been taught in a realistic and meaningful manner. This notion is supported by Stratton and Wright (1991), who stressed the importance of building a broad base of experience for conceptualizing the content of stories.

Some of the storybook modules will require more creativity than others when it comes to bringing a real-life perspective to a young child with a visual impairment. *The Rainbow Fish,* for example, is a book about a beautiful fish with sparkling scales. For the child who cannot see the pictures, the concept of a fish might be very foreign. The child's experience with four-legged creatures cannot help suggest what a fish looks like. Fish sticks at lunch time do not facilitate an understanding of how fish swim in the water or what scales feel like! A plastic replica or paper art project fish does not represent the real-life counterpart. To learn about fish, the child needs to experience a real fish. This is where your ingenuity comes in, and your entire classroom or center should benefit! Bring in an aquarium or minnow pond fish, and encourage the children to hold the fish. Or examine a taxidermied fish or a whole, fresh fish purchased from the market. Now the children can build a more concrete perspective of the fish in the story. Once the child with a visual impairment has a baseline understanding of "fish," the pretend activities within the classroom will take on more meaning.

Remember to take care not to assume that a child has a true understanding of a concept or an activity just because he or she can provide a verbal description. Use of associated language may turn out to only be rote memorization, and full understanding may not be mastered at all. Sara, a 3-year-old with optic nerve atrophy, could label many of the parts of a shape puzzle. Her instructor, impressed that she had correctly used the word "oval," paused a moment, though, to probe her understanding of the word. When she asked, "Tell me about the oval," Sara broke into a smile and said, "Oval, oval Redenbacher [of popcorn fame]!" A true understanding of the spatial dimensions of an oval was not the goal of Sara's preschool program, of course, but this example illustrates the influence of two limiting language-learning experiences: being drilled on a shape puzzle without the benefit of finding the shapes in real-life settings and passive listening to television commercials!

Remind parents and other team members to not assume that the audio or verbal narrative associated with a film or story alone provides complete and meaningful information to a young child with a visual impairment. Ground the child's understanding of the content of the story in real-life experiences; otherwise, you may have children who can reproduce commercial jingles and rattle off associative vocabulary but have not expanded or deepened their conceptual framework.

Sighted children glean information from pictures to supplement the verbal narrative. Miscellaneous information not even mentioned in the story is conveyed to the sighted child by the illustrations. Pictures help to increase visual recognition and memory skills and aid in interpreting the direction of the story. For the child who cannot benefit from visual images, the words may be empty of context and the chance for expanded knowledge lost, unless hands-on experience with the key concepts in the book is offered (Henderson, 1960).

If you can, preview each book you elect to use for its visual language. Close your eyes, and have another person read the book to you as a way to hear the words without the opportunity to see the accompanying illustrations. This method often highlights at what point props are needed and which real-life experiences can be associated with the storytelling.

In *Somebody and the Three Blairs*, an abundance of information in the pictures gives particular meaning to the story's words. When the visiting bear announces, "This game is too noisy," the illustration shows him knocking over a pile of canned goods. As he sorts through food in the freezer, he says, "This game is too cold." Unless you deliberately narrate what is in the pictures, the child without sight misses information that is readily offered to the other children. Even with the verbal description, the words may not be meaningful unless the child has the opportunity to handle canned goods from the cupboard or feel the cold of freezer food. Dramatic play can be especially useful as a tool for the child with a visual impairment to learn about an activity. A center that has real canned goods in a cupboard offers an excellent role-play opportunity. Later, the canned goods can be used in a real-life setting: Ask the children to select a can of fruit for their afternoon snack.

Some storybook concepts will be particularly challenging to "bring to life" when a child cannot benefit from the pictures in a book. A story about a rocket ship and outer space may not have full meaning to children with sight, but the pictures on the pages will help build their understanding of the topic. When a story involves more abstract concepts, such as space travel, you can first introduce something more familiar and concrete to preschool children, such as a car to represent the idea of a moving vehicle. Then you can lift up some of the children, especially those with visual impairments, one at a time and ask them to reach overhead and "feel" the air above them. With this kind of simple dramatization, space beyond touch can begin to be understood. These experiences will help give more meaning to words that do not have direct tangible experiences easily associated with them.

IDENTIFY PREFERRED LITERACY MODES

Literacy mode refers to the sensory channel(s) that the child will ultimately use for reading and writing (Koenig & Holbrook, 1995). The literacy modes of some children with visual impairments will be obvious. The child who is blind will undoubtedly learn best from tactile and auditory modes. The child with low vision, however, may or may not use vision as a primary literacy mode. Careful assessment is necessary; assumptions should never be made based on diagnosis or visual acuity alone. All available sensory channels should be developed and refined in the early years; the goal is to enhance *all* learning avenues and build future options for literacy access.

INTRODUCE CLASSROOM ROUTINES

Deliberate exposure to and participation in the daily routines associated with the family's home and the preschool or kindergarten program offer an important backdrop for hands-on learning. The storybook curriculum approach supports learning through modules, or units, and routines. The curriculum offers the child multiple opportunities to learn by touching, interacting, and doing. Although hands-on learning with real objects is important for all young children, it cannot be emphasized enough for the child who has a visual impairment.

The classroom routine further provides the child with "a predictable reality" of the sequence of learning activities (Drezek, 1995). Routines provide a clear understanding of when an activity begins and when it ends. Even though the content of the day changes with new storybook activities, the structure of the day can remain the same. This framework lets you provide the child with an important vehicle to know what, when, and where something is happening.

One recommended strategy is to examine what aspects of a classroom routine might be missed by the child with a visual impairment. For example, the child who is blind cannot see the classroom teacher getting the snack materials from the cupboard. Without this information, the snack may seem to appear on the table "from out of nowhere." The child should have the opportunity to assist in getting the snack from the cupboard, disseminating the items to classmates, cleaning up the table, and putting the items away. This full experience certainly does not need to happen during every snack period, but it should be built into the child's repertoire early in the school year.

Verbal and physical cues can also assist with the process of anticipating and participating in the sequence of the routines. Object cues can be used to announce an activity; for example, you could give the child the magic wand to announce a singing activity associated with *Abiyoyo*. Whenever the classroom routines are altered, be sure to let the child know about the change. For example, if outdoor play needs to be moved inside, you could let the child feel the cold windows and explain that because of the weather, you are going to play inside where it is warm.

STRUCTURE THE ENVIRONMENT

Specific attention to the physical features of the environment is needed. Every time you or your team makes changes in the classroom layout or rearranges setups to introduce a new storybook module, the child with a visual impairment should be provided an opportunity to experience or become familiar with the change. For example, as the contents or locations of the learning centers are altered, the child should be shown the changes. If feasible, let the child physically assist with moving items from one place to another.

Drezek (1995) suggested that once a child is familiar with an area's arrangement, the teaching staff can engineer a "problem," such as locking a cupboard that is usually unlocked. The child must then find a solution, such as requesting assistance or locating and using the key kept in a nearby location. This is an important skill for all children as it encourages problem solving.

Visual Adaptations

What visual adaptations you decide to use will depend on individual needs. Some children with visual impairments will benefit from enhanced visual displays, such as enlarged or simplified pictures. For others, specific colors and contrast may be especially helpful. Children with CVI, for example, often demonstrate increased visual attention to bold colors. You might designate a red drinking cup at snacktime for a child with this condition. You may help another child improve reaching accuracy by putting a dark cup on a light-colored table or providing pastel-colored flannel cutouts on a dark flannel board.

Depending on the eye condition, *increased* or *decreased* lighting may assist the child. For a child who needs increased lighting, consider setting up storytime in a part of the room where an overhead light can fall on the pages of the book. Be mindful, though, that for some eye conditions or when certain anticonvulsant medications are taken, a child might experience light sensitivity or poor light/dark adaptation. If overhead lighting is suddenly darkened or illumination is quickly brought up for a specific activity, you will want to be aware of its effects on the child. If the storybook activity involves a dark place like a pretend blanket cave, a child with poor light/dark adaptation may need a moment or two to get used to the difference in lighting while crawling into or out of the cave.

A tool called the Lightbox can be used to illuminate transparent objects or to highlight the silhouettes of solid objects. Colors and shapes can be visually displayed for the child who benefits from the illuminated colors and contrast provided by the Lightbox. Equipment such as a Lightbox should be discussed by your team with the teacher certified in the area of visual impairment to determine its potential benefit to the child.

Attention to the clarity and size of pictures is important to children who can use some visual information. Reducing visual clutter can make a tremendous difference in the ability of a child to discern a picture or an object from its background. Enlarging visual materials may be appropriate for other children with visual impairments. As with other decisions, what to do should be determined on an individual basis. For one child, the use of a slide projector to show big pictures on a wall may help compensate for reduced vision, but if a child has, for instance, a significant visual field loss, then enlargement of pictures or other visual symbols may actually be a detriment to the child's ability to take in the whole picture.

It might be helpful to have a variety of magnification devices in your classroom. A bar or stand magnifier may help a child see a small picture or a detail within an illustration. A closed circuit television can be used to enlarge items that are too small or too fragile to touch in the classroom, such as a ladybug or a tiny flower. It can also be used as a tool for the child to observe his or her own scribbling, drawing, or writing.

Attending to the position of the child also assists with visual access to presented materials. Observe the child's self-determined distance or position from a visual display. Inquiring about an aspect of a picture will invite the child to move as close as he or she needs to answer the question. By asking, "What is the mommy holding in this picture?" you can learn important information about the degree of visual detail the child can discern and the preferred distance for viewing certain types of pictures.

Lack of attention to the focal range of the child can have frustrating consequences for both the child and classmates. For example, Wayne, a preschooler with Down syndrome and a visual impairment, was thought to have a behavior problem because of his fidgety and disruptive behavior during storytime. After a few minutes of listening to the story, Wayne would begin touching and talking to his nearby peers. By moving Wayne closer to the teacher while the story was being read, however, this "problem behavior" was easily rectified. The staff had not been fully aware of Wayne's poor distance vision; when he was 5 or more feet from the teacher, he was not able to see the storybook and props. Without the concrete visuals to reinforce his auditory attention, Wayne had found other things to do at the expense of the storytime activity.

Auditory Adaptations

Listening to stories and storytelling are vital parts of **Read, Play, and Learn!** You may want to challenge the children to fill in the missing words of a familiar story or encourage families to read aloud to their children at home. These activities and other listening-related games can promote auditory, comprehension, and problem-solving skills.

To further highlight listening skills, Miller (1985) recommended an "auditory experience album" in which the sounds of learning events are recorded. The tape can be played at a later time much like a storybook would be read. The class can remember the activity and build on the vocabulary associated with the environmental and vocal sounds of the tape.

An example of a book that might be used for an auditory experience album is *The Little Old Lady Who Was Not Afraid of Anything*. There are a variety of sounds associated with the story, such as shoes that "CLOMP, CLOMP" and gloves that "CLAP, CLAP." To illustrate how clothing can make such sounds, the children can collect each item and work to replicate the sound. Specific fabrics and floor surfaces can be used to figure out the best sound effect. Once the items have been selected, the story can be recorded with the accompanying sounds.

Consider the acoustical environment of your classroom, too. All children need opportunities to have quiet time. The child with a visual impairment may be distracted by too much auditory information. Sara, a busy and precocious 4-year-old, complained to her teacher that the bathroom light was on. This occurred during a quiet table time task 2 days in a row. On the second day, it dawned on the preschool teacher that Sara (who is blind) was telling her that the bathroom light was on.

Before she jumped up to turn off the light in the nearby room, she paused to ask Sara how she knew the light was on. Sara replied, "When the light is on, the fan is on and it is driving me *crazy*!" The teacher realized that she had habituated to the fan's sound, even though it was an obvious deterrent to Sara who relied so heavily on auditory input.

INTRODUCE READING AND WRITING STRATEGIES

The child with a visual impairment is at risk for lack of exposure to written materials (Rex et al., 1995; Swenson, 1988). If the child is not deliberately exposed to people reading or writing at home and at school, these concepts may not be understood. Care should be taken to show the child how others read and write. Include the child in note taking tasks such as making lists of items needed for the next activity or reading a snack recipe together.

Braille

Information typically presented in print is of limited value to the child who is blind unless there is a braille counterpart. When a child in your classroom has a visual impairment, you will want to be sure that braille is introduced as a mode to literacy just as important as the sight reading of print. Braille "should be given its rightful place as a tool in the language arts program" (Henderson, 1960, p. 261). Think about ways to naturally introduce all of your preschoolers to braille. Invite a volunteer who reads braille to read stories to the children. What a great role model! During a field trip, show the children braille in an elevator or on signs. Ask for a braille menu at a restaurant. Since the passage of the Americans with Disabilities Act (ADA) of 1990 (PL 101-336), there have been many more opportunities to see (and touch) braille in our everyday environment.

Braille can be added to any of the commercial storybooks by using transparent overlay material right on the book. There are specific readiness programs for a child who will be a braille user. Rely on the member of your team who is certified in the area of visual impairment to suggest activities with prebraille instructional materials, which can be incorporated in the storybook routines of the classroom. This individual will also be an important resource when ordering books with both print and braille from a variety of commercial sources; some suggestions are listed in the appendix at the end of the chapter.

Tactile Adaptations

In addition to introducing braille in your classroom, you can also use tactile books or "book bags" to promote early literacy (Miller, 1985). Tactile books can be purchased commercially through the American Printing House for the Blind (see the appendix at the end of this chapter) or made by hand. The latter is an especially nice way to capture the objects associated with a learning activity. For example, a "touch book" can be made out of all the textures described in *A Porcupine Named Fluffy*. As the children find materials that reflect the tactile characteristics in the story, the materials can be placed in a book format. Or you and the children could make a tactile book from a collection of items found on a field trip. These items can be glued into a book format or placed in a paper bag reserved for the items pertaining to a certain story or activity. The videotape *Discovering the Magic of Reading: Elizabeth's Story* (1995) offers another way to "bag a story" by placing the items in Ziploc plastic bags that have been stapled at the seams to form a book. The module based on *Picking Apples & Pumpkins* offers a fun opportunity for a field trip. The children can learn firsthand about where and how the produce grows. Branches, leaves, vines, seeds, a sandwich bag of dirt, and other tangibles can be collected for a tactile book or bag.

Plan to send tactile books home to facilitate home–school literacy experiences. Some families of young children who have visual impairments are less likely to read commercial books to their children because of their concern that their child will not understand the magnitude of the visual information (Crespo, 1990). Tactile books can assist families in feeling more confident about reading to their child and creating their own "touchable" stories, if they are worried that the child might be confused by a story that relies on illustrated pictures.

One note of caution when making touch books is to select items that truly feel like the tactile characteristic that is being sought. Sometimes tactile books are made with items that look a certain way but do not feel a certain way. For example, corduroy fabric may feel more bumpy than soft. The actual gluing of the item down into the book can also create a completely different tactile display. If the glue dries in a clump in the middle of the fabric, the cloth can go from being *smooth* to *lumpy!*

In general, it is a good idea to close your eyes and touch a tactile display before introducing it to a child. Otherwise, you might get a quite unintended reaction. Miller (1985) expressed her dismay after using sandpaper in a book that she made for her daughter. The sandpaper accomplished exactly what she was not looking for: Her daughter did not want to touch it! You will want to stay away from items that are tactually aversive. Be aware of the child's reaction to certain textures, and note what both invites and hinders the child to touch and explore.

You can mark books used often in the classroom with special tactile symbols to assist the child with a visual impairment in identifying them. The symbol might be a piece of fabric, a line of dried glue, or another tactile marker. A thin stick representing the magic wand in *Abiyoyo* or sequins representing the fish scales of *The Rainbow Fish* could be glued to the covers of these books. These tactile markers are designed to allow all of the children, including those with visual impairments, equal opportunities to locate a desired book.

You can also use tactile adaptations to highlight certain concepts in commercial storybooks. Not everything on a page needs a tactile adaptation; the idea is to highlight a visual aspect that has a tactile counterpart. For example, one of the main characters in *Friends* is Charlie the Rooster. A feather could be glued to those pages featuring Charlie. This simple adaptation invites children with and without visual impairments to physically connect with the book while learning that roosters have feathers.

Art or learning activities can be designed to include tactile adaptations, such as different types of fabrics or papers and raised lines using puffy paint, dried glue,

Wikki Stix (bendable strands of wax), or pipe cleaners. The Swail dot inverter (available from the American Printing House for the Blind [see the appendix at the end of this chapter]) or a tracing wheel can be used to make lines of dots. The embossed dots from a braillewriter can also be incorporated into the children's artwork or learning materials. The idea is to reinforce the child's creativity and expression through art and heighten learning from tactile input.

Writing Activities

During scribble activities in which the children "write" their stories, the child who is blind can scribble using the braillewriter, slate and stylus, or other tools that leave tactile markings. If a teacher certified in the area of visual impairments or another person with braille skills is in the classroom, he or she can model brailling the story as you are writing the story for the children.

A small window-type screen can be placed under a piece of paper for crayon activities. As the child runs the crayon over the paper, the screen creates tactile markings on the paper. For the child with low vision, scribbling can occur with writing instruments that leave bold markings.

Swenson (1988) recommended that a child with a visual impairment be provided with a variety of opportunities to see the purpose of writing. The goal is to connect the act of marking on paper as a means to tell a story, record a list, send a note to someone, and so forth. Let the child with a visual impairment feel the action of the pen or pencil on the paper to learn how someone writes in print. Then model using a braillewriter or slate and stylus to write the same item in braille. As the child sees others writing, the child will have a reason to experiment with writing independently (Stratton, 1996).

WORK AS A TEAM

It is important to remember to use a team approach to determine how best to meet the needs of the child with a visual impairment. The team should identify what primary and secondary sensory systems are used to gather information and to complete tasks. This information helps to define how information, including emergent literacy materials, is presented to the child. Rex et al. recommended a team approach to repeatedly provide "meaningful interactions with braille literacy materials" in the early years (1995, p. 10).

Early intervention staff can work with the family to ensure that all of the child's sensory avenues are addressed at both a medical and an educational level. An orientation and mobility (O&M) specialist can help structure the environment for optimal exploration, support gross and fine motor activities, and determine the need of adaptive mobility devices and/or a long cane (Anthony, 1993). A teacher certified in the area of visual impairment will greatly assist the team in selecting individualized adaptations and recommendations for specialized equipment.

The teacher certified in the area of visual impairment should also work directly with the family and early childhood personnel to determine the preferred literacy modes of the child and, as appropriate, embed braille into both the home and classroom environment. Ensuring that the home environment has access to equipment and materials that support the child's literacy mode(s) is very important (Craig, 1996). Parents may want to know more about how to read and write braille, use magnification aids, or order books on tape. Ongoing input from parents as well as specialist consultations should be an integral part of your planning.

USE THE CURRICULUM'S DEVELOPMENTAL LEVELS

Following is a discussion of strategies that may be employed for children at different ability levels to promote sensory awareness and understanding in the classroom. Use of these strategies will assist in encouraging thinking skills, increasing social interactions, promoting literacy skills, and improving quality of movement.

Sensorimotor Level

The child's focus during the sensorimotor stage is on learning to move independently and acting on the environment for sensory reward. Take extra care to provide opportunities for purposeful movements that invite active exploration. Encourage the child to reach out and touch the surrounding items in the environment. A reach can later be expanded to a step or a walk across the room to retrieve a requested item.

As the child participates in the daily routines of the classroom, be sure the child has opportunities to interact with the objects involved in the storybook curriculum. Real-life objects should be used at all three learning levels but are especially important in the sensorimotor stage.

Objects should be used in their natural context so that their meaning is reinforced through experience. As you or another team member is reading the story at the beginning of the day, ask the child with a visual impairment to hold an item that is key to the story line. Throughout the daily routine, a variety of objects can be highlighted for the child, such as the cup at drink time, the backpack at the end of the preschool day, and so forth.

Functional Level

Labeling objects is a big part of the functional stage. The best way for children to learn the names of objects in their world is by having hands-on experience with the item. The language exposure can follow. It is wise to balance how much verbal information is offered when the child is involved in active play with the object. It is important that the offered words do not incessantly interrupt the active exploration of the child. Timing is critical. For example, if the child is busy exploring a new item, you may want to wait for a natural pause to offer information about the object (e.g., "You're holding the bell. It makes a nice sound when you shake it." Later, "You're ringing the bell; ring, rrrinnng").

The child at this stage is better able to listen and remember the story. Stories with predictable sequences or key words are great. Encourage the child to fill in the blank as you pause for a moment. If a story invites a motor response, this may be an excellent way to invite the child's participation. For example, as the Billy Goats Gruff make it across the bridge, the children can pound their feet on the floor.

Invite curiosity by reading the title of the book and encouraging the children to guess what the story might be about based on the title. This is a good way to learn more about the child's past experiences that may relate to the content of the book. If the title does not yield much information (as in *Abiyoyo)*, the children with sight can be encouraged to look at the cover of the book for more information. This will allow the child who has a visual impairment to hear what his or her classmates think about the cover. If something is mentioned that is familiar to the child with a visual impairment, encourage the child to elaborate on this personal experience by talking about the items on the cover.

Symbolic Level

As noted previously, the developmentally younger or more inexperienced child needs real-life objects to learn concepts and to model language. Replications or miniatures of objects are only appropriate for the child who is at a symbolic level of thought. Even if the child has the capacity for symbolic thought, actual objects should be used whenever possible when initially introducing a new concept. For example, if the child understands that a stuffed toy puppy represents the family pet at home, this does not mean that the child will have a similar conceptualization that a plastic bunny represents a real bunny, if the child has never touched a live rabbit.

As the level of abstraction increases, be sure that the child with a visual impairment understands the presented materials. Too often tactile books include cutout silhouettes of objects. The sighted child can immediately decode the felt outline of a bird, but the tactile version is not so easily discernible.

In addition to sensitivity about the level of abstraction required of the child, it is important to foster a wide range of experience specific to a concept. Drinking from one cup, for instance, does not bring an understanding of the many different types of objects that can be called "cups." It is important to provide the child with comparisons to ensure conceptual learning (in this example, cups made from plastic and glass, cups with and without handles, cups with different visual and tactile markings, etc.).

The Three Billy Goats Gruff provides ample opportunity for comparison learning: the voices soften and deepen, the clothing sizes grow from smaller to larger, and the sounds on the bridge become louder and louder. Engage the children in finding different size shoes to try on to tromp over the bridge. Encourage matching by asking which shoes are the same and which are different. Comparisons can also be made about other qualities: which shoes make the loudest noises on the bridge or whether slippers and hard-soled boots make similar or different sounds.

Try pausing during the reading of the story to request that the children at this level predict what events might occur next. The child who has a healthy repertoire of real-life experiences will have a more realistic sense of what might happen next in a story (Castellano & Kosman, 1997). This further highlights the importance of a classroom environment that provides rich hands-on experience.

The child at the symbolic level can begin to remember and retell stories from the props. The *Abiyoyo* wand reminds the child of the song in the story, just as a feather represents Charlie the Rooster in *Friends*. As the child becomes more familiar with a story, role-play can be encouraged with and without props.

NOW YOU'RE READY

Children with visual impairments can both contribute to and learn from the many experiences available in the storybook modules presented in this curriculum. Communication among team members and the inclusion of parents in the activities will help make the entire process of learning an exciting and enjoyable one. Keep in mind that most of the suggestions discussed in this chapter will also benefit children in the class who do *not* have visual impairments. Adding the auditory and tactile cues, the preparatory comments, and verbal explanations will benefit all children.

REFERENCES

Americans with Disabilities Act (ADA) of 1990, PL 101-336, 42 U.S.C. §§ 12101 *et seq.*

Anthony, T. (1993). Orientation and mobility skill development. In *First steps: A handbook for teaching young children who are visually impaired* (pp. 115–138). Los Angeles, CA: Blind Children's Center.

Castellano, C., & Kosman, D. (1997). *The bridge to braille.* Baltimore: National Organization of Parents of Blind Children.

Craig, C. (1996). Family support of the emergent literacy of children with visual impairments. *Journal of Visual Impairment & Blindness, 90,* 194–200.

Crespo, S. (1990). Storybooks for blind infants and children. *Journal of Visual Impairment & Blindness, 84,* 39–40.

Drezek, W. (1995). *Move, touch, do.* Louisville, KY: American Printing House for the Blind.

Groenveld, M., Jan, J.E., & Leader, P. (1990). Observations on the habilitation of children with cortical visual impairment. *Journal of Visual Impairment & Blindness, 84*(1), 11–15.

Henderson, F. (1960). Little bumps that say something. *Exceptional Children, 26,* 261–266.

Individuals with Disabilities Education Act Amendments of 1997, PL 105-17, 20 U.S.C. §§ 1400 *et seq.*

Koenig, A.J., & Holbrook, M.C. (1995). *Learning media assessment of students with visual impairments* (2nd ed.). Austin: Texas School for the Blind and Visually Impaired.

Levack, N. (1991). *Low vision: A resource guide with adaptations for students with visual impairments.* Austin: Texas School for the Blind and Visually Impaired.

Menacker, S.J., & Batshaw, M.L. (1997). Vision: Our window to the world. In M.L. Batshaw (Ed.), *Children with disabilities* (4th ed., pp. 211–239). Baltimore: Paul H. Brookes Publishing Co.

Miller, D. (1985). Reading comes naturally: A mother and her blind child's experiences. *Journal of Visual Impairment & Blindness, 79,* 1–4.

Morgan, E. (Ed.). (1994). *Resources for family centered intervention for infants, toddlers, and preschoolers who are visually impaired: Vol. II.* Logan, UT: SKI*HI Institute.

Rex, E.J., Koenig, A.J., Wormsley, D.P., & Baker, R.L. (1995). *Foundations of braille literacy.* New York: American Foundation for the Blind.

Sacks, S.Z., & Silberman, R.K. (Eds.). (1998). *Educating students who have visual impairments with other disabilities.* Baltimore: Paul H. Brookes Publishing Co.

Stiles, S., & Knox, R. (1996). Medical issues, treatments, and professionals. In M.C. Holbrook (Ed.), *Children with visual impairments: A parents' guide* (pp. 21–48) Bethesda, MD: Woodbine House.

Stratton, J.M. (1996). Emergent literacy: A new perspective. *Journal of Visual Impairment & Blindness, 90,* 177–183.

Stratton, J.M., & Wright, S. (1991). On the way to literacy: Early experiences for young visually handicapped students. *RE:view, 23,* 55–62.

Swenson, A.M. (1988). Using an integrated literacy curriculum with beginning braille readers. *Journal of Visual Impairment & Blindness, 82,* 336–338.

Wright, S. *Discovering the magic of reading: Elizabeth's story* [Videotape]. (1995). Louisville, KY: American Printing House for the Blind.

Appendix

RESOURCES PERTAINING TO
YOUNG CHILDREN WHO ARE BLIND
OR WHO HAVE VISUAL IMPAIRMENTS

The following is a listing of national resources for parents and professionals who want to learn more about young children with visual impairments. Many of the agencies offer free written information. Others have subscription fees for newsletters or other publications. Also included are resources for children's books in braille.

The American Foundation for the Blind

11 Penn Plaza, Suite 300
New York, New York 10001
(212) 502-7600
FAX: (212) 502-7777   www.AFB.org

The American Foundation for the Blind publishes a multitude of books and pamphlets on literacy, early childhood, and other topics related to visual impairment. There are four regional offices across the United States. They are located in Atlanta, Chicago, Dallas, and San Francisco.

American Printing House for the Blind

1839 Frankfort Avenue
Post Office Box 6085
Louisville, Kentucky 40206-2405
(800) 223-1839
FAX: (502) 899-2274   www.aph.org

The American Printing House for the Blind produces materials and books for people who have visual impairments. There are two publications specific to the literacy of young children with visual impairments: *Discovering the Magic of Reading: Elizabeth's Story* [videotape and brochure] (Wright, 1995) and *On the Way to Literacy: Early Experiences for Visually Impaired Children* [handbook and tactile storybooks] (Stratton & Wright, 1991). There are other early childhood–related publications and a large variety of materials (e.g., braillewriters, slates and styluses) that may be appropriate for a preschool classroom. A teacher certified in the area of visual impairments can assist a preschool program with securing these materials through the American Printing House for the Blind quota fund program.

The Blind Children's Center
4120 Marathon Street
Los Angeles, California 90029
(800) 222-3566   www.info@blindchildrens.org

The Blind Children's Center has created several pamphlets on topics pertaining to language, movement, play, socialization, and transition strategies for young children with visual impairments.

Blind Children's Fund
311 West Broadway, Suite 1
Mt. Pleasant, Michigan 48858
(989) 779-9966   www.blindchildrensfund.org

This nonprofit organization provides information and materials specific to the development of young children with visual impairments. It publishes a newsletter and sells books on visual impairments, including children's stories with characters who have visual impairments.

Council of Families with Visual Impairments
c/o American Council of the Blind
1515 15th Street NW, Suite 720
Washington, DC 20005
(800) 424-8666   www.acb.org

The American Council of the Blind is composed of individuals with visual impairments, family members, and professionals. The Council of Families with Visual Impairment is a national support group.

DB-Link
c/o Teaching Research
345 North Monmouth Avenue
Monmouth, Oregon 97361
(800) 438-9376

A federally funded clearinghouse that offers a wealth of free written information on all topics related to individuals, from birth through age 21, who have vision and hearing loss.

Hadley School for the Blind
700 Elm Street
Winnetka, Illinois 60093
(800) 323-4238

Free home study correspondence courses are offered to both parents and professionals through the Hadley School for the Blind. There are courses specific to young children with visual impairments.

National Association for the Visually Handicapped
22 West 21st Street, 6th Floor
New York, New York 10010
(212) 889-3141

The National Association for the Visually Handicapped provides informational literature, guidance and counseling in the use of visual aids, emotional support, and referral services for parents of children who have low vision and those who work with them.

National Association of Parents of the Visually Impaired
Post Office Box 317
Watertown, Massachusetts 02272-0317
(800) 562-6265

A national support agency that serves as a clearinghouse of information related to visual impairment of children and youth. They provide a quarterly newsletter (*Awareness*) to its members, a listing of publications, and referral services.

National Braille Press
88 St. Stephen Street
Boston, Massachusetts 02115
(888) 965-8965

The National Braille Press offers a catalog of braille books for young children and other items.

National Federation of the Blind
1800 Johnson Street
Baltimore, Maryland 21230
(410) 659-9314

The National Federation of the Blind publishes monthly and quarterly publications. Parents of Blind Children is a parent organization sponsored by the National Federation of the Blind.

National Library Service for the Blind and Physically Handicapped
1291 Taylor Street, NW
Washington, DC 20542
(202) 707-5100

A national library service that provides braille and recorded books and magazines on free loan to anyone who cannot read standard print because of visual or physical disabilities.

SEEDLINGS
Post Office Box 51924
Livonia, Michigan 48151-5924
(800) 777-8552

SEEDLINGS offers a catalog of print-braille and braille books that are produced for children of all ages.

Visually Impaired Preschool Services
1906 Goldsmith Lane
Louisville, Kentucky 40218
(502) 636-3207

This early intervention program for children with visual impairments has produced an excellent set of 11 videotapes on early childhood topics and a newsletter. The first five in the series were completed in 1991 and the last six in 1996. Many of the following videotapes discuss topics pertinent to literacy development:

1. *Seeing Things in a New Way*
2. *Learning About the World: Concept Development*
3. *Becoming a Can-Do Kid: Self-Help Skills*
4. *Making Friends: Social Skills and Play*
5. *Going Places: Orientation and Mobility*
6. *Through Their Eyes: An Introduction to Low Vision*
7. *Moving Through the World: Gross Motor Skills and Play*
8. *Hands-On Experiences: Tactile Learning and Skills*
9. *Successfully Adapting the Preschool Environment*
10. *Power at Your Fingertips: An Introduction to Learning Braille*
11. *Look How Far We've Come*

Chapter 7

THE EMERGENCE OF LITERACY

Malinda Etzler Jones
and Karen Crabtree

Preschool and kindergarten provide critical developmental opportunities, not only for the development of cognitive, social, communication and language, and motor skills but also for the emergence of basic literacy abilities. As a teacher of preschool and kindergarten children, you need to be able to recognize and acknowledge the understandings that these young, "emerging" readers and writers have constructed about oral and written language, no matter how incomplete their behaviors and ideas might appear to be. How have their conceptualizations been developing, and how can these conceptualizations be extended toward conventional understanding and usage of written language? The information in this chapter is provided specifically to help you learn more about the important relationship between oral language and literacy and to help you become familiar with the various stages of reading, writing, and spelling development. This knowledge will be useful when you are reading to children, planning individualization for activities, and assisting children in moving to a higher level of understanding of the form and function of print.

In a curriculum like **Read, Play, and Learn!®,** children's knowledge about written language and children's oral language development are acknowledged and enhanced as adults and children explore the pictures and illustrations in concept books, alphabet books, and other picture books. With the repeated reading of favorite stories, young children begin to notice that the content and language of books remain constant from one reading to the next. If parents and teachers make reference to the print as they read (e.g., "If you move your hand, I can see the words") or if they track or point to the words, children may notice that print rather than the pictures conveys the story and that books are read from front to back, top to bottom, and left to right. They may even begin to understand how one spoken word is represented by one printed word (sequence of marks between spaces). Such concepts may develop even more rapidly if children have the opportunity to watch their parents and teachers demonstrate and talk about the form and function of writing, for example, by writing the child's name or pointing out the form and function of print in their environment (e.g., "This is where you hang your coat. See, this is your name under the hook. Your name begins with the letter M").

As children begin to understand that written symbols are used to represent messages, labels, and ideas, they begin both on their own and with adult mediation to make sense of the forms and functions of print in their environment and attempt to decipher the code.

The degree and richness of children's oral language development are influenced by the quantity and quality of the stimulation, responses, opportunities, and encouragement children receive from those who are more language proficient. This is also true with regard to the development of children's understandings about written language. In the following examples, facilitators in a *Read, Play, and Learn!* classroom provide opportunities for children to demonstrate their level of understanding so that they can then provide scaffolding to support new learning:

- Jasmine sits beside her preschool teacher looking at books. The teacher prompts, "I see a pig. I see a mouse. I see a chicken." Jasmine demonstrates her developing receptive language and understanding of symbolic representations by touching the corresponding picture in the book *Friends.* "You found the . . . !" the teacher responds, reinforcing the newly acquired vocabulary terms.

- As the teacher finishes reading *Friends,* she might provide an opportunity for developing phonemic awareness by saying, "I am thinking of other animals I saw in the book. I am going to say the name of the animal I am thinking about in a special way. When you know the name of the animal I am saying, raise your hand. I will let you whisper it in my ear. Then you can choose where you want to play. Listen carefully. Here's the first one, '/c/ /o/ /w/.'"

- Ellis is in the Literacy Center searching for his favorite book, *The Three Billy Goats Gruff.* He locates the book by using the illustrations and colors on the cover. "Goats, trip-trap. Read me," he says as he hands the book to his teacher. He anticipates the familiar story of the three billy goats when he selects this book, indicating that he understands that stories remain constant.

- During outdoor play, Jacob, wearing a police hat, chases after a friend on a speeding tricycle. Approaching his friend, Jacob shouts, "You're going a hundred miles an hour! I'm going to give you a ticket." Jacob proceeds to scribble out a speeding ticket. Although the ticket is written with a series of scribbles rather than with conventional print, Jacob demonstrates that he understands one of the functions of print. The fact that his scribbles go from the left of the paper to right and from top to bottom indicates that he is developing understandings about directionality.

- Karissa tugs on her teacher's shirt and says, "I want to paint and I can't 'cause Kevin's picture is still there." The teacher accompanies Karissa to the easel. "How did you know that was Kevin's picture?" the teacher asks. "'Cause his name has a K in it like mine." Karissa's comments indicate that she is able to identify some letters by name and is able to recognize them in different contexts.

WHAT IS EMERGENT LITERACY?

Emergent literacy is the term used to describe the literacy behaviors and conceptualizations demonstrated by children from infancy until they begin to read and write conventionally (Clay, 1966). As reflected in the previous examples, emergent literacy implies that the development of reading and writing begins to evolve long before children reach elementary school age and represents a wide range of understandings. Literacy development is affected by children's interactions with their environment, including the degree and quality of modeling, stimulation, and instruction within their environment. Emergent literacy also implies that through accommodation and assimilation (equilibration) during these interactions, children's literacy understandings become increasingly sophisticated and move toward the ability to read and write conventionally.

The concept of *emergent literacy* is based on several assumptions:

1. Children begin critical, cognitive work as infants and toddlers when they begin to understand the functions (power) and structure of oral language (e.g., crying; cooing; babbling; the use of developing labels, such as "ba" for bottle).

2. Children in literate societies begin to develop literacy long before they start formal reading and writing instruction. Children learn about and develop dispositions toward oral and written language through active engagement in literacy experiences. They learn through social interactions with adults in writing and reading situations, particularly when adults answer questions, provide new information about print, and encourage children to use what they already know about print. Children profit from modeling by significant adults, particularly their parents, primary caregivers, and preschool teachers. They construct and refine literacy understandings as they explore print independently in their play and have opportunities to experiment with developing understandings in informal and formal settings within their home, school, and community.

3. Children's early reading and writing behaviors are a legitimate phase of, not a precursor to, their literacy development.

4. Emerging understandings about reading, writing, and oral language development are mutually supportive. Listening, speaking, reading, and writing development are interrelated and develop concurrently rather than sequentially. For example, the notion that reading must precede writing, or vice versa, is a misconception.

5. Literacy development is enhanced when children have opportunities to use reading and writing purposefully and playfully to communicate specific information, share thoughts and ideas, organize and learn about their environment, locate or record important information, and learn about or document events. Opportunities to learn about and explore the many functions of reading and writing are as critical during early childhood as are opportunities to experiment with the forms of written language.

6. Although children's literacy development can be described in terms of generalized stages, children can pass through these stages in a variety of ways and at different ages. Any attempts to "scope and sequence" development or instruction should take this developmental variation into account (assumptions adapted from Teale & Sulzby, 1986).

CREATE A SUPPORTIVE LITERACY ENVIRONMENT

The ability to read and write does not develop naturally without careful planning and instruction (International Reading Association [IRA] & National Association for the Education of Young Children [NAEYC], 1998). Whether children are at school or at home, their interest in and competence with language and print are directly related to 1) the quantity and quality of literacy interactions they have with more literate others, 2) the opportunities they have to watch their parents and teachers engage in reading and writing activities and then participate with them, and 3) the variety of print materials available to them. Studies have found that parents play a vital role in their children's learning to read by informally and intentionally incorporating into daily family life pleasurable opportunities for their children to notice, talk about, explore, use, and play with print (Durkin, 1966). Effective teachers incorporate Durkin's conclusions by providing these same types of daily literacy opportunities and enthusiastic adult–child interactions during language and literacy events.

Ensure Quantity and Quality of Interactions

You can increase the *quantity* and *quality* of interactions that the children have with those who are more literate as they share and discuss real and vicarious experiences and as they explore books and print together. You, the parents or caregivers, and other team members should do the following:

- Demonstrate genuine interest when you share literacy events with children.
- Model appropriate grammar and use precise vocabulary as you interact with children.
- Engage children in language play with rhymes, chants, songs, rhythms, and alliteration to develop phonemic awareness (see pages 126 & 136–137 for more information on phonemic awareness).
- Invite children to share, attend to, and respond to books in developmentally appropriate ways (e.g., touching pictures in response to labels, labeling, storybook reading, shared reading). "It is the talk that surrounds the storybook reading that gives it power, helping children to bridge what is in the story and their own lives" (IRA & NAEYC, 1998, p. 7).
- Direct children's attention to print in their environment. For instance, when reading *Abiyoyo*, you might say, "Abiyoyo is a long name. It has lots of letters. Sam is a short name. It has just three letters." On a field trip to the airport during the module based on *First Flight*, you might point out the letters in various signs: "Look, Garrett, that sign says 'GATE 21.' It has the letters G and A, just

like in your name, G-A-R-R-E-T-T." When setting up the environment in the classroom, add elements that encourage children to use print (e.g., "Someone is using the computer right now. Let's put your name on the sign-up sheet, so you will be next"). By enthusiastically and frequently inviting children to "figure out" and use print in their day-to-day lives, adults have a significant influence on children's confidence and competence as literacy learners.

- Answer children's questions about print. Respond to their attempts to read (pretend storybook reading) and write (scribbles, letter-like marks, or letter strings) with enthusiasm and genuine interest while encouraging them to use what they know to explore new books and print. Each of the centers and areas in *Read, Play, and Learn!* provides opportunities to incorporate print. For example, use picture and word charts in the Science and Math Center; label materials and work in the Art Area; make books in the Literacy Center; and make signs in the Floor Play area, such as "Do Not Move" so that the custodian will leave the miniature scenario intact. In addition, print can be used for many functions in the Dramatic Play: Theme Area. For example, menus can be used for the restaurant during the module based on *The Knight and the Dragon*, mileage and road signs may be used for *A Porcupine Named Fluffy*, airline tickets can be included during the module on *First Flight*, and receipts can be used for *Picking Apples & Pumpkins*. Each of the stories in the curriculum presents opportunities for reading and writing in every center.

  How you respond to children's questions about print is important. In the following dialogue, Kevin is constructing an adobe house, as in *The Three Little Javelinas*, in the Floor Play area with blocks:

  Kevin: My house keeps getting knocked over. How do you write "KEEP OUT"?

  Teacher: What a good idea to make a sign to tell people not to walk through the Block Area! There are two words. The first word, "KEEP," begins with K. You know how to make a K. You write it everyday when you write your name.

Provide Opportunities

You can set up many *opportunities* for children to watch teachers and parents participate in reading and writing activities and to interact with their teachers and parents as they demonstrate reading and writing. The following are some good examples:

- Read and write for authentic purposes when the children are watching. Let them know that adults enjoy reading and writing and that they make time for reading and writing in their lives. Tell them about the reading and writing a teacher or parent does. For example, at the Literacy Center, the teacher modeled writing when she wrote a note home to the parents. She commented, "Look, Brenda. I'm writing a letter to your Mom and Dad. It asks them to send in a picture of your family. Listen so that you can help them read it when you get home."

- Read a variety of developmentally appropriate books (fiction and nonfiction), rhymes, and songs aloud to children frequently. Share the books with enthusiasm and energy. Invite the children to participate in the story as they are able. Demonstrate the pleasure of reading—the rhythm of a rhyme or song and the excitement of a good story. Assist children in noticing concepts about print and the conventions of written language as appropriate for each child. For example, during the module based on *Night Tree*, the teacher chose to read to a small group of children for shared reading. The book she selected was *Brown Bear, Brown Bear*, one that the group knew by heart. As she read, the teacher moved her hand left to right under the words, and they "read" together.

- Demonstrate the purposes and processes of writing for children. Take frequent opportunities to record children's thoughts and to use writing for reasons that are meaningful to children. Help children to notice the conventions of written language, and invite them to participate in the actual writing as they are able. For example, when making an experience chart about their trip to the airport, the teacher wrote down the children's words: "We went to see planes." After writing down several sentences containing the word *plane*, she underlined each word *plane*. As she began to write, "The planes were very big," she paused at the word *plane* and asked, "Does anyone want to try to write the letters in the word *plane*?"

Introduce Variety

You can provide a wide *variety* of print materials for children to play with and to use in their play (e.g., storybooks, writing materials, maps, cookbooks, plastic or magnetic letters, magazines). "Literacy materials that reflect life outside the classroom help children see the purpose and necessity of reading and writing" (Patton & Mercer, 1996, p. 13). You, the parents or caregivers, and other professionals should do the following:

- Gather and make readily available reading and writing materials (literacy props) related to current experiences, interests, storybooks, or topics under exploration. For example, for the module based on *The Rainbow Fish*, books related to going to the beach or to an aquarium (something the children might have experienced), books about raising fish at home, books about various types of fish, and other storybooks about fish should be available for the children to examine and share.

- Observe how, and if, children use the literacy materials in their play. If needed, appropriately step in and out of the children's play to model ways to incorporate literacy experimentation into the play. Some examples might include writing a check for fruits and vegetables in the module based on *Picking Apples & Pumpkins*, making airline tickets for passengers during the module based on *First Flight*, and using a telephone book to call the police in the module based on *Somebody and the Three Blairs*.

FOUNDATIONS OF LITERACY: CONCEPTS ABOUT PRINT

Studies that have attempted to determine predictors of school achievement have found that early childhood experiences with print are significantly related to later achievement and that it is the frequency with which children are being read to from a variety of books during their early childhood years that is the most significant predictor of later school success (Bus, van IJzendoorn, & Pellegrini, 1995; IRA & NAEYC, 1998; Taylor, 1983; Wells, 1986). Children who are read to frequently and begin to acquire favorite stories often incorporate reading-like behaviors into their play by pretending to read (i.e., emergent storybook reading, Sulzby, 1985) to themselves, to others involved in their play, or to dolls and stuffed animals. Holdaway (1979) has indicated that this reading-like behavior is one of the most important events in literacy development. In addition, the most common thread throughout all of the home literacy experiences of children who have learned to read "naturally" is frequent one-to-one reading of storybooks.

Children who have been immersed in frequent and rich storybook reading as well as other appropriate interactive literacy experiences may have been exposed to—even before they reach your classroom—some very important concepts about print (Clay, 1979, 1991; Ollila & Mayfield, 1992; Wells, 1986) necessary to learn to read and write proficiently:

1. **They may be familiar and comfortable with the structures and cadences of written language**, recognizing that they are distinctly different from those of spoken language. Children who have been read to frequently often "read" favorite stories to their dolls or stuffed animals using the language patterns and intonations of "storybook talk."

2. **They discover that it is the print, not the pictures, that the parent or teacher is reading and that print carries the author's message.** When pretend reading, children often track the print with their finger as they "read" even though there may be little relationship between their spoken words and the print.

3. **They may be familiar with many functions of print.** They may have discovered that with books they can learn about dragons, dangerous animals, trucks, and the moon. They may begin to understand that they can experience feelings of silliness, love, anger, success, failure, hope, loss, and happiness through stories such as *The Three Billy Goats Gruff* and *The Kissing Hand*. They may have learned that written language can help them make pancakes during the module based on *Somebody and the Three Blairs*, find a friend's house for *Franklin Has a Sleepover*, or select favorite foods from a menu for *The Knight and the Dragon* (Ollila & Mayfield, 1992). They may have come to appreciate the value of leaving a note for a parent when the babysitter has taken them to the park or on an errand.

4. **They may be familiar with some of the many forms of print.** They may have noticed how preparing for a trip to the grocery store requires a column of words (a list), whereas a letter to Grandma is written left to right and top to bottom, in "sentence" form (connected text), with a greeting at the beginning and a closing at the end.

5. **They may have begun to hypothesize about some of the conventions of print.** As they observe parents and teachers writing and/or rereading familiar books, they may begin to develop the concept of a *word*, that words are separated by spaces, and that one written word corresponds with one spoken word. They may begin to observe the relationship between sounds and symbols (letters) as they watch their parents puzzle over the spelling of "broccoli" for the shopping list. As they encounter favorite books again and again, they begin to relate key words to pictures and to notice the constancy of words.

6. **They may recognize that texts are organized in consistent ways and that storybooks are presented in a style that differs from books about real topics (expository books).** If children have had opportunities to experience both storybooks and informational books, they may begin to notice that storybooks have pictures that relate to the story whereas informational books seem to have more diagrams with labels. They expect one to begin with something like, "Once upon a time . . . ," and the other with something like, "There are several kinds of sharks. . . ."

7. **As a result of being read aloud to from books, they will have much greater breadth of vicarious experiences,** beyond their own world into the world of other people, places, and times, as well as into the world of "might happen" and "could have been." With these new "experiences," children are introduced to new vocabulary for talking about them. They will draw on these "experiences" and the vocabulary as they become readers and writers (Ollila & Mayfield, 1992).

8. **When they are engaged in frequent and pleasurable storybook reading experiences, they begin to anticipate becoming actively involved in meaning making.** When children become engaged in a story, they construct mental pictures of the characters and events. With engagement comes increased anticipation; with increased anticipation comes increased comprehension and enjoyment; and with increased enjoyment comes the desire and ability to attend to and to listen. The active listener becomes the active reader.

BE PREPARED FOR DIFFERENCES IN EARLY LITERACY EXPERIENCES AND DEVELOPMENT

The children who enter your classroom are likely to do so with vast differences in their experiences and abilities with written language. Experientially, some children enter school having been read to practically every day of their lives. They may have had more than 1,000 hours of informal literacy experiences before they enter the classroom (Adams, 1990). Others have had virtually no interactions with storybooks or other print (Allington & Cunningham, 1994). Others will be somewhere in between. Developmentally, some children may enter the classroom functioning cognitively, socially, and/or emotionally far below their chronological age for a variety of reasons. Regardless, it is critical for teachers to *determine* the understandings the children do have about vocabulary, syntax, phonemic awareness, and the form and function of print in order to build on them. Keep in mind that all children, even those who have developmental delays or who have had limited literacy experiences, come to school with *some* knowledge about the form and function of print.

By observing the children in the classroom, you can determine who labels pictures in books, who chimes in as a familiar, predictable book is read aloud, who writes the first few letters of his or her name, and who simply indicates an understanding that pencils and crayons are used to make marks on a piece of paper. Through observation of individual children's functional literacy awareness and skills, you can begin to determine what level and type of support is needed for each child for his or her continued literacy development. Do not forget to ask what type of print materials are in the home, what books and other materials are read to the child, and how the parents and children interact around books and environmental print. Ascertaining this information, through an informal discussion with parents or a simple questionnaire (perhaps to help avoid having a family believe that it is being judged), can help you distinguish experiential characteristics from possible individual abilities or disabilities while also giving you an easy way to remind parents of the importance of sharing print in various forms with children.

STAGES OF LITERACY DEVELOPMENT

The wide range of literacy understandings the children in your class have may overwhelm you. The task of helping children build new understandings based on what they already know (schema theory) can seem like a formidable task unless you have a framework for understanding the developmental continuum of learning to read.

When Do Children Begin to Acquire Literacy Skills?

Children's literacy journeys actually begin at birth as they respond to the voices, touches, and physical presences in their environments. Most infants soon learn that crying results in feeding and/or attention and that cooing or babbling (emergent speech mechanisms) brings pleasant responses from those around them. Toddlers quickly learn that the word *no* can be used to control behavior, just as they learn that certain utterances result in the appearance of certain objects, for example, a bottle or a ball. The motivation for learning and using language comes from the functions it can serve. As children become increasingly mobile, their needs, desires, interests, and worlds expand. The demands on their language faculties, both listening and speaking, expand concurrently.

As with other aspects of human development, oral language learning is a result of interactions between nature (what children bring to the task by way of biological endowment) and nurture (the oral language interactions they experience, particularly those in which they participate) (Wells, 1986). Children learn the oral language of their community as they interact with more language-proficient others. They modify their language understandings, interactions, and behaviors according to the quantity and quality of the stimulation provided and the responses they receive from their efforts with others. If the responses are negative or the attempts are unsuccessful, children construct new hypotheses and try them out in future language interactions. If the responses are positive and their attempts are successful, they maintain the modifications.

Oral language interactions with more language-proficient others are crucial not only to the children's oral language development but also to their reading and writing development. Children initially develop and extend their receptive vocabulary and their understanding of English syntax through oral language interactions with those around them. The greater their receptive vocabulary and the more diverse the syntactical patterns they understand, the greater their potential for reading achievement.

The role of oral language "play" to develop phonological and phonemic awareness has been further heralded as a major contributor to the reading and writing development of children. As defined by the International Reading Association Board of Directors (1998), *phonological awareness* refers to an understanding of large units of sound, such as syllables, onsets (the part of the word before the first vowel sound; e.g., /gr/ in grape), and rimes (the first vowel sound and everything that follows; e.g., /ape/ in grape) (Durica, 1998). *Phonemic awareness* reflects an understanding of phonemes, the smallest units of sound that make up the speech stream. Phonemic awareness is not the same as phonics (letter–sound relationships). A learner's ability to isolate and manipulate the phonemes in spoken language provides a basis for associating sounds with letters as children begin to interact with printed language. Without phonemic awareness, it is very difficult for learners to visually map speech onto print or to decode print into speech. Children with the ability to segment words into sounds are likely to become better readers than those who cannot do so (Adams, 1990; Blachman, 1989, 1991; Bradley & Bryant, 1983, 1985; Griffith & Olson, 1992; Lundberg, Olofsson, & Wall, 1980; Stanovich, 1986; Yopp, 1995a).

Some children may have developed phonemic awareness prior to interactions with print. Others may develop phonemic awareness concurrently as they develop understandings about written language. Some children may develop phonemic awareness through informal language play with more language-proficient others. Others require varying degrees of intentional language interactions selected or designed specifically to assist children in developing phonemic awareness. The range of intentional oral language interactions includes sharing nursery rhymes, songs, chants, and children's literature containing alliteration or phoneme substitution; bringing children's attention to the specific position or manipulation of sounds within rhymes, songs, chants, and books; providing and modeling opportunities for the children to substitute beginning sounds in rhymes, blend phonemes into words, and/or segment spoken words into sounds (e.g., Elkonin boxes; Clay, 1993); and providing intensive, structured programs such as Auditory Discrimination in Depth (Lindamood & Lindamood, 1969).

The following continuum of literacy development is presented in terms of stages. Children, as they experience uneven bursts of understanding, will sometimes demonstrate behaviors characteristic of more than one stage or may seemingly be between stages. Such discrepancies are also apparent as learners focus on using a new source of information and appear to ignore other sources that they had previously used consistently. Still, a knowledge of the broad continuum will be useful as a teacher develops skills for observing children.

The stages presented in the following sections[1] (see Table 1) incorporate research and observations of several authors and researchers, including Clay (1991); Hart-Hewins and Wells (1990); Jones and Crabtree (1994); Sulzby (1985); Teale (1982); and Wishon, Crabtree, and Jones (1998).

STAGE 1: BEGINNING WITH BOOKS

Children at the first stage of literacy development, Beginning with Books, tend to be infants and toddlers or children with developmental delays who are at the sensorimotor/exploratory level of development. During this stage, children's receptive and expressive language skills (e.g., vocabulary, syntax, phonemic awareness) are developed, refined, and extended as more language-proficient children and adults interact with them. Vocabulary development often begins with simple labeling by others and by the children themselves of objects or people important to the infant or child (e.g., *mama, bottle*). A child's understanding about syntax will develop as others interact with infants and children in complete sentences. Children's phonological awareness evolves as parents or caregivers engage their children by reciting nursery rhymes or by playfully creating nonsensical rhymes and rhythms. Adults knowingly or unknowingly begin to stimulate visual attention to pictures and shapes by sharing black-and-white and primary-colored mobiles and photographs with their infants.

Parents and caregivers often initiate a child's literacy journey into written language by reading nursery rhymes or simple board books to their infant as they feed, cuddle, change, and rock him or her. The infant may not be aware of the function of the book or the meaning of the words but over time comes to associate books with the enjoyable cadence of oral literacy language and a pleasant encounter with the parent or other significant adult.

The first books that seem to maintain children's attention tend to be board books containing simple, discrete, colorful photographs of familiar objects, people, characters, or animals. Children's familiarity with these objects, people, charac-

Table 1. Stages of literacy development

Stage 1:	Beginning with books
Stage 2:	Immersion in storybooks, patterned books, and rhymes
Stage 3:	Role-playing "the reader"
Stage 4:	Developing inner control
Stage 5:	Becoming independent
Stage 6:	Independent reader

---

[1]The content in the following sections on the stages of literacy development has been directly quoted, revised, adapted, and expanded from Jones and Crabtree's chapter "Development of Literacy in the Primary Years: The Interdependence of Reading, Writing, Listening, Speaking, and Thinking" in *Curriculum for the Primary Years: An Integrative Approach,* by Wishon, Crabtree, and Jones © 1998; adapted by permission of Prentice-Hall, Inc., Upper Saddle River, NJ.

ters, or animals may be due to real-life experiences, due to play experiences with toys and other children, or due to vicarious experiences through television or videotapes. Adults encourage attention and interaction with the books by pointing to and labeling the photographs (e.g., "Car, truck, bus"; "Cow. A cow says 'moo'"; "There's Cookie Monster!"). As the children begin to understand and enjoy this receptive experience, parents begin to encourage them to respond in some way (e.g., "What does the lion say?" "Where's the doggie?" "Touch the cow," "Find Cookie Monster"). Children begin to relate concepts and labels from the world around them to the familiar pictures (symbols) in the books and to develop new concepts and labels from the less familiar illustrations to apply to their world.

Some adults become frustrated when infants, toddlers, or young children with special needs appear disinterested in sharing books. Some children may grab the book and chew on it, others may turn the pages before the reader has finished, whereas others may simply walk away to find a more interesting activity. Resist drawing the conclusion that these children are simply not ready for interactions with books.

When sharing books with children at this stage of literacy development, regardless of their age, it is important to consider the previous experiences the child has had with books to answer the following questions:

- Is sharing a book a new or infrequent experience for the child?
- Does the child's behavior demonstrate familiarity with and appreciation of books? Does the child eagerly bring books to the adult to read? Does the child voluntarily attend to the reader as well as to the illustrations in the book?
- Have previous book-sharing experiences been appropriate and positive?

The frequency and quality of the experiences the young child has had with books will have a significant impact on the way the child responds to your attempts to share a book. The child who has not been read to or who has not been read to appropriately may not become engaged as quickly or to the same degree as a child who has. In addition, you must carefully consider the following questions when choosing the place and time of day that books should be read:

- Are there noisy or distracting activities going on nearby?
- Are there new or interesting materials or activities competing for the child's attention?
- Is the adult reader able to give complete attention to the book experience?
- Is being physically active the child's more immediate need?
- Is the child physically comfortable during the reading?

During high-energy times, a developmentally young child may not be able or willing to engage or stay engaged with a book. The longing to be physically active may be more compelling. This does not mean that the child is not ready for books. It may simply mean that you have not chosen the appropriate time or circumstance. The following may be appropriate times to share books with a child in this stage:

- The child is most relaxed or willing to give attention to books (e.g., before or after nap, while taking a bottle, after lunch, after strenuous physical activity).
- The child is in need of a calming or distracting activity and may welcome the opportunity to manipulate the pages, examine the colorful illustrations, and engage with an adult with books (e.g., when being administered medication, when in a plane or in a car, during a diaper change).
- The child is not engaged in play or center activities with other children and seems to be having difficulty finding an activity of personal interest.

Then, ask yourself about the type of book:

- Is the book visually appealing to the child?
- Does the book contain colorful illustrations or photographs of familiar objects, characters, animals, people, actions, and concepts?
- Is the book no more than 10–12 pages, with very few words per page?
- Does the book contain simple words and language familiar to the child and directly connected to the illustrations?

These characteristics are common to concept books, counting books, nursery rhymes, songs, poems, and wordless picture books rather than to storybooks with elaborate text. Some adults believe that sharing books with very young children means reading stories to them. Children at this stage of literacy development, however, are not yet able to attend to or to understand stories. A child will quickly lose interest and seek other activities if you are not in tune with the child's cognitive development by adjusting your reading and/or interactions with individual children. Consider what your expectations should be for each child when sharing a specific book (each module contains recommended modifications for children at various ability levels):

- Have you thought about the child's cognitive development, previous experiences with books, and attention span?
- What is the nature of a child's cognitive and language development and your role in supporting this process?
- Are you taking cues from the child to know when and where to share a book, what book to select, when to move on to a new book, how much to read or talk about on each page, when to turn the page, which words or concepts to identify or ask questions about, and when to initiate a different activity?

By carefully considering all of the factors described in this section and responding to the child during book sharing based on your astute observations, the child will be able by the end of this stage to attend to simple nursery rhymes; to patterned, predictable books; or to short, appealing stories with interest and mental participation. Adults can help the child at this stage of literacy development to construct new and more sophisticated schema both about the world and about book-reading experiences. Books appropriate for book sharing interactions with young children at Stage 1 are listed in the appendix at the end of this chapter.

Although none of the books in Collection 1 or Collection 2 are board books, or simple picture books, these types of books should be included in the classroom. The adults sharing the books listed in Collection 1 and Collection 2 with children should keep in mind the factors listed in this section and adapt their reading accordingly. You may need to emphasize the pictures or labels for some children as you read, let them point to objects or characters, and have the children relate pictures to real items.

Aural (Receptive) and Oral (Expressive) Language Connections

During Stage 1 of literacy development, a child's receptive and expressive vocabulary and syntax are developing rapidly. Books provide a rich source of material to support a child's language development. By selecting books with colorful photographs of objects, people, or animals familiar to the child from real-life experiences, you can easily support the child's developing receptive vocabulary by providing the verbal label while touching the corresponding illustration. This confirms and reinforces the language label for the child. Gradually the child is able to touch the appropriate illustration in response to the verbal label you provide.

These same interactions or how the adult uses the vocabulary from the storybook can be used to further extend the child's receptive vocabulary when used with concepts that are new to the child or as the adult uses the vocabulary of the author along with the child's to extend the child's vocabulary (e.g., "It is a horsey. A baby horse called a foal"). In **Read, Play, and Learn!**, the teacher provides actual objects and demonstrates action words in order to support vocabulary development. Parents can do the same in the home environment. As words become integrated into the child's receptive vocabulary, they may also become incorporated into the child's expressive vocabulary. Incorporation of these words into the child's expressive vocabulary can be encouraged by inviting the child to identify illustrations while sharing books, by conversing with the child about the books, and by providing related props in the child's play and learning environment.

Writing Connections

During Stage 1, children observe and come to appreciate the function of writing tools. With demonstrations, guidance, and support, they learn to grasp these tools themselves and experience the wonder of marking on various surfaces, eventually learning to confine their experimentation to the appropriate surfaces. A child's first fascination may be simply to remove and replace the cap of a marker or to click an ink pen in and out. The child's curiosity is piqued by watching other children and adults use these tools to make intriguing marks. You should support this curiosity by assisting the children in grasping the tools in a way that will result in creating marks and responding positively to their attempts. The perceptive adult will invite children at this stage to "write" or "draw" along with children at more advanced stages of literacy development, providing a writing surface large enough to capture the broad sweep of these children's first efforts.

Mediation

As you converse with the child, it is important to model conventional syntax. Restate the single word or kernel sentences used by the child in complete and conventional syntax. For example, the child's sentence, "Go Papa's house," is restated, "Yes, we are going to Papa's house." The books you choose to share with children in this stage of literacy development should be selected intentionally not only to support the child's vocabulary but also to support and extend the child's developing understandings of syntax patterns within the child's zone of proximal development. You will have many opportunities in **Read, Play, and Learn!** to adapt the environment and activities for all levels of ability. Particularly in the Literacy Center and during the shared reading time with peers, you can select books and materials related to the theme that reinforce vocabulary and concepts yet are at the appropriate level for each child.

During this stage it is also important to engage children intentionally in language play that will facilitate the development of phonemic awareness. The most appropriate language play activities for children in the sensorimotor stage are those using rhymes, rhythms, songs, and alliteration. During oral-motor time or during music and movement activities, you can introduce fingerplays, nursery rhymes, and songs that match the themes of the storybooks. For instance, for *Night Tree* or *The Kissing Hand*, the song "Twinkle, Twinkle Little Star" can be related to the stories. Rhymes can also be changed to fit with stories. Or, "Mary Had a Little Goat" may be more appropriate than "Mary Had a Little Lamb" during the module based on *The Three Billy Goats Gruff.* You can assist children to attend to rhyme and rhythm, especially if you intentionally emphasize them using clapping or tapping to note rhythm and tone, intonation, or loudness to highlight the rhyming words. Sharing and playing with alliteration and nonsensical sequences can also help children to develop an ear for beginning sounds, rimes, and onsets and to perhaps begin to imitate the same.

STAGE 2: IMMERSION IN STORYBOOKS, PATTERNED BOOKS, AND RHYMES

Children at the second stage of literacy development (which is similar to the functional level in **Read, Play, and Learn!**) enjoy listening to beginning storybooks, nursery rhymes, traditional folktales, and patterned predictable books. At the beginning of this stage, children believe that the "story" is generated solely from the pictures. They do not yet realize that there is a relationship between the words on the page and the talk that comes from a reader's lips. Frequent reading aloud to children in a one-to-one setting, as well as in group settings, is imperative for children in this stage. Once children are immersed in storybook reading experiences, they learn that a story remains the same each time it is read.

A positive sign that children are moving beyond this stage and developing critical attitudes and concepts about print is when they begin to "pretend read" (emergent storybook reading) very familiar storybooks by using their memory of the story and the pictures. Concepts about reading that children are developing, such as you read a book from front to back and turn the pages right to left, can be observed during emergent storybook reading. Print materials appropriate for shared readings and demonstrations in this stage are listed in the appendix at the end of this chapter. All of the books used in **Read, Play, and Learn!** are appropriate for children at this level.

Aural and Oral Language Connections

(*Note:* Oral language connections for each stage are cumulative. Connections from all previous stages apply to each future stage.) Continuation of the experiences and activities from Stage 1 is appropriate and important during Stage 2. During this stage, however, it is essential to create ways for children to develop phonemic awareness by becoming more actively involved both physically and cognitively. When the children become physically involved with the rhymes, rhythms, and songs, they learn to recognize segmentation in words, the meaning of intonation and pauses, and memory of sequences. For example, the finger, hand, and arm movements accompany rhymes, rhythms, and songs, such as *The Itsy Bitsy Spider* (Traponi, 1993) for the module based on *The Little Old Lady Who Was Not Afraid of Anything,* and an adaptation of *Where Is Thumbkin?* (Schiller & Moore, 1993) for *The Kissing Hand.* A variety of such songs and fingerplays can be adapted for many different modules. When reciting, singing, or reading rhymes and songs with the child, invite the child to recite the rhyme with you and pause appropriately to encourage him or her to fill in the rhyming word.

Writing Connections

Children learn about written language in a global way. That is, "they experiment and approximate, gradually becoming aware of the specific features of written language and the relationships between symbols, sounds, and meaning. They form their models of how written language works as they encounter it in specific settings" (Genishi & Dyson, 1984, p.30), and they compare it to encounters they have had in other settings.

Children appear interested in the *functions* of writing first, then the *forms,* and finally the *conventions.* They become aware of what writing can be used for and attempt to use it long before they can produce it in conventional form (Morrow, 1989; Taylor, 1983; Teale, 1986). Consequently, the first words children write, as well as those they first speak and read, are those that are meaningful and purposeful to them (e.g., their names, names of their family members, signs, labels).

Children very naturally incorporate the *functions* of print that they have observed in their environment into their play. When the class is reading *The Knight and the Dragon,* the child may find a paper and pencil at home to take orders at dinner time. At preschool, they may initiate leaving a note for the janitor to prevent him from throwing away a rotting pumpkin the class has been observing while reading *Picking Apples & Pumpkins.* Initially children are unconcerned about the end product of their labors, focusing solely on its purpose and on the act of accomplishing it.

After experimenting with and developing understandings about the functions print can serve, children become interested in the *forms* of print. That is, they begin to extract generalizations about what writing should look like and the features that characterize the marks (words and letters) on the page. They hypothesize that written language runs horizontally and that the same mark cannot just be repeated over and over again. A variety of different marks are required.

As they test out and begin to conceptualize the functions and the forms of print, children seek to learn about the conventions of print. The conventions include directionality, wordness, and the understanding that punctuation serves a purpose in reading and writing (Morrow, 1997).

Sulzby (1986) suggested the following description of developmental writing behaviors. She encouraged teachers, however, to keep in mind that children's writing may not proceed systematically from one stage to another, that children may skip a stage or revert to a previous stage for a specific writing purpose, and that children develop at individual rates:

1. Random scribble (no message): There is no apparent differentiation between writing and drawing.

2. Using drawing as writing: Illustrations represent a message, story, or label. Children may "read" their drawings with the cadence and intonation of written language.

3. Scribble writing: Symbolic of writing, the "act" looks like the child is actually writing (left to right and top to bottom). The "writing" is linear, repetitious, uniform in size, and sometimes wavy; it "looks" like writing. Children are focusing on the functions, the "feel," and the general "look" of writing.

4. Writing using letter-like forms: Children create shapes that resemble letters. They have begun to notice that writing consists of a variety of marks with specific characteristics.

5. Writing using well-learned units or letter strings: Children use random strings of letters or letter sequences learned from familiar words such as their names or the names of family members. There is no evidence of knowledge of sound–symbol relationships.

6. Writing using sound-spelling: Children create the spelling of a word by isolating a sound(s) within the word and assigning the appropriate letter(s) to it. A continuum of invented spelling proceeds from one letter representing an entire word to letters representing all sounds and incorporating visual memory of phonograms and/or conventionally spelled words. (See the section "Stages of Spelling Development.")

7. Writing using conventional spelling: Children write with correctly spelled words and incorporate the conventions of written language. (List adapted from Morrow, 1997, and Sulzby, 1986.)

Mediation

In order for children to progress to the next stage of literacy development, they need opportunities to become aware of how literacy is related to their everyday lives. It is especially important for them to have the opportunity to see adults use print in a variety of ways for a variety of purposes. It is equally important that children have the opportunity to "play" with literacy materials and to experiment with using print in their play. The adult not only must make literacy materials available to children but also suggest or demonstrate how the materials could be used in their play. The following example demonstrates this:

During the reading of Somebody and the Three Blairs, *Allison and her mother made oatmeal together. They read the back of the oatmeal box to see how much oatmeal and how much water to put in the pan. Later, Allison was overheard in the bathtub saying, "The recipe says 1 cup of water," as she poured water back and forth between two containers. This statement illustrates Allison's awareness of the use of print. The next day, Allison's mother suggested that she make oatmeal in her play kitchen. As Allison watched, her mother carefully printed the recipe on a card. She knew that Allison could not really read the card, but for several days, Allison took out the card, "read" it, and made pretend oatmeal.*

You must be aware of the ways literacy is used in the children's environments and provide the materials, time, and mediation needed for children to "play" with written language.

For children at this stage of literacy development, it is important to make readily available materials directly related to the rhymes, songs, and stories they know. **Read, Play, and Learn!** provides many suggestions for cues and prompts that will assist children in remembering words and sequences and using pictures, symbols, and print. Wall charts with printed text and illustrations that children can associate with particular songs, nursery rhymes, or fingerplays will stimulate children to sing or recite the material. Props, such as bowls and spoons of three distinct sizes, will assist the children in revisiting the story of *Somebody and the Three Blairs* in their play. Puppets and flannel board materials for each module can serve a similar function. You can mediate by supporting the children's efforts to recall the story and the vocabulary specific to the story. As the children attempt to reenact a fingerplay or story, you can mediate by joining in with the fingerplay actions and/or supporting the children's recall of the accompanying "story." This facilitates children's vocabulary understandings, their memory for text (rhyme or story), and their sense of constancy of story—all crucial to subsequent reading and writing development.

STAGE 3: ROLE-PLAYING "THE READER"

"Children learn a lot about reading from the labels, signs, and other kinds of print they see around them" (IRA & NAEYC, 1998, p. 7). Although some children may not have had many experiences with storybook reading prior to entering the classroom, they may have had environmental experiences with print, such as reading cereal boxes, signs, and menus, as well as opportunities to observe their parents reading letters, newspapers, magazines, messages from school, and directions on microwavable foods. Appropriate environmental print can be incorporated into daily classroom experiences. In **Read, Play, and Learn!,** each of the centers and areas offers opportunities for exposure to print. For example, in the Dramatic Play:

Theme Area, a mailbox labeled with "Fluffy" can be placed outside the playhouse during the module based on *A Porcupine Named Fluffy*. The children can then be encouraged to use the mailbox to send Fluffy notes, pictures, advertisements, or coupons, which can then be retrieved and "read." For many of the stories, a book can be made in the Literacy Center relating to the story theme or their experiences. Bulletin boards can be used to display the children's, parents', and staff's writing. For instance, during the module on *The Three Billy Goats Gruff*, letters from parents about how their children are brave and special can be shared with all of the children and then posted on a bulletin board at the children's eye level. Children can then find their letter and "read" it to the staff, parents, or other children. These activities allow professionals an opportunity to observe what a child might know and to help the child see the relationship between the print with which he or she are familiar and the print in the classroom.

Children at Stage 3 are entering the broad symbolic level designated in **Read, Play, and Learn!** They realize that print carries the meaning, and they can often be found pretending to read (emergent storybook reading) familiar books to a favorite stuffed animal or doll, to a friend, or to themselves. They rely heavily on previous experiences with that book; memorization of patterns within the text, such as repeated words or phrases; and the association of text sequences with the illustrations. They sometimes memorize the entire text if it is clearly supported by the pictures and their auditory memory is good. Children at this stage are developing understandings of such conventions as *wordness* (there is one spoken word for every written word), *directionality* (print is read from left to right and from top to bottom), and *sound–symbol relationships* (graphophonics). If asked to count the number of words on the page, they may indicate confusion of the task by counting the letters. In fact, they often do not yet understand the instructional vocabulary (terminology) of *letter, word, sentence,* or *sound.* They may mimic the directionality and wordness of a parent or teacher even though their sense of wordness may still not be fully established. Although they may appear to have only memorized the text, they know not to "read" when the illustration is not accompanied by print. Print materials used with children at this Role-Playing "the Reader" stage are not only to help them think like a reader and to "feel" like a reader but also to support them as they begin to notice some very basic features of print. These materials continue to include Stage 1 and Stage 2 materials and are extended to include the materials listed in the appendix at the end of this chapter.

Creating reading materials from children's dictation about familiar and memorable experiences also serves this purpose. Dictated language experience (DLE) materials consist of one to several sentences that a child, or group of children, dictates to an adult after a discussion of an event. The adult serves as a scribe to record exactly what is said. Because children are being supported in their attempts to make the connection between oral language and print, their exact words must be recorded. The adult reads each word while writing it slowly and clearly, then reads the entire message back, pointing to each word while reading. Children are often encouraged to illustrate their dictation. The picture then becomes a cue to support their rereading. Each time the children reread their dictation, they are reinforcing and refining their understandings about print.

A DLE can be a very powerful demonstration and source of initial materials for children to "try out" reading. Directionality, familiarity with the look and conventions of written language, and the functions of print are often concepts that children in this stage begin to grasp after repeated DLE opportunities. Because the print has been generated from the children's own experience and in their own language, their memory will support their attempts to reread what was written. As with all Stage 2 materials, children at Stage 3 should be provided with opportunities to read and reread these dictations. *Read, Play, and Learn!* offers you many occasions in the Literacy Center to transcribe the children's dictation of experiences into print so that children can see their words in print and share them with others.

Children in this Role-Playing "the Reader" stage are further encouraged to experience what being a reader is like through the technique of Shared Reading (Holdaway, 1979). *Shared Reading,* as described by Holdaway, is different from the reading experience shared at the beginning of each day in *Read, Play, and Learn!* Books selected for a Shared Reading require a pattern or predictability that children can easily chime in with and memorize. (For examples, see *Getting the Most from Predictable Books* [Opitz, 1995].) The teacher first reads the book aloud to the child or children (making certain the pictures and print are clearly visible), so they can enjoy the story, rhyme, and/or rhythm. The children are then invited to participate during subsequent rereadings. In *Read, Play, and Learn!,* Shared Reading can be done in the Literacy Center with related stories using memorizable books that have only one or two lines per page, in reading time after center play is completed, or as a transition between daily routines.

If the book is to be shared with a group, an enlarged copy (big book) is required for the children to be able to see the print and pictures clearly. The book may be reread several times in this way in order for the children to become completely familiar with the story (develop memory for text). Once familiarity is established, the book is read again, slowly and clearly, yet fluently, while you point to each word as it is read (demonstrating directionality and wordness). Children may spontaneously chime in during any of these rereadings or should be encouraged to do so by pauses at appropriate points. For example, when doing the module based on *A Porcupine Named Fluffy,* the children have an opportunity to role-play and engage in many activities related to textures and self-image. Williams's (1998) *Let's Go Visiting* ("Let's go visiting. What do you say? Four _____ _____ are ready to play") presents an opportunity to do a Shared Reading. During these readings, you may demonstrate how to use illustrations and text to reconstruct or create a story. Concepts about print are further developed and reinforced when frequent opportunities are provided for children to "reread" these books independently, to friends, or to an adult.

Aural Language Connections

A large body of research indicates that phonemic awareness bears an important relationship to achievement in reading (Adams, Foorman, Lundberg, & Beeler, 1998). *Phonological awareness,* and specifically phonemic awareness, is the conscious awareness that words are made up of phonemes and the ability to manipulate those phonemes. Phonological awareness develops along a continuum ranging from the ability to recognize rhymes and alliteration to the ability to segment words into syllables, rimes, onsets, and finally into phonemic units (Swank & Catts, 1994). An inability to hear the phonemes and the subsequent inability to relate them to the printed word appears to be a common problem of many children who experience difficulty learning to read, particularly if you begin reading instruction at a level that assumes children have already developed this skill.

Some children do not develop phonemic awareness naturally. This may be due to the absence of the types of experiences, both informal and structured, that facilitate the development of phonemic awareness. Phonemic awareness typically develops as children playfully participate in poems, songs, and stories filled with rhymes and alliteration (Adams et al., 1998; Griffith & Olson, 1992; Yopp, 1992, 1995b). Some children may require more directed experiences, such as stretching words slowly, making and breaking words, or participating in activities using rimes and onsets (Castle, Riach, & Nicholson, 1994; Clay, 1993; Cunningham, 1995; Gastins, Ehri, Crass, O'Hara, & Donelly, 1997). Studies have indicated that phonemic awareness can be taught to children 5 years and older but that training for children younger than 5 is highly suspect (Bradley & Bryant, 1983; Byrne & Fielding-Barnsley, 1991). A small percentage of elementary children may require even more intensive interventions in order to develop phonemic awareness. If a child continues to experience problems with phonemic awareness and conventional reading appears to be impeded, you should collaborate with a special education or language specialist for ideas to increase the child's phonemic awareness.

Oral Language Connections

It is important to remember that children at all stages of reading development can listen to, understand, and enjoy books that are at a higher level than those they can read. At Stage 3, however, it is particularly important that you provide children many opportunities on a daily basis to listen to different kinds of books, both fictional and informational, to help develop very crucial concepts and attitudes about stories, books, and print. Sharing of a variety of quality literature, fiction and nonfiction, narrative and expository, is critical to the continued development of oral language, syntax (grammar), and semantics (vocabulary). In *Read, Play, and Learn!* you can provide such opportunities through reference and picture books in the Science and Math Center; through adding various related poetry books, informational books, and storybooks to the Literacy Center; and through the books made available for the peer-paired reading time. Opportunities to read aloud to children are considered critical to the *Read, Play, and Learn!* curriculum.

Children should be encouraged to ask questions and to discuss concepts and vocabulary reflected in the illustrations and text of the materials read. Take the opportunities spontaneously provided in conjunction with storybook reading to build and extend the children's language base and to stimulate their thinking while you or another child reads the book. Whenever possible, reading aloud to the children should be related to the learning that takes place during the day and should not be an isolated experience. *Read, Play, and Learn!* incorporates the vocabulary and concepts presented in a story throughout the day and throughout the curriculum with purposeful intent.

Writing Connections

Children in Stage 3 of literacy development may demonstrate vastly different writing behaviors depending on their experiences with writing, the quality and quantity of developmentally appropriate adult mediation they have received, and the purpose for which they are writing. They may use scribble writing, letter-like marks, random strings of letters, or even sound-spelling, depending on their intent and understanding of the form of written language. They are still exploring the various functions print can serve, the roles print plays in their everyday lives, and the various forms it can take. Writing children's names and messages on pictures and helping them to notice the significance of labels, signs, directions, letters, notes, and so forth facilitate these understandings and provide children with opportunities to discover the consistent features of written language. Bringing in examples of environmental print to stimulate discussions and sociodramatic play guides children to recognize the presence and power of literacy in their own culture and helps to bridge possible gaps between home literacy and school literacy. For the module on *Abiyoyo,* the adults might bring in actual sheet music to show the children how notes and words on the page tell us what to play and sing. During the module on *The Snowy Day,* an empty (or even full) box of hot chocolate packets can be added to the Dramatic Play: Theme Area for "Peter" to have when he comes in from playing in the snow. You can read, or some of the children can pretend to read, the directions for making the hot chocolate on the box. In the Science and Math Center, the children can follow a recipe chart on the wall to actually make some hot chocolate and study the effects of the hot water on the chocolate powder. Coupons could be given to children to take home for hot chocolate, hot soup, or other items that are warming.

Even very young children must have opportunities to observe the process of writing as well as to use writing in informal settings, for a variety of purposes. Encouraging and modeling for children ways to incorporate print into the Dramatic Play: Theme Area serves this purpose particularly well. Teachers may demonstrate various ways in which children "write" (scribble strings, letter-like marks, random letters, sound-spelling, etc.) in order to encourage children to use whatever written form they like. This often gives children opportunities to explore with writing and has been shown to increase their attempts to write independently.

When children begin to understand that writing is a means of encoding speech and begin to incorporate letters into their writing, they have made a remarkable breakthrough. Teachers and parents should celebrate children's attempts to use letters to represent their talk—even if their use of graphophonics is nonexistent, fledgling, and not yet conventional (Clay, 1979).

The alphabetic knowledge (the ability to discriminate between and identify individual letters) of children at this stage of literacy development is still developing as is their phonemic awareness (the ability to hear discrete sounds or sound units in words even though they may not be able to identify the letters that represent them). Early in this stage they often write using a random string of letters that reflect no sound–symbol correspondence. Gradually, with appropriate adult mediation and instruction, children begin to represent the sounds they hear (ones that sound dominant to them) with the letter(s) they associate with these sounds (invented or sound-spelling). The number of sounds children are able to hear within a word and to represent appropriately depends on their knowledge of graphophonics and how discriminating their ears have become. Children at this stage profit from the informal yet intentional introduction of information about sound–symbol correspondence. What is taught and how it is taught must be determined by what the child already knows. Therefore, you must work within each child's zone of proximal development. In *Read, Play, and Learn!*, computer software, letter stamps or stencils, alphabet puzzles, magnetic letters, electronic alphabet and word games, and so forth are incorporated into the Literacy Center, Table Play area, and Floor Play area. You can also provide information informally and answer children's questions about print as you demonstrate the writing process during dictation. (For specific suggestions, see Clay, 1991, and Fisher, 1991.)

Stages of Spelling Development

Children at this stage of literacy development may be at the prephonemic (marks or random strings of letters) or at the early phonemic stage of spelling. If these children use letters, then they may use one or more letters to represent words or syllables. For example, TRUCK might look like T or TK. These children still may not demonstrate control of the concept of *wordness* in their writing or in their reading.

Prephonemic Stage

Children at the prephonemic stage do not use spaces to set apart words and do not yet grasp the concept that words are composed of sound units (phonemes) represented by letters. They frequently use a random string of letters and numbers to represent a complete thought or thoughts. Sometimes, however, they include symbols to represent people or objects that they are writing about. Their writing cannot be "read" by adults because there is too little information on the page for them to interpret. Children may or may not be able to reread their writing depending on its meaningfulness and if it is accompanied by an illustration or other contextual association.

Example: $STN3vSEll$

What the child is spelling: "I went to two Rockies games, and I'm going to go again on my birthday."

Early Phonemic Stage

At the early phonemic stage, children spell words based on the dominant sounds that they are able to isolate and identify. At the beginning of this stage, they may use only one letter to represent a word and not attempt to sound through the entire word. They often stop after identifying a letter that they believe represents the most dominant sound within the word, usually the initial consonant. As teachers, other children, and parents help them or model for them how to stretch a word to hear its additional phonemes, and as their auditory discrimination becomes more developed, they begin to add other letters. Typically these are the final and then medial consonants. Again, these are the dominant sounds the child hears. Children at this stage still may not have the concept of wordness and may not use spaces between words, although they may use spaces to differentiate between thoughts or sentences.

Example: T, TK, TRK

What the child is spelling: Truck

Phonemic Stage

At the phonemic stage, children still base their spelling on what they hear versus any visual memory of the word. They include a letter for every phoneme (sound unit) contained in the word, and all sound features are represented. Endings such as -ed begin to appear, and wordness is in evidence. Vowels begin to appear in this stage, but they may not be the correct ones. Children at this stage may benefit from being introduced to word families, spelling patterns, and word structures (Gentry, 1982).

Example: PLAN

What the child is spelling: Plane

Example: TRUK

What the child is spelling: Truck

Transitional Stage

Children at the transitional stage tend to blend their visual memory of words with their knowledge of sound–symbol relationships. Sometimes their memory for words overrides their graphophonic (sound–symbol relationships) awareness. Vowels appear in every syllable, and many words are correctly spelled. Knowledge of the silent e rule and inflectional endings are evident.

Example: YOUNITED

What the child is spelling: United

Example: SUMTIME

What the child is spelling: Sometime

Conventional Stage

Children at the final stage of spelling development, the conventional stage, demonstrate a basic knowledge of their native system of spelling and its rules. They have an extensive knowledge of word structures (e.g., affixes, contractions, compound words) and are growing in their accurate use of silent consonants, doubling consonants, and irregular words. They have a large written vocabulary (number of words that they can write and reread accurately). Children at this stage often sense when words do not "look right."

Mediation

Children should have daily opportunities to participate in situations in which they can see the print and observe the processes of reading and writing demonstrated and mediated by those who are more literate. A DLE story, a morning message, a shared reading from an enlarged text, and a class schedule can help children understand that the print holds the message. Opportunities to reread these familiar texts, such as those suggested in **Read, Play, and Learn!**, help young children understand that print remains constant and encourages children to search for familiar features or conventions and to make new discoveries.

The more frequent and the more personally significant the opportunities children have with print, the more likely their writing will come to resemble conventional print. Teachers need to provide even very young children with opportunities to try writing and to see their personal attempts as authentic and valuable.

As mentioned previously, DLE is a powerful and very personal medium with which to model for children the process of writing as well as the process of reading. It can be used to demonstrate very general or very specific concepts and is, therefore, used at subsequent stages with different intent and mediation. When children are encouraged to participate in the actual physical writing of the text to any extent that they can, the activity is called *supported writing*. During supported writing, children of varying levels of cognitive and literacy development can contribute by actually doing some of the writing. If children's names are included in the text, for example, children can contribute the writing of their own name or several of its letters, even if you must guide their hands. Children with more advanced literacy understandings can contribute letters to words, entire words, punctuation, and so forth. For example, during the module on *The Three Billy Goats Gruff*, you can provide the children with an opportunity to help compose, dictate, and "write" a letter filled with blanks, which they can then take home for their parents to read. The parents then fill in the blanks with answers about their children and send the letters back to school. This involvement in letter writing makes the message that was sent home personally meaningful to the children and the parents. The children will want to "read" it to their parents and will take an interest in what the parents write back in the blanks.

Although many ideas are presented in **Read, Play, and Learn!,** there are obviously an infinite number of opportunities to put words into print that present themselves each day for the adults in the classroom to seize. The creative professional will look for these situations and take advantage of them as they arise. Always have pencils and blank pieces of paper handy!

Dictation can be constructed as a group, such as by setting up a chart and calling it *The Daily News*, which can be used to announce any plans or special notices for the day, a summary of an experience such as a trip to the aquarium, a thank-you note to a visitor, a summing up of new information gleaned from a theme exploration, or thoughts generated from the **Read, Play, and Learn!** curriculum. Children can also dictate and contribute their efforts to brief individual messages to accompany their drawings, to communicate information to others (e.g., "Don't use this side of the sink. It gets you wet!"), or to add individual contributions to a group book.

Teachers of emerging readers and writers can model sounding out a word by saying the word slowly and pretending to stretch it out like a rubber band (using index fingers to indicate the stretching motion) to listen for its sound units (Calkins, 1986). Teachers can also model the process of stretching out a word as children write. Children may recognize different sound units in a word. For example, in the word *cat*, the children may hear /c-at/ or /ca-t/ or /c-a-t/. Many children may be able to segment sound units and yet cannot identify which letter(s) should represent the units. At this point, the teacher can provide the print for the sound unit or may provide the appropriate letter tiles to make the sound unit. This helps the child begin to make appropriate graphophonic (sound–symbol) associations.

Children at this stage also need others who are more literate to stimulate their interest in the forms print takes and to answer their questions about how print works. Children at this stage need to observe print being used for a variety of purposes, such as to organize the environment, to record experiences and information, to communicate information, and as a source of enjoyment. Literacy props should be incorporated into the Dramatic Play: Theme Area, and possible uses should be modeled and discussed. As children are provided with opportunities to dictate their experiences, to read and reread familiar stories and messages, to observe writing, to use literacy in their play, and to write, they construct new understandings about literacy. You can use these opportunities to observe what the children know, to answer questions that children might have, and to mediate the children's efforts to read and write. You can nurture independence and problem solving by encouraging the children to use what they know to figure out the unknown.

INITIATING SEARCHING BEHAVIORS

The children had been reading *The Rainbow Fish*. The teacher had set out vinyl letters along with the plastic fish and sea creatures in the water table. A table with a tray on it was placed next to the table. David pulled several letters from the water and placed them on the tray as follows: M, R, and Q . "Fish. This says 'Fish,'" the boy said. The teacher replied,

"Fish starts with an F. Let's find the letter F that says, /fffff/." Together they found the letter F and placed it on the tray. The teacher continued, "Each letter makes a different sound. The letter D in your name makes a /d/ sound for D-avid. /F/ is the first sound we hear in 'fish,' so we put the letter F first." David rapidly began retrieving letters from the water. "What sound does the R make?" David asked. "What sound does this one make?" David made a literacy connection and was eager to explore new ones.

STAGE 4: DEVELOPING INNER CONTROL

Children at the Developing Inner Control stage of literacy development are beginning to construct an increasing amount of knowledge about graphophonics, constancy of word, and strategies to derive meaning from print (Clay, 1991). They have developed the concept of *wordness* (one written word for each spoken word, although not necessarily the "correct" word) and use a reading-like voice to "read" their version of the text.

They can point to print accurately across the page as they "read" (tracking print) and often do so to keep their place. Self-monitoring behaviors appear as children begin to reread a familiar story or dictation, pointing to each word as they read, and then run out of print before the story is finished. They may, on their own or with prompting, start the process over to solve the mismatch problem, which initiates further analysis of the print.

Children at this stage are encouraged to use tracking to find individual words on a page. That is, they use their memory of the text and wordness to locate specific words. As they track and identify specific words, they continue to develop hypotheses about, and refine their knowledge of, graphophonics and begin to develop a small sight-word vocabulary as they notice that the print representing a particular spoken word looks the same every time (constancy of words). They are prompted to use picture cues in conjunction with meaning (memory of the story and anticipation of the story line), syntax (sentence structure), graphophonics, and other audiovisual cues to help them make sense of print.

Shared reading materials from Stage 3 can now be read independently or through supported reading in which you read only enough to help the child begin to anticipate the language or pattern of the book instead of shared reading in which you familiarize the child with the book by reading it completely. Reading materials now can be extended to books that are slightly less predictable and may have more than one word that changes in the pattern. The illustrations do not support the text in a word-for-word fashion.

Reading less predictable books with less directly supporting pictures requires the children to "read" less familiar content and to identify less familiar words by using their knowledge of syntax and semantics. Children must generate words with similar meanings that might make sense in a particular part of the story and in a particular place in the sentence. Although children at this stage *may* not yet use print to narrow or to confirm their hypotheses, this is a good time to demonstrate how print can help in this process and to encourage the children to stretch their vocabulary at the same time. For example, when a child "reads" *flower* instead of *rose,* you can take this opportunity to show the child what the word "flower" looks like and assist the child in comparing it with the author's word, "rose." You may also take this opportunity to focus the child's attention on the initial consonants and tell the child what the sounds for /r/ and /fl/ represent. Children should not be expected to remember these generalizations about print at this time. It is the process and not necessarily the specifics that are being modeled.

Children at this stage of literacy development should be encouraged to create innovations of predictable books with which they have become familiar. Innovations of a text are new versions of patterned, predictable, or language-predictable books created by the children. For example, when reading *Somebody and the Three Blairs*, you might use *Brown Bear, Brown Bear* (Martin, 1983) as a pattern for an innovation. You may then encourage the children to substitute personally selected words for targeted words in the original text. For example, children might substitute "Green frog, green frog," for "Brown bear, brown bear"; "Andrea wore her striped socks," in lieu of "Mary wore her red dress" in *Mary Wore Her Red Dress and Henry Wore His Green Sneakers* (Peek, 1985); or "The important thing about my sister is that she has curly hair" instead of "The important thing about snow is that it is cold," in *The Important Book* (Brown, 1949). These innovations obviously maintain their pattern and predictability but now also possess the added intrigue and support of the children's own language. For example, while reading *The Little Old Lady Who Was Not Afraid of Anything*, the children can make up their own version, such as "Two hands go CLAP, CLAP" or "Three bears go GRR, GRR."

Innovations such as these can be written on chart paper to share with the whole class (big-book style), or they can be prepared as individual booklets and illustrated. Both should remain accessible to children for rereading. The rereading of these materials will help the children develop a sight-word vocabulary and read more fluently. Rereading will also provide them with the opportunity to construct new hypotheses about graphophonics and other visual aspects of print. Books appropriate for this stage are listed in the appendix at the end of this chapter.

Interactive charts (Schlosser & Phillips, 1992) are an excellent way to help children construct relationships between oral and written language, to reinforce their concepts of directionality and wordness, and to help guide their development of effective reading strategies. An interactive chart consists of a familiar poem, song, fingerplay, chant, and so forth written on a chart and/or sentence strips in such a way as to present children with an opportunity to physically manipulate the print in a concrete way. An example of an appropriate poem to use as an interactive chart during the module based on *Picking Apples & Pumpkins* is "A Dime":

A DIME

My father gave me a dime
To buy a lime.
But I didn't buy a lime,
I bought some _____.

Food word cards can then be created for use in the final blank of the chart. Cards may include an appropriate picture, if necessary, to help children identify the words. In the above poem, the children could substitute other items they could buy at a farm or market. (For further information about interactive charts, see Schlosser & Phillips, 1992.)

The word/phrase/sentence that the children can manipulate (exchange for interchangeable words/phrases/sentences) is selected by the teacher based on its meaningfulness to the text, the ability of the child or children, and the objective of the chart. "By effectively guiding children in focusing on the print [of interactive charts], teachers can assist children in integrating semantic, syntactic, and grapho-phonic cuing systems" (Schlosser & Phillips, 1992, p. 11). Concepts of varying sophistication, such as directionality; differences among letters, words, and sentences; wordness; punctuation; letter recognition; graphophonics; and rhyming words can be easily developed for individual children or groups of children through the use of both interactive charts and innovations of text.

Toward the end of Stage 4 and the beginning of Stage 5, it is important to provide children with language-predictable books. Language-predictable books usually have one or two sentences per page and are written in the natural language (syntax and vocabulary) of the child rather than in literary language. The meaning of the text is clearly supported by the picture, but not in a word-for-word fashion. An example of a language-predictable book that could be used with the module on *Night Tree,* in which a family drives to the forest in a pickup truck, is *Joshua James Likes Trucks* ("Joshua James likes trucks. He loves big trucks. He loves . . ."; Petrie, 1982). Other language-predictable books include many selections written by Byron Barton, Brian Wildsmith, and Harriet Ziefert. Books appropriate for this stage are listed in the appendix at the end of this chapter. Again, these types of books are appropriate to include in the Literacy Center.

Oral Language Connections

Asking children to dictate innovations of a predictable text encourages them to listen for patterns and rhymes with more intent and focus than they would during shared reading. Creating innovations of a text also encourages children to play with language. They must often not only search but stretch their language repertoire to find just the right word to fit the pattern both in terms of syntax and semantics. Some children will "work hard" to find words for their innovation that will make the reader laugh. They literally begin to play with words. Innovations may also provide opportunities for children to refine and extend their developing understandings about print and their phonological and phonemic awareness.

Writing Connections

When children at this stage write, they typically use sound-spelling; that is, they spell primarily based on what they hear. They gradually develop the understanding that certain letter combinations make certain sounds. The word *truck* may now be spelled "TRK" rather than "TK" as their ear for sounds (phonemic awareness) has become more refined and as they have internalized more sound–symbol correspondences. They may demonstrate an understanding of wordness in their writing by leaving spaces between words or by clearly pointing to words as they read. Children at this stage of literacy development may also be developing a writing vocabulary (words they can write, read, and spell correctly) of personal words. They also reexamine already familiar environmental print from a new, more analytical perspective. They seem to enjoy searching for and copying specific words from familiar books, wall charts, and environmental print. In this process they confirm or reject hypotheses about print and construct new hypotheses as they search for new connections.

The way in which the learning environment is designed has a marked impact on whether children will perceive themselves as writers. Children at all levels of literacy development should see their own writing prominently displayed and should see print produced and used to organize the classroom (labels, instructions, helping charts, daily schedule, etc.) and to communicate with others (message boards, planning charts, newsletters, etc.). In addition, you should always have writing materials available for all of the children in a location with which the children are familiar so that they will know where they can find, use, and return the materials.

Materials available in the Literacy Center might include markers, pencils, erasers, crayons, pens, lined and unlined paper, correction fluid, glue, blank booklets, staplers, art supplies to construct and decorate their books, tape, and scissors. Similar materials should also be strategically placed in other areas of the classroom (sociodramatic play, science, math/manipulatives, etc.) to spark the inclusion of writing into the play or study in progress.

Mediation

At this stage of literacy development, you should provide children with instruction and mediation to help them move beyond memorizing predictable text as they begin to incorporate print cues with mediation (wordness, length of word, sight words, and some initial consonants) into their current repertoire of reading strategies (memory and the use of illustrations). Ask the children to look more closely at print. Let the children know that the words they predict may or may not be exactly what they or the author wrote (e.g., I spent the night at my cousin's *versus* I spent the night at my cousin's house, Planes fly in the air *versus* Planes fly in the sky) and that they can confirm or challenge their prediction by looking at and crosschecking with the print.

Many times during this process, you should informally, yet intentionally, provide children with information about sound–symbol correspondences (as the children need or request it), which the children may or may not internalize at the time. As this type of mediation occurs over time with a variety of texts (and in supported writing experiences), children make connections that lead to generalizations. Once children notice that a certain letter represents a certain sound or that a certain sequence of letters represents a word, they search for even more connections independently. They make hypotheses about connections and initiate the search for confirmations.

STAGE 5: BECOMING INDEPENDENT

The Becoming Independent stage of literacy development is a very exciting stage for everyone—parents, teachers, peers, and especially the children. All of the previous literacy experiences seem to come together like pieces of a puzzle, and the children seem to understand how the pieces work together to form the whole picture.

Children at this stage of literacy development read for meaning. Appropriate instruction delivered in a literacy-rich classroom has enabled them to strategically use several sources of information to identify unknown words. Although they still need the support of pictures, clearly printed text, and familiar concepts and vocabulary, they are now able to use print cues effectively as part of this problem-solving process. Classroom instruction and mediation have helped them to begin to use various strategies to identify unknown words independently. Their problem-solving processes (crosschecking) become less tedious and more fluent. Instruction supports their rapidly expanding sight-word vocabulary, their ability to recognize and use patterns in words, their knowledge of graphophonics, and their vocabulary concepts. Instruction is considered effective if children begin to independently integrate this knowledge into attempts to identify unfamiliar words. Books appropriate for children at this stage of literacy development are listed in the appendix at the end of this chapter.

As children are provided with time to read new books and to reread old favorites independently, the automaticity and fluency with which they are able to effectively use these sources of information continue to increase while new knowledge is simultaneously constructed. The readers rapidly exert inner control over the print and become increasingly independent.

Children at this stage can begin to develop personal word banks. A personal word bank is a notebook or box consisting of words from familiar materials (including DLE) and words that are personally significant to the child. These words may be familiar and/or significant within the context of a DLE, a memorable portion of a storybook curriculum book, or a significant personal life experience. As the child reads and rereads his or her bank of words and refers to the words when writing, the words gradually become part of the child's sight-word vocabulary and/or writing vocabulary. These words then become the "known," which can be used as bridges to new literacy learning during instruction or informal "teachable" moments. For information on key words, refer to Ashton-Warner (1963).

Oral Language Connections

Reading aloud to children from storybooks and informational books (stretching books) containing less familiar concepts, rich vocabulary, more complex sentence structures, and illustrative literary elements is particularly important at this time. Picture reading these stretching books together before children attempt to read them independently is also important. Both situations provide opportunities for engaging children in stimulating (language and thought) conversations and contribute to their aural and oral language development. This is accomplished by listening carefully as children respond to stories and books in their own language and by skillfully and unobtrusively interjecting new information and new vocabulary into responses to children's questions.

These conversations also provide you with an opportunity to listen to the children's syntax, to determine their sense of story, to note their expressive and receptive vocabulary, and to extend their understandings of the concepts presented and the related vocabulary. By anticipating possible stumbling blocks, teachers increase the children's ability to read stretching books with greater success. Children at this advanced stage of the symbolic level can be actively involved in reading the stories in *Read, Play, and Learn!* and reading the print around the room and in the various areas and centers. It is not anticipated that many children in preschool or kindergarten will be at this stage, but for those who are, you will need to provide opportunities for continued literacy development.

Writing Connections

Children at this stage of literacy development consistently use spaces between words and have begun to use vowels (correct or incorrect) along with the more dominant consonant sounds. You will notice more and more conventional spelling in the children's writing as they use visual memory of words and patterns with words they have seen in books and in their environment. The word "truck," therefore, may be spelled "trak," "track," "truk," or "truck." Children at this stage may benefit from spelling instruction that introduces them to word families, spelling patterns, and word structures.

Toward the end of this stage, children should be provided with opportunities to explore different genres of writing and to begin to tackle longer pieces. Children should be taught how to revise and edit selected pieces before "publishing" them and be guided through the process of doing so. Teachers should provide self-help tools, such as checklists, to assist children in revising and editing their work. These tools will help children become independent and to internalize conventions of punctuation and grammar. For related information on the writing process, see Calkins (1994) and Graves (1994).

Mediation

The goal of literacy mediation at this stage is to help children become strategic readers who are able to use independently what they know to figure out and solve print problems. You should support their reading only to the extent that it is needed (scaffolding) and continue to nurture independence and problem solving (Clay, 1991; Fountas & Pinnell, 1996).

A combination of supported reading and independent reading is recommended depending on the difficulty of the text for a particular reader. The teacher's observations and instructional decisions are especially critical at this point because the children are at the jumping-off point, ready to read independently if provided with the appropriate materials and mediation to make those next connections. When children come to a difficult word, for example, rather than tell them the word, you may demonstrate strategies to use available information and prompt them to do so. These prompts may include, "Look at the picture to see if that would help," "Think of what would make sense there," or "What would make sense and start with that first letter?"

Once children are instructed in the use of various strategies to identify unknown words, you must provide them with wait time (quiet time at the point of the reader's hesitation or confusion) to allow them to apply known strategies to solve the problem independently. If necessary, more general prompts should be used to help the children apply the strategies they already know. For example, "What could you do to figure out that word? What else could you try?" Reinforcement of strategic reading is an important aspect of the mediation that you supply in this and every stage. Children who are at this stage and at Stage 6 should be encouraged to do independent reading at the Science and Math Center and the Literacy Center on areas of interest. Just because a very young child can read well, however, does not mean that book, paper, and pencil tasks should replace play and interaction with peers. Dramatic play, movement in the Motor Area, play at the Floor and Table Play areas, and so forth are still vitally important.

STAGE 6: INDEPENDENT READER

Although few preschoolers and kindergartners will be at this stage, you need to understand how to encourage children who have achieved this level of ability. Readers at the Independent Reader stage of development depend more on themselves than on others when reading. They have learned to rely on themselves to employ a repertoire of problem-solving strategies to make sense of whatever they are reading. Their preference has shifted from the more public arena of oral reading to the more personal monitoring of silent reading. The problem-solving process has become internalized and automatic. Readers are able to use various sources of information to anticipate a word and do not have to correct as many inappropriate, spontaneous responses after the fact. Consequently, the reading process becomes more efficient and fluent. Reading has become less "work" and more pleasurable. Children at this stage now have more energy for and derive more pleasure from reading longer, more substantive stories and books. They are eager to share with others the vicarious experiences they are having with books. Books appropriate for this stage are listed in the appendix at the end of this chapter.

Oral Language Connections

During this stage, you should continue to include read alouds, as well as appropriate materials for independent reading, from all genres. Stories should be selected that reflect diverse social and cultural contexts as well as situations or problems to "stretch" the children. Such variety will provide models and vicarious experiences and help the children expand their knowledge of the pragmatics of language. Selections should be made with the intent to build on and expand the children's informational and conceptual knowledge base.

The read alouds (both fiction and informational) shared with children should become longer with varied themes, have more complex text structures, and have increasingly more challenging concepts and vocabulary. Fiction books should be filled with literary embellishments. You should continue with the rich prereading predictions and conversations and with discussions during and after the reading to stimulate thinking about the content of the material.

Writing Connections

When independent readers write, they usually use conventional spelling except when tackling long words. For these words, they use their knowledge of graphophonics or their knowledge of similar words to attempt to spell the word, or they substitute shorter words to avoid the conflict of spelling words "incorrectly." Your response or a parent's response to incorrectly spelled words will have an effect on which decision the child makes. Instruction and guidance in the writing process (Graves, 1994), familiarity with a variety of literature to provide models of writing forms and styles, and peers and self-help tools to assist with revising and editing will alleviate stress and facilitate the children's writing and spelling development.

Mediation

Children at this stage of literacy development begin to take on more responsibility for their reading and writing habits. They need guidance in selecting books based on their personal interests and capabilities. Monitoring the repertoire of strategies children use as they read and write is your responsibility as well as the individual child's responsibility.

Teachers need to plan periodic opportunities to hear children orally read both familiar and new texts. As each child reads, teachers should record the number and type of deviations from print (miscues). This information is used to determine whether the child is self-correcting for meaning, overrelying on one source of information, or using a variety of cues appropriately (crosschecking). Children need to be reminded of what strategic readers do when they read as well as of their personal strategies for reading (metacognition). This allows you and the students to continue to work as a team to nurture the children's literacy development.

In order to guide and support these children's efforts, you need to plan for opportunities to 1) monitor the reading strategies each child uses with familiar and unfamiliar text; 2) evaluate the reading and conceptual levels of the texts each child selects; 3) observe whether each child is appropriately challenged but not frustrated by the material he or she consistently selects; 4) help each child to monitor both the quantity and quality of his or her reading; 5) observe and guide each child's understanding of the author's message; and 6) consider and further stimulate each child's critical thinking, which, it is hoped, is being stimulated by the text.

SUMMARY

Emergent literacy forms the basis from which all subsequent literacy evolves. Failing to nurture and develop expressive and receptive language, attitudes, and skills early in a child's life imparts a heavy price on the child, the child's family, and society (Mitchell, 1989). The richer and more nurturing the literacy environment of young children, the more likely they are to explore language and print and the more creative and competent their literacy usage will become. All teachers, but especially those working with very young children and children with special needs, must be knowledgeable about and have internalized the developmental continuum of reading and writing in order to set developmentally appropriate literacy goals. Teachers must also be skilled in a variety of instructional strategies to assess and support individual children's development and learning across the curriculum and to be able to adapt these strategies for children whose development and learning are advanced or delayed. Although children with special needs may be chronologically within the age range of their peers, they may be at a stage of literacy development significantly below their peers. But, do not assume that these children are not ready for a curriculum that includes literacy interactions and mediation (just as many teachers assume very young children are not ready for literacy interactions and mediation). Consider the previous literacy experiences and cognitive development of each child in order to provide interactions with language, books, and print that will facilitate the continued emergence and development of the children's literacy understandings and performance.

REFERENCES

Adams, M. (1990). *Beginning to read: Thinking and learning about print.* Cambridge, MA: MIT Press.

Adams, M.J., Foorman, B.R., Lundberg, I., & Beeler, T. (1998). *Phonemic awareness in young children: A classroom curriculum.* Baltimore: Paul H. Brookes Publishing Co.

Allington, P., & Cunningham, R. (1994). *Classrooms that work: They can all read and write.* New York: HarperCollins College Publishers.

Ashton-Warner, S. (1963). *Teacher.* New York: Simon & Schuster.

Blachman, B. (1989). Phonological awareness and word recognition: Assessment and intervention. In A.G. Kamhi & H.W. Catts (Eds.), *Reading disabilities: A developmental language perspective* (pp. 138–158). Needham Heights, MA: Allyn & Bacon.

Blachman, B. (1991). Early intervention for children's reading problems: Clinical applications of the research in phonological awareness. *Topics in Language Disorders, 12,* 51–65.

Bradley, L., & Bryant, P. (1983). Categorizing sounds and learning to read: A causal connection. *Nature, 271,* 746–747.

Bradley, L., & Bryant, P. (1985). *Rhyme and reason in reading and spelling.* Ann Arbor: University of Michigan Press.

Bus, A., van IJzendoorn, M., & Pellegrini, A. (1995). Joint book reading makes for success in learning to read: A meta-analysis on intergenerational transmission of literacy. *Review of Educational Research, 65*(1), 1–21.

Byrne, B., & Fielding-Barnsley, R. (1991). Evaluation of a program to teach phonemic awareness to young children. *Journal of Educational Psychology, 83,* 451–455.

Calkins, L. (1986). *The art of teaching writing.* Portsmouth, NH: Heinemann.

Calkins, L. (1994). *The art of teaching writing* (2nd ed.). Portsmouth, NH: Heinemann.

Castle, J., Riach, J., & Nicholson, T. (1994). Getting off to a better start in reading and spelling: The effects of phonemic awareness instruction within a whole language program. *Journal of Educational Psychology, 86,* 350–359.

Clay, M. (1966). *Emergent reading behaviour.* Unpublished doctoral dissertation, University of Auckland, New Zealand.

Clay, M. (1979). *The early detection of reading difficulties* (3rd ed.). Portsmouth, NH: Heinemann.

Clay, M. (1991). *Becoming literate: The construction of inner control.* Portsmouth, NH: Heinemann.

Clay, M. (1993). *Reading recovery: A guidebook for teachers in training.* Portsmouth, NH: Heinemann.

Cunningham, P. (1995). *Phonics they use* (2nd ed.). New York: HarperCollins.

Durica, K. (1998). A "sound" foundation for reading: The importance of phonemic awareness. *Colorado Reading Council Journal, 9,* 11–14.

Durkin, D. (1966). *Children who read early.* New York: Teachers College Press.

Ericson, L., & Juliebo, M. (1998). *The phonological awareness handbook for kindergarten and primary teachers.* Newark, DE: International Reading Association.

Fisher, B. (1991). *Joyful learning.* Portsmouth, NH: Heinemann.

Fountas, I., & Pinnell, G. (1996). *Guided reading: Good first teaching for all children.* Portsmouth, NH: Heinemann.

Gastins, I., Ehri, L., Crass, C., O'Hara, C., & Donelly, K. (1997). Procedures for word learning: Making discoveries about words. *The Reading Teacher, 50,* 312–327.

Genishi, C., & Dyson, A.H. (1984). *Language assessment in the early years.* Greenwich, CT: Ablex Publishing Corp.

Gentry, J. (1982). An analysis of developmental spelling in GYNS AT WRK. *Reading Teaching, 36,* 192–200.

Graves, D. (1994). *A fresh look at writing.* Portsmouth, NH: Heinemann.

Griffith, P., & Olson, M. (1992). Phonemic awareness helps beginning readers break the code. *The Reading Teacher, 45,* 516–522.

Hart-Hewins, L., & Wells, J. (1990). *Read books for reading: Learning to read with children's literature.* Portsmouth, NH: Heinemann.

Holdaway, D. (1979). *The foundations of literacy.* Portsmouth, NH: Heinemann.

International Reading Association (IRA) & National Association for the Education of Young Children (NAEYC). (1998). *Learning to read and write: Developmentally appropriate practices for young children. A joint position statement of the International Reading Association (IRA) & National Association for the Education of Young Children (NAEYC).* Newark, DE: Author.

International Reading Association Board of Directors. (1998). IRA board issues position statement on phonemic awareness. *Reading Today, 15*(6), 28.

Jones, M., & Crabtree, K. (1994). Guide for observing emerging readers and writers. In K. Crabtree, *Accelerated reading: Early prevention for emerging readers and writers at risk* (pp. 26–30). Unpublished manuscript, University of Northern Colorado, Greeley.

Lindamood, C., & Lindamood, P. (1969). *Auditory discrimination in depth.* Boston: Teaching Resources.

Lundberg, I., Olofsson, A., & Wall, S. (1980). Reading and spelling skills in the first school years, predicted from phonemic awareness skills in kindergarten. *Scandinavian Journal of Psychology, 21,* 159–173.

Mitchell, B. (1989). Emergent literacy and the transformation of schools, families, and communities: A policy agenda. In J.B. Allen & J.M. Mason (Eds.), *Risk makers, risk takers, risk breakers: Reducing the risks for young literacy learners* (pp. 284–285). Portsmouth, NH: Heinemann.

Morrow, L. (1989). *Literacy development in the early years: Helping children read and write* (2nd ed.). Upper Saddle River, NJ: Prentice-Hall.

Morrow, L. (1997). *Literacy development in the early years: Helping children read and write* (3rd ed.). Needham Heights, MA: Allyn & Bacon.

Ollila, L., & Mayfield, M. (Eds.). (1992). *Emerging literacy: Preschool, kindergarten and primary grades.* Needham Heights, MA: Allyn & Bacon.

Opitz, M. (1995). *Getting the most from predictable books.* New York: Scholastic.

Patton, M., & Mercer, J. (1996, Fall). "Hey, where's the toys?" Play and literacy in 1st grade. *Childhood Education,* 10–16.

Schlosser, K., & Phillips, V. (1992). *Building literacy with interaction charts.* New York: Scholastic Professional Books.

Stanovich, K. (1986). Matthew effects in reading: Some consequences of individual differences in the acquisition of literacy. *Reading Research Quarterly, 21,* 360–407.

Sulzby, E. (1985). Children's emergent reading of favorite storybooks: A developmental study. *Reading Research Quarterly, 20,* 458–481.

Sulzby, E. (1986). Kindergartners as writers and readers. In M. Farr (Ed.), *Advances in writing research: Vol. 1. Children's early writing development* (pp. 127–199). Greenwich, CT: Ablex Publishing Corp.

Swank, L., & Catts, H. (1994). Phonological awareness and written word decoding. *Language, Speech, and Hearing Services in Schools, 25,* 9–14.

Taylor, D. (1983). *Family literacy.* Portsmouth, NH: Heinemann.

Teale, W. (1982). Toward a theory of how children learn to read and write naturally. *Language Arts, 59,* 555–570.

Teale, W. (1986). The beginning of reading and writing: Written language development during preschool and kindergarten years. In M. Sampson (Ed.), *The pursuit of literacy: Early reading and writing.* Dubuque, IA: Kendall/Hunt.

Teale, W., & Sulzby, E. (Eds.). (1986). *Emergent literacy: Writing and reading.* Greenwich, CT: Ablex Publishing Corp.

Wells, G. (1986). *The meaning makers: Children learning language and using language to learn.* Portsmouth, NH: Heinemann.

Wishon, P., Crabtree, K., & Jones, M. (1998). *Curriculum for the primary years: An integrative approach.* Columbus, OH: Merrill/Prentice-Hall.

Yopp, H. (1992). Developing phonemic awareness in young children. *The Reading Teacher, 45,* 696–703.

Yopp, H. (1995a). A test for assessing phonemic awareness in young children. *The Reading Teacher, 29,* 20–29.

Yopp, H. (1995b). Read-aloud books for developing phonemic awareness: An annotated bibliography. *The Reading Teacher, 48*(6), 538–543.

Appendix

SUGGESTED MATERIALS
FOR THE DIFFERENT STAGES
OF LITERACY DEVELOPMENT

MATERIALS FOR STAGE 1: BEGINNING WITH BOOKS

Concept Books (to share with children)

- One word/short phrase per page
- One directly related picture
- Describes color, shape, size, place, and so forth

Hoban, T. (1978). *Is it red? Is it yellow? Is it blue?* New York: Greenwillow Books.
Hoban, T. (1983). *Big ones, little ones.* New York: Greenwillow Books.
Oxenbury, H. (1981). *Family.* New York: Simon & Schuster.
Rockwell, A. (1976). *My nursery school.* New York: Dutton's Children's Books.

Wordless Picture Books (to share with children)

- Wordless
- Picture communicates a story

Ormerod, J. (1981). *Sunshine.* New York: Lothrop, Lee & Shepard.
Rathmann, P. (1994). *Goodnight gorilla.* New York: Scholastic.

Nursery Rhymes, Songs, and Poems (to share with children)

- Traditional and contemporary

Christelow, E. (1989). *Five little monkeys.* New York: Clarion.
Frank, J. (1982). *Poems to read to the very young.* New York: Random House.

Glazer, T. (1983). *Music for ones and twos: Songs and games for the very young.* New York: Doubleday.

Prelutsky, J. (1986). *Read-aloud rhymes for the very young.* New York: Alfred A. Knopf.

Raffi. (1988). *Songs to read: Wheels on the bus.* New York: Crown.

Warren, J. (1991). *Piggyback songs for school.* Everett, WA: Warren.

Counting Books (to share with children)

- One word and one number per page
- Pictures clearly represent the number

Hoban, T. (1985). *1, 2, 3: A first book of numbers.* New York: Greenwillow Books.

Peek, M. (1981). *Roll over! A counting song.* New York: Clarion.

Siegler, K. (1997). *Ten fat hens.* New York: Random House.

Wells, R. (1979). *Max's toys: A counting book.* New York: Dial Books for Young Readers.

MATERIALS FOR STAGE 2: IMMERSION IN STORYBOOKS, PATTERNED BOOKS, AND RHYMES

(Continue with all of the materials for Stage 1.)

Fingerplays (to share with children)

- Simple movements to accompany rhymes

Dutton, M. (1980). *Finger rhymes.* New York: Doubleday.

Dutton, M. (1985). *Hand rhymes.* New York: Doubleday.

Dutton, M. (1987). *Play rhymes.* New York: Doubleday.

Glazer, T. (1973). *Eye winker tom tinker chin chopper: Fifty musical fingerplays.* New York: Doubleday.

Traditional Fairy Tales and Folktales (to read to children)

- Simple story lines
- Familiar concepts

Ahlberg, J., & Ahlberg, A. (1978). *Each peach pear plum.* Toronto, New York: Penguin Books.

DePaola, T. (1986). *Tomie DePaola's favorite nursery tales.* New York: G.P. Putnam's Sons.

Galdone, P. (1970). *The three little pigs.* New York: Scholastic.

Galdone, P. (1973). *The little red hen.* New York: Scholastic.

Beginning Storybooks (to read to children)

- Familiar concepts
- Supporting pictures

Hill, E. (1980). *Where's Spot?* New York: G.P. Putnam's Sons.
Jonas, A. (1982). *When you were a baby.* New York: Greenwillow Books.
Kunhardt, D. (1940). *Pat the bunny.* New York: Golden Books Family Entertainment.
Tafuri, N. (1984). *Have you seen my duckling?* New York: Greenwillow Books.

Patterned, Predictable Books (to read to children)

- Repeated patterns
- Supportive illustrations
- Rhyme and/or rhythm

Cowley, J. (1980). *Mrs. Wishy Washy.* Auckland, New Zealand: Shortland Publications.
Martin, B. (1983). *Brown bear, brown bear, what do you see?* New York: Henry Holt and Co.
Wildsmith, B. (1988). *Whose shoes?* New York: Oxford University Press.
Williams, S. (1998). *Let's go visiting.* New York: Harcourt Brace & Co.
Wood, A. (1990). *Quick as a cricket.* Singapore: Child's Play.

MATERIALS FOR STAGE 3: ROLE-PLAYING "THE READER"

(Continue with all of materials for Stages 1 and 2.)

Patterned, Predictable Books (for shared reading and independent reading)

- Repeated patterns
- Supportive illustrations
- Rhyme and/or rhythm

Cowley, J. (1980). *Mrs. Wishy Washy.* Auckland, New Zealand: Shortland Publications.
Martin, B. (1983). *Brown bear, brown bear, what do you see?* New York: Henry Holt and Co.
Wildsmith, B. (1988). *Whose shoes?* New York: Oxford University Press.
Wood, A. (1990). *Quick as a cricket.* Singapore: Child's Play.

Dictations of Children's Own Language

- Several sentences dictated by one or more children to an adult

The children relate an experience, tell a story, or summarize a learning

Innovations of a Text

- Newly created versions of patterned, predictable books with substituted words provided by children

Brown, M. (1949). *The important book.* New York: Harper & Row.
Martin, B. (1991). *Polar bear, polar bear, what do you see?* New York: Henry Holt and Co.
Peek, M. (1985). *Mary wore her red dress and Henry wore his green sneakers.* New York: Clarion.
Williams, S. (1998). *Let's go visiting.* New York: Harcourt Brace & Co.

MATERIALS FOR STAGE 4: DEVELOPING INNER CONTROL

(Continue with all of the materials for Stages 1, 2, and 3.)

Less Patterned and Less Predictable Books (for shared reading and independent reading)

- More than one change in the pattern
- Less direct support from illustrations

Brown, M. (1991). *Goodnight moon.* New York: HarperCollins.
Gerstein, M. (1985). *William, where are you?* New York: Crown.
Wildsmith, B. (1988). *My dream.* New York: Oxford University Press.
Wood, L. (1991). *Bump, bump, bump.* New York: Oxford University Press.

Language-Predictable Books (for supported reading and independent reading)

- Syntax patterns and vocabulary predictable by the child
- Becoming more like "book talk"
- May include simple dialogue
- May have one or two lines of print per page

Campbell, R. (1982). *Dear zoo.* New York: Penguin Books.
Petrie, C. (1982). *Joshua James likes trucks.* Chicago: Children's Press.
Wildsmith, B. (1987). *If I were you.* New York: Oxford University Press.
Ziefert, H. (1985). *Where's the Halloween treat?* New York: Penguin Books.

MATERIALS FOR STAGE 5: BECOMING INDEPENDENT

(Continue with all of the materials for Stages 3 and 4.)

Stretching Books (for supported reading and independent reading)

- Concepts are familiar, but vocabulary is extended
- Less direct support from illustrations (illustrations support the story but not necessarily individual words)
- Story and syntax become more complex
- Syntax pattern within reader's reach
- May have two or three lines of print per page

Asch, F. (1981). *Just like Daddy.* New York: Simon & Schuster.
Barton, B. (1981). *Building a house.* New York: Mulberry Books.
Barton, B. (1982). *Airport.* New York: Harper & Row.
Perkins, A. (1970). *The nose book.* New York: Random House.
Stadler, J. (1984). *Hooray for snail!* New York: Harper & Row.

MATERIALS FOR STAGE 6: INDEPENDENT READER

Easy Storybooks

- Same characteristics as stretching books (above) except with more print per page
- Some pages may not have an illustration

Eastman, P. (1960). *Are you my mother?* New York: Random House.
Joyce, W. (1987). *George shrinks.* New York: Harper & Row.
Minarik, E. (1986). *Kiss for little bear.* New York: Harper & Row.
Slobodkina, E. (1968). *Caps for sale.* New York: HarperCollins.

Challenging Picture Books

- Illustrations may not tell the whole tale
- Informational books
- Some unfamiliar vocabulary concepts
- More literary language

Christelow, E. (1991). *Five little monkeys sitting in a tree.* New York: Clarion Books.
Fowler, A. (1994). *When you look up at the moon.* Chicago: Children's Press.
Kerr, J. (1968). *The tiger who came to tea.* London: Picture Lions.
O'Connor, J., & Alley, R. (1986). *The teeny tiny woman.* Toronto, Ontario, Canada: Random House, Canada.

ADDITIONAL SUGGESTED RESOURCES

Base, G. (1988). *Animalia.* Toronto, Ontario, Canada: Stoddart.

Butterworth, N. (1990). *Nick Butterworth's book of nursery rhymes.* New York: Viking.

Lobel, A. (1970). *Frog and Toad are friends.* New York: Harper & Row.

Ochs, C. (1991). *Moose on the loose.* Minneapolis, MN: Carolrhoda Books.

Parrish, P. (1963). *Amelia Bedelia.* New York: Harper & Row.

Rylant, C. (1987). *Henry and Mudge: The first book of their adventures.* New York: Bradbury Press.

Scarry, R. (1970). *Richard Scarry's best Mother Goose ever.* New York: Western.

Schiller, P., & Moore, T. (1993). *Where Is Thumbkin?* Mt. Rainier, MD: Gryphon House.

Sendak, M. (1991). *Chicken soup with rice.* New York: Harper Trophy.

Sesame Street. (1982). *One rubber duckie: A Sesame Street counting book.* New York: Children's Television Workshop.

Seuss, Dr. (1965). *Hop on pop.* New York: Random House.

Traponi, I. (1993). *The itsy bitsy spider.* New York: Scholastic.

Chapter 8

ENCOURAGING FAMILY INVOLVEMENT WITH READ, PLAY, AND LEARN!

Susan M. Moore and Toni W. Linder

Children learn more and progress faster when both home and school are cooperating to ensure that a child has a good learning environment and is exposed to a broad range of learning experiences. By letting families know about the modules you are using from *Read, Play, and Learn!*®, families can have a chance to read the same books at home as you are reading at school, share in their child's school experiences, have additional topics to talk about with their child, and better observe their child's progress as new skills are acquired. Throughout the year, an ongoing dialogue with the families of the children in your classroom is important. This chapter provides you with the following:

1. Guidelines for developing a family involvement component tailored to your program
2. Guidelines for conducting workshops that introduce parents and others to the importance of emerging literacy, provide strategies for interactive storybook reading at home, and offer guidance on other topics of concern to families
3. Reproducible handouts to share with parents, caregivers, and other family members, including basic information about skill building and suggestions for supporting children's reading, playing, and learning

Most families naturally support their children's development by playing with and reading to them. Most families also recognize just how important reading and writing will be to their children's success in school; yet, many may not realize that the development of literacy is dependent on language skills, cognitive skills, fine motor abilities, and social growth. Qualities of the *Read, Play, and Learn!* curriculum, such as its emphases on repeatedly reading the same stories and engaging in developmental play based on the stories' themes and ideas, allow easy carryover to home activities. Parents are typically pleased to learn that, as part of their regular family routines, they can support their child's development and learning at home *without sitting down to teach* their child.

You will want to help parents and caregivers see how literacy experiences are embedded in each day and reinforced throughout the 2–3 weeks of activities in each module. The daily rereading and discussing of the story provide children with an understanding of how to read a book, build vocabulary, and lead to an appreciation of the structure and sequence of a story. Dramatizing the story reinforces these concepts through concrete actions and use of literacy props. The science and math activities provide not only opportunities to experiment with numbers and concepts but also additional exposure to the uses of print and its relationship to speech. Making books and exploring forms of print make the components of books personally meaningful. Art activities combine practice with drawing and representing ideas in picture form with representation through symbols and writing.

DEVELOPING A FAMILY INVOLVEMENT COMPONENT

With your guidance, parents and caregivers can acquire an awareness of what is taking place in their children's classroom and learn natural interaction strategies that they can easily incorporate into their day. Morrow (1997) recommended communicating with parents through formal and informal methods, both written and oral, as well as individually and in groups. Following are numerous suggestions and strategies from which you and other team members can select to plan a family involvement component for your program. How you communicate and interact with families will be influenced by many factors, including the time of year, the backgrounds of your children and their families, whether a second language is spoken in the home, the literacy level of parents and caregivers, the availability of parents to participate in different activities, and the structure of your program. Remember to monitor your family involvement component throughout the year; use your team to evaluate how well you are staying in touch with the families. Help parents understand that it is in the *developmental* nature of their child's early learning that they will see progress toward building the foundations for conventional writing. If you are not seeing the results you want, use your weekly team meetings to introduce modifications.

Share Your Program's Philosophy

At the beginning of the year, describe to the parents and caregivers of the children in the classroom what a transdisciplinary play-based curriculum is. Tell them how **Read, Play, and Learn!** is organized. Communicate in writing your classroom philosophy and goals for overall development and emerging literacy. Let families know how cultural and language diversity are integrated in the classroom. For example, when reading *A Rainbow of Friends*, which discusses diversity of all types, tell parents how they can talk about how people are the same in many ways and yet they have different strengths, and when reading *Abiyoyo*, let families know that you are reading an old African folktale. Suggest that they recount folk stories from their own cultural background to their children. Relate to the families how reading experiences are integral to the broader communication processes, which include speaking, listening, and writing as well as other communication systems, such as art, music, and math. Point out how language and literacy development are linked to other areas of development. For example, when a child goes home and "Trip, Traps" across the bridge, as in *The Three Billy Goats Gruff,* let the families know how the repeated role play helps the child to remember the story sequence, acquire a memory for sounds and patterns, and perhaps recognize simple word patterns. Your program philosophy can be part of the handbook you assemble for families, described in more detail in the next section.

Some parents will be interested in the rationale for a curriculum like **Read, Play, and Learn!,** and you may want to provide some of the following information found in the research literature. It is important for parents to understand that repeated readings of the same story increase the number and kind of children's response to books (Morrow, 1987). In addition, children who have successive exposure to the same storybook provide higher level responses to questions than do children who are exposed to different books. They are better able to interpret the meaning of the story, predict outcomes, make associations and judgments, and give more detailed statements. Recurrent readings also encourage children to begin their first attempts at "reading" through storytelling as well as to focus on the print related to the storytelling. Children may begin to ask names of letters and words. Practice in retelling the story helps children to acquire the concepts of story structure, such as setting, theme, plot episodes, and resolution. Comprehension of story details also increases, and the child begins to attribute expression to the characters' voices (Morrow, 1985). Roser and Martinez (1985) found that children of lower abilities also demonstrate growth through repetitive readings. Not only do such research conclusions reinforce the use of storybooks as a foundation for early curriculum, but they also have implications for the repeated reading of storybooks at home.

Although your goals and philosophy should be available in written form for families, a personal discussion with parents and caregivers is also recommended. When possible, home visits are especially valuable; you can clarify a parent's questions, learn about each family's daily routines, and determine how reading and writing and other developmental issues are currently incorporated into the child's life. Personal communication at parent conferences (see page 165) is another option, but home visits tend to be more informal and comfortable.

Create a Set of Program Handouts

A set of handouts is intended to help parents and caregivers support their child's development in the **Read, Play, and Learn!** curriculum. In addition to your program's philosophy and goals, your handouts can include information about child development, emerging literacy, and parenting. Each handout should be brief and to the point, with lots of specific ideas for what families can be doing at home to help their child learn. You could also list other available community resources, such as storytime at the local public library, performances at children's theaters, and concerts.

Your handouts can be distributed to families one at a time or bound together as a handbook and given to families at the beginning of the school year. Handouts can be individualized for families or reproduced in the same format for everyone. Provide them at one-to-one parent conferences or during group meetings, or send them home with the children. If necessary, handouts can also be mailed to families. A sample set of handouts is provided in the next section of this chapter. Users of **Read, Play, and Learn!** are granted permission to photocopy this material or modify it for their purposes, but credit lines to **Read, Play, and Learn!** (like the ones at the bottom of each handout sample) must appear on every page borrowed or adapted from this curriculum.

Use Journals and Communication Notebooks

Much of the communication between educator and parent or caregiver takes place when children are dropped off or picked up; when parents' schedules prohibit them from participating in this routine, a personal journal or communication notebook that goes back and forth between school and home can be particularly helpful. This type of journal is also very useful for children who have special needs or who have many specialists in their lives.

Coordinating goals and sharing progress and challenges can be accomplished effectively by using a notebook in which you write a note and/or the child draws or "writes down" something special about the day to share with parents or others in the child's life. For instance, Nika was sent home with the following note to her parents: "Nika loves the story of *Somebody and the Three Blairs*. She particularly likes the humor in the pictures of Somebody making a mess." Just these two sentences provided Nika's parents with information about their child's enjoyment of school, the book the class was reading, and insight into her sense of humor. Parents often find these notes useful as they learn about their child's activities and then have a basis for talking to their child about those activities. Parents can also communicate with you about events influencing their child at home. "We have relatives visiting, so Nika's schedule has been irregular. She got to bed late last night. Just thought you might like to know why she is falling asleep while playing!" This back-and-forth journal can quickly become part of the daily routine and can help professionals and families monitor a child's growth and change.

Share "Good News" Messages

Parents love to hear something good about their child. Call parents or send home "good news" messages when the child has done something well or accomplished a new milestone. These calls will also provide a reason for the parents to communicate this positive feedback to their child. These positive messages also have the added advantage of making the parents feel more positive about their child's learning experiences, which, in turn, builds advocacy for your program.

Write to Families on a Regular Basis

It is important that you continue to communicate with the families throughout the school year. Send home with the children a letter or newsletter on a regular basis (weekly is best) to inform families of what is taking place at school and what the families can do at home to strengthen their children's learning. These letters can give ideas for promoting all areas of development. The parents' role is to determine which of the suggestions offered they can implement. Even if the families choose not to use the ideas presented, some of the suggestions may stimulate parents to think of other things that they can do.

Each module in the *Read, Play, and Learn!* collections includes two sample letters to the families, one to let families know of the new storybook you are starting and one for the second week to give families a further overview of the kinds of activities in which the class is engaging. You can embellish these letters with further suggestions for activities that parents and children can do together (that relate to the current storybook theme), benefit the child's development and promote emerging literacy, and are just plain fun. In a newsletter, you might also include lists of suggested books for children and parents related to specific topics or themes, lists of predictable books, poetry or rhyming books, books in different languages, and whatever else you think will be helpful for the families. A "More Suggestions" section in each module will give you some ideas for newsletter content, but teams should be thinking of other ideas, too. It is also wise to consider separate communications or a translation for individual children or groups of children when their first language is not English, when there are special considerations or adaptations for a child, or when the language skills of the family may call for an individualized approach in the communication.

Although not all parents will have computers, many families will have access to e-mail. You may be able to e-mail parents to share announcements, answer questions that caregivers raise, and provide families with information about their child and how they can be supported in their learning. As the areas of technology and communication continue to evolve, there will certainly be even more options for parent–professional communication.

Have Discussions with the Children and Families

Before and after class is a great time to meet with the parents and caregivers of the children in your class. A 2-minute catch-up between you and a parent or caregiver at drop-off and pick-up times can be critical for information sharing. Family members can touch base, find out about a special happening that day, hear a quick story about their child's accomplishments, and/or set up a meeting or telephone call with you during this time. This obviously cannot happen every day for each child in your class, but the occasional extended greeting can go a long way in connecting what is happening in the classroom with what is happening in a child's home environment.

Schedule Conferences

Schedule conferences and/or home visits on a regular basis to review each child's progress and jointly problem-solve with the parents about how learning can be further advanced at school and at home. Conferences provide an opportunity to deliberately discuss a child's progress at a specified time, but they should be informal dialogues, with conversation flowing between you and a parent or caregiver, not a teacher-directed, prepared presentation. For children with disabilities, you will, of course, need to be sure that the appropriate individualized family service plan (IFSP) or individualized education program (IEP) team meetings are scheduled throughout the year. Parents or caregivers are recognized by law (in the Individuals with Disabilities Education Act Amendments of 1997, PL 105-17) as key members of the team.

Make Your Classroom Informative for Families

Many parents will come into the classroom on a regular basis; others may drop in occasionally. Take advantage of these brief moments. Even when you cannot take time to talk to every parent, they may be able to glance at your colorful, informative bulletin board. Develop these bulletin boards (they are not just for the children!) and table displays that highlight that week's story. Post schedules of classroom activities and pictures of what is happening in the classroom. For example, when reading *A Rainbow of Friends,* have the children make a similar book of themselves engaged in activities with their friends. This book could be left in a special place entitled "Our Rainbow of Friends." Both children and parents love looking at the pictures and having the children point out their friends or activities.

Written suggestions for home can also be available on the bulletin board. Staple an envelope on the board that contains "recipes for fun" that parents can pick up and take home. The ideas can include actual recipes of materials or foods prepared in the class as part of the module, vocabulary to emphasize at home, and ideas for fun activities for the family to try that are related to the current theme and story and that foster the child's development. For example, during the module based on *A Porcupine Named Fluffy,* some of the following "recipes for fun" might be offered:

- Use the word "fluffy" to describe things in your house, such as towels, pillows, marshmallows, cotton balls, clothes out of the dryer, mashed potatoes, and popcorn.
- Use similar words to explain "fluffy," such as fuzzy, furry, soft, and light.
- Put bubble bath in the tub, and let your child blow bubbles with a straw. Talk about the fluffy bubbles.

Provide Opportunities for Story Reading and Family Sharing

Invite parents to participate in story reading time at school. First let them observe how the story is read. They will then see a model for interaction with children around books. You may also want to let parents be the story readers or storytellers as they become comfortable with the interactive process. (Books can be translated for families whose first language is not English.)

You may also provide opportunities for parents, grandparents, or siblings to visit the classroom and read to the children at individual book reading time. Relatives may also share a family story or cultural experience, introduce new brothers and sisters, or share their special skills or talents (e.g., computer skills, visual or performing arts skills, construction ability) with the children individually, in groups, or in centers. For example, family members might be invited to come to a "reading day" during the module on *The Snowy Day* (preferably on a snowy day if your area gets snow). The children (and family members, if they want) could come in their pajamas with their stuffed animals. The family members could read to the children as long as desired and share hot chocolate.

Create a time for parents or caregivers to introduce a new child to your classroom. Ask them to talk about their family, share pictures or stories, and describe what is special about their child and family. This may lead to a discussion among the children about how their families are alike or different. Include parents in observing and noting their child's developmental progress, including emerging literacy.

Family members may volunteer to prepare snacks consistent with storybook themes. Many parents have creative recipes to share and would love to help to make them in the classroom. For example, during the module based on *The Three Little Javelinas,* one mother helped the children make tortillas and then showed them how to use different fillings at snacktime.

Involve Families in the Centers

Invite parents to participate in literacy and other developmental activities in the classroom, including those in the Dramatic Play: Theme Area, the Literacy Center, and the Science and Math Center. Family members may also enjoy making books or doing projects with individual children. Give the parents specific instructions about what their roles are to reduce misunderstandings. Make a list of guidelines for parents so that they know how to interact with children in the classroom.

Involve Families in Class Projects

Parents may want to help with various school or classroom projects. One option is to have a parent help set up the Family Resource Room and collect books and toys for all of the children to check out and take home (see "Create a Family Resource Room" later in this chapter). Book, videotape, and toy lending libraries provide a convenient way for parents to augment the materials they have at home. The Family Resource Room can provide otherwise unavailable resources to families, particularly those with limited economic means. You can also provide opportunities for parents and family members to be involved in classroom or school projects, such as "book fairs," "book shares," holiday festivities, clean-up days, and school fairs.

Enlist parents to help develop "book bags." Book bags are special bags or backpacks that are filled with module-related items, including the book, a tape of the book being read, puppets, dolls, stuffed animals or miniature characters for role-playing the story, and activities for family members to do together. For example, a book bag for *The Kissing Hand* might include the book, a blank tape for a parent to tape-record the story, raccoon puppets that represent Chester and his mother, plastic forest animals, pieces of fur to make raccoon art pieces, and heart stickers.

The children covet these book bags, and being able take one home is a real treat. Parents may also offer to add something to the book bag for other children or for the classroom. You might be surprised at what a few creative parents can contribute! (One parent made a dragon suit complete with shiny scales for the module on *The Knight and the Dragon!*)

Conduct Group Programs

Determine what information is of interest to the children's families through a needs assessment (formal written survey or informal verbal survey), and provide informational and interactive workshops for parents on topics of interest. Implementing parent workshops, such as the one described in the next section of this chapter (see "Conducting Workshops for Families"), can help parents understand emerging literacy and what they can do at home to help facilitate their child's development. Workshops might also focus on "How to Play with Your Child," "How to Cope with Difficult Behaviors," and other developmental topics. Give parents options about topics, formats, who presents or leads the workshops, whether children are involved, and whether child care is needed.

Parents especially like child-involved parent programs. You can show them videotapes of their children that your team has made in the classroom. As you watch the classroom videotapes, discuss what is happening, why, and how development is being facilitated. Parents also love to watch their children in a live performance. For example, a reenactment of *The Little Old Lady Who Was Not Afraid of Anything* is great fun. Each of the children can have a role in the story (e.g., shaking a glove, stomping a boot).

One successful program option has been to set up parent-led discussion groups on topics of interest to many of the parents. For example, as children are "graduating" to the next class, parents and caregivers are often interested in what this change will mean, how they can best communicate with their child about the change, and what they should talk about with their child's new teacher. Sharing experiences and ideas with parents who have previously gone through such changes may be helpful.

Bring Families Together

Formal gatherings are not the only option for including parents and caregivers. You could also have social gatherings to highlight a story theme and extend what is happening in the classroom to family fun. Families may be included on field trips, such as the barbecue in the park during the module on *The Knight and the Dragon*. For families who cannot participate in day activities, Family Fun Nights can be planned. Family Fun Nights can incorporate activities related to the story theme in which all of the family can participate. For example, a Family Fun Night during the module on *Picking Apples & Pumpkins* might include making apple pies and carving pumpkins to take home. These evenings enable families to meet each other, to experience the types of activities their children are doing in school, and to learn how to carry out similar experiences at home. Children and their families can also work on projects together. Projects, such as building a puppet theater for the classroom, can be fun for everyone involved and benefit the classroom.

You may want to hold occasional parent "coffees" to share information about child development, literacy, community resources, and so forth. These can be held in the relaxed atmosphere of a Family Resource Room (described in more detail below). Be flexible with the times you schedule these, taking into consideration the work hours of the parents and caregivers; a "coffee" does not have to be the traditional mid-morning chat.

Make sure that parents have the telephone numbers of the other children and parents in the class. This will encourage play dates for the children and networking among parents. Establish a "telephone tree" to help the parents contact other parents to pass on important information, share resources, or make social connections.

Create a Family Resource Room

Create a Family Resource Room for all of the classrooms in your school to share. Such a room can provide opportunities for parents and families to share with each other; to have access to books, toys, articles, and other resources; and to just have a place to relax for a few minutes and connect with other parents. If possible, have a computer and Internet hook-up available in the Family Resource Room to allow families who do not have a computer at home to search for information and resources. One option is to have a parent be in charge of setting up and keeping this room filled with useful resources.

Establish Parent–School–Community Contact

Establish an advisory board to meet quarterly to provide feedback, solve problems, be involved in program planning and evaluation, and promote parent participation. Advisory boards may consist entirely of parents or may include alumni parents and community members, such as people from community agencies or representatives of specific disciplines that can provide expert consultation (legal, medical, public relations, funding, etc.). Advisory boards not only provide input and feedback but can also serve as a valuable connection to the community. A community advocacy base is a critical element in successfully finding funding when budgets are tight and measuring up to standards of accountability.

Add a Parent Consultant to Your Team

If funding is available, establishing a position on your early childhood team for a parent consultant is a good idea. This individual might be a veteran parent of a child with special needs, an experienced parent with a background in early childhood education, or a parent with experience with agencies serving children and families. The role of this individual is to be a mentor and resource consultant to families in your program. A parent consultant might also determine families' interests and needs, organize parent programs and interactions, maintain the telephone tree, coordinate the newsletter, maintain the Family Resource Room and lending library, convene the parent advisory board, and evaluate the parents' perceptions of the program. This person could also enhance the use of community-based services and supports through information sharing, connecting families to resources in the community, and providing information on and facilitation of transition planning for families. The consultant can be a link with families that helps keep them involved in the program, a link to the community and parent resources, a link with service organizations for funding and special projects, and a link to volunteer organizations.

A parent consultant can also be valuable in the role of *parent as trainer*, during which he or she mentors or co-teaches components of the parent workshops. This person has credibility with other parents and, thus, can sometimes be a more effective trainer than early childhood professionals who may not be as comfortable relating to groups of parents as they are to groups of children. The person who is the parent consultant can be an invaluable member of the team and can make the program more meaningful to families.

Ask Families for Their Opinions

Obtaining feedback on the effectiveness of your family involvement efforts is important. Using surveys, such as the "Things We Do at Home" survey (see Figure 1) and reaction and feedback sheets that you create using a rating scale can provide information about the effectiveness of activities and workshops. Program satisfaction questionnaires are also an effective way to keep the communication lines open between you and the families. These will help you to evaluate your program efforts, to plan for future events, and to ensure that you are meeting the individual needs of each child and family.

CONDUCTING WORKSHOPS FOR FAMILIES

Setting up a series of workshops for family members to heighten their awareness of emergent literacy activities and how they can be implemented and adapted to meet the needs of individual children can be an excellent way to reinforce the material that you send home in handout format. Emergent literacy for children "depends upon reading role models, opportunities to explore, and interaction with adults" (Saint-Laurent, Giasson, & Couture, 1997, p. 52). When you offer educational workshops for families, you help parents, caregivers, and other family members become better role models.

It is important to begin any program designed to support families' learning and participation with a discussion of what the families know and what they want more information about. Before the first workshop, ask families to complete a "Things We Do at Home" survey; by considering the items on this survey, they will have a basis for discussion and information sharing at the workshop. The survey (see Figure 1) asks parents to notice things their child likes to do at home that have to do with emergent literacy (e.g., scribbling, drawing, reading, playing, talking). It also highlights the interactions between parent and child that are critical to the interactive reading process. Answering the survey's questions helps family mem-

THINGS WE DO AT HOME

A Survey for Families

Child's name: _____ **Parent name(s):** _____

Your child is growing and learning all the time. It will help us to know more about how your child plays at home and the kinds of things you do together. Then we can be sure we help your child with learning at school in the best ways possible.

Things My Child Likes to Do at Home

1. Scribbles or draws pictures: ❑ yes ❑ no
    (If yes, then check the following that apply to your child.)
    ❑ pencils   ❑ pens   ❑ crayons   ❑ chalk   ❑ markers

2. Has had experiences using (check the following that apply to your child):
    ❑ coloring books   ❑ scissors   ❑ stamp pads   ❑ clay or playdough
    ❑ stencils (drawing around shapes)   ❑ tracing   ❑ alphabet letters or numbers

3. Plays educational games: ❑ yes ❑ no
    (If yes, then check the following that apply to your child.)
    ❑ matching pictures (Lotto)   ❑ color games   ❑ counting games

4. Talks about what he or she is playing or tells stories about the action of figures
    (e.g., toy people, animals, cars/trucks):   ❑ yes ❑ no

5. Likes to look at books or have stories read to him or her: ❑ yes ❑ no
    (If yes, then check the following that apply to your child.)
    ❑ pretends to read books   ❑ remembers the story and tells part of it
    ❑ talks about the pictures   ❑ can retell the whole story
    ❑ asks questions about the story

6. Knows some words or signs in the environment (e.g., a stop sign, McDonald's
    golden arches, cereal boxes):   ❑ yes ❑ no

7. Asks for help in knowing about signs or words he or she sees: ❑ yes ❑ no

8. Recognizes his or her name in print: ❑ yes ❑ no

9. Knows some or all of the letters in his or her name: ❑ yes ❑ no

10. Asks you to write words or letters for him or her: ❑ yes ❑ no

11. Pretends to write (by scribbling or making some letters):   ❑ yes ❑ no

_____
continued

Figure 1.   Use a survey, such as the one shown in this figure, to help ascertain what families know and what they would like more information about. Asking participants to complete the "Things We Do at Home" survey before the first workshop helps prepare family members for discussion and information sharing. (Adapted and reproduced by permission for the ***Read, Play, and Learn!*®** curriculum from S. Moore, S. McCord, & D. Boudreau. [1997]. *Things we do at home survey.* Child Learning Center, University of Colorado at Boulder.)

Figure 1. (*continued*)

Things I Do with My Child

1.	Talk with my child about what he or she is playing:	❑ yes ❑ no
2.	Talk with my child about family plans or things he or she will be doing:	❑ yes ❑ no
3.	Ask questions to help my child think about what he or she sees or is doing:	❑ yes ❑ no
4.	Play "pretend" or "make-believe" with my child:	❑ yes ❑ no
5.	Tell stories about our family or culture:	❑ yes ❑ no
6.	Sing songs, tell nursery rhymes, or play rhyming games:	❑ yes ❑ no
7.	Look at books or magazines, read stories, or look at story videotapes with my child:	❑ yes ❑ no
8.	Take my child to the library to hear stories or choose books:	❑ yes ❑ no
9.	Point out a sign or a word and tell my child what it means:	❑ yes ❑ no
10.	Tell my child the names of colors, alphabet letters, or numbers:	❑ yes ❑ no

11. Read with my child:
❑ daily at bedtime   ❑ daily at bedtime as well as other times during the day
❑ two or three times per week   ❑ less than two or three times per week

When We Read Together, My Child . . . (Please use scale.)

		Not at this time	Occasionally	Often	All the time
1.	Pretends to read the story	❑	❑	❑	❑
2.	Fills in words or lines from the text of the story	❑	❑	❑	❑
3.	Asks questions about the story	❑	❑	❑	❑
4.	Answers yes and no questions about the story	❑	❑	❑	❑
5.	Comments on the story, labels, or names and talks about pictures, characters, and so forth	❑	❑	❑	❑
6.	Points to pictures	❑	❑	❑	❑
7.	Turns pages or indicates when you should turn them and performs other actions (e.g., lifts flaps)	❑	❑	❑	❑
8.	Comments about something other than the story or related experiences	❑	❑	❑	❑
9.	Follows and attends to the story	❑	❑	❑	❑
10.	Identifies letters and sounds	❑	❑	❑	❑

continued

Figure 1. (*continued*)

	Not at this time	Occasionally	Often	All the time
11. "Reads" or recognizes words and phrases	❑	❑	❑	❑
12. Makes up new story line or endings	❑	❑	❑	❑
13. Other_____	❑	❑	❑	❑

When We Read Together, I . . .

	Not at this time	Occasionally	Often	All the time
1. Relate the story to my child's own experiences (e.g., "That looks like your truck," "We saw one like that at the zoo")	❑	❑	❑	❑
2. Label or name pictures and events in the story	❑	❑	❑	❑
3. Ask my child yes/no questions about the book (e.g., "Is that a truck?")	❑	❑	❑	❑
4. Ask wh- questions during storybook reading (e.g., "What is that?")	❑	❑	❑	❑
5. Require my child to contribute in some way: ❑ to point to pictures ❑ to turn pages ❑ to request attention ("Look at . . .")	❑	❑	❑	❑
6. Use conversational "fillers" (e.g., make noises/sound effects)	❑	❑	❑	❑
7. Confirm my child's attempts to communicate	❑	❑	❑	❑
8. Offer a choice of books	❑	❑	❑	❑
9. Read story/text	❑	❑	❑	❑
10. Identify letters and sounds that my child points out	❑	❑	❑	❑
11. Wait for my child to "fill in" words or phrases	❑	❑	❑	❑
12. Other _____	❑	❑	❑	❑

I Would Like More Information About . . .

1. What types of stories/books my child might like:	❑ yes	❑ no
2. Resources and information about how children learn to talk:	❑ yes	❑ no
3. Resources and information about how children learn to read and write:	❑ yes	❑ no
4. Toys, games, and other resources to help my child learn:	❑ yes	❑ no
5. Strategies and activities appropriate for my child as he or she develops language and literacy:	❑ yes	❑ no

Thank you for taking the time to complete this survey.

bers get a better idea of what is meant by emergent literacy and a better understanding of the level of learning in which their child may be engaged. Most important, the survey requests that family members think about questions they have or resources and information they need to help their child in the learning process. This will assist you, the other members of your team, and your parent consultant (if your classroom has one) individualize the subsequent learning that happens in the workshops.

Designing a Workshop Agenda

Based on the survey results, discussions you and your team members have, and the needs and objectives of your program, you will then be ready to design the content of your workshops. A sample agenda for one workshop is displayed in Figure 2. This agenda focuses on literacy and language learning as an interactive process that occurs within a context of daily routines, play, and interactive storybook reading. Activities in which parents are asked to participate are designed to model the interactive nature of the learning process. In addition to providing an orientation to the **Read, Play, and Learn!** curriculum, you will want to plan small group and large group activities that last no longer than 2 hours. Each section of the sample agenda is described below.

What Is Read, Play, and Learn!?

After family members have had an opportunity to meet each other and/or talk informally, open the session with a brief description of **Read, Play, and Learn!** The extent of this overview will depend on the timing of your first workshop in relation to the start of the school year and how familiar the family participants are with the curriculum. Select for the group to read one of the books from **Read, Play, and Learn!** or another predictable or repetitive story you are using in your classroom. A storybook like *Abiyoyo* is a good choice. Have everyone join in and be involved in the reading. Explain that this is how the children start each day at school, reading the storybook together.

What Is Literacy?

In this segment of the workshop, lead attendees in brainstorming about "What do you think about when you think about literacy?" Having parents and caregivers call out words or phrases, which you can capture on a flipchart, is helpful in clarifying parental perspectives, thoughts, questions, and viewpoints. It is especially fun to look at words that denote similar meaning across languages. For example, family members often list key words such as "listening," reading," and "writing" at first and then begin to add more qualitative descriptors such as "quiet time," "sharing," "bedtime," and so forth. From there you can move into the literacy environment in their home (McCord, 1995; Moore, McCord, & Boudreau, 1997).

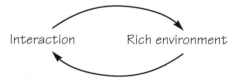
Figure 2.   If possible, consult with other team members and your parent consultant to design the agenda for your first workshop. Include overview information and small and large group activities, like the example shown here. (Adapted and modified by permission for the *Read, Play, and Learn!*® curriculum from Moore et al. [1997]. Child Learning Center, University of Colorado at Boulder.)

How to Create a Literacy-Rich Environment (Small-Group Activity)

Break attendees into small groups of four to six based on similarities in their children's literacy level. In this way they can share common experiences. Brainstorm the many ways they can pull literacy into daily routines such as going to the bank, shopping at the market, driving in the car, straightening up at home, working in the kitchen, taking baths, or whatever activities the parents and caregivers suggest. It is often helpful to set the stage for this part of the workshop by collecting items that you can set out in stations to stimulate ideas and help trigger parents' thinking (e.g., old checkbooks, deposit slips, and receipts help create a bank area;

toy cars, miniature road signs, and road maps provide the basis for traveling in the car area). Store these collectibles in plastic bags with labels denoting their routine (e.g., "BANK," "AIRPORT," "MARKET"). It is also helpful to choose a book to be included in each setup that illustrates the theme. While one small group is talking about daily routines, another group might be brainstorming opportunities for literacy building around holidays or customs (e.g., birthday parties); use invitations, wrapping paper, name cards, and so forth to get the small group discussions going.

Give the small groups sufficient time to create their lists of ideas, and then bring everyone together again. Participants have fun sharing all of the creative and "real" ideas that family members come up with. Participants quickly realize it is the interaction that happens with their child that supports growth in language and literacy learning, rather than literacy artifacts made available in the home (Moore et al., 1997).

Indeed, the daily routines in work and play, in the give and take between parent and child, will create an environment rich in opportunity for emergent literacy and other developmental skills:

> Talking with young children is very much like playing ball with them. What the adult has to do for this game to be successful is, first, to ensure that the child is ready, with arms cupped, to catch the ball. Then the ball must be thrown gently and accurately so that it lands squarely in the child's arms. When it is the child's turn to throw, the adult must be prepared to run wherever it goes and bring it back to where the child really intended it to go. Such is the collaboration required in conversation, the adult doing a great deal of supportive work to enable the ball to be kept in play. (Wells, 1986, p. 50)

This is an apt analogy that also describes what happens during interactive storybook reading.

How to Foster Interactive Storybook Reading (Large-Group Activity; Videotape Viewing)

Watching videotapes of caregivers reading to young children is an excellent strategy to illustrate good ways of reading to children that foster interaction and build a literacy-rich environment. Watching a videotape of a dad, mom, or older sibling reading with a young child brings to life just how critical the type of interaction is to successful literacy skill building. By watching the videotapes, participants readily see that the children behave in many ways, from touching or snuggling, to occasionally turning a page or pointing to a picture, to *filling in* words and phrases, to demanding to hold the book and read it themselves. Engaging the child in interaction will depend on the child's state (e.g., is he or she tired or ready to "read"?), age, and level of literacy learning as well as the relationship between caregiver and child. Children may quickly lose interest if a reader sticks only to the text without matching the child's level of interest and ability.

Parents and caregivers quickly recognize the natural strategies that promote interactive storybook reading. Use of these strategies allows time for the child to initiate questions, make comments, and expand his or her world knowledge. For many parents, it is comforting to see fathers and mothers struggling with the squirming child who is not necessarily interested in looking at a book at that moment or the "talker" who interrupts so often that it seems reading time will never end. Recognizing that a child's demands to have the same story read over and over again are natural is also reassuring.

Watching videotapes of interactive storybook reading not only provides a model for family members of strategies they might use effectively but also allows participants time to formulate additional questions about the reading process. Parents quickly recognize that there is no one "blueprint" for how you read with a young child. Give each participant a worksheet that allows them to jot down answers to the following questions: "What do you see?" "What was helpful to keep the child interested?" (and other questions you might want to pose). The worksheet is a helpful tool to elicit comments about the videotapes and focus your group's discussion. Point out the individual ways of interacting, and draw parallels to young children's individual learning styles and pace of interaction.

So start developing your library of videotaped interactive storybook reading now and be sure to collect stories with different age children and a variety of readers and children with challenges so that you can present a full array of variations on the theme. Friends and colleagues reading to their children may be a productive resource for starting up your video library.

Where Do We Go from Here? . . . Our Next Session

Close your workshop with a look ahead at what topics could be covered in later workshops. Be sure to ask attendees about their preferences. If possible, announce the date and time for the next meeting. It is a good idea to vary the day and time of the week so that family members who were not able to attend this workshop because of a regularly scheduled conflict can make another meeting.

Additional Ideas for Workshops

With the families and your team members, you will find it easy to identify topics for additional workshops. Some specific ideas, tested at the Child Learning Center at the University of Colorado at Boulder (Moore et al., 1997) follow, but be sure to personalize the content for your own group.

Individualize Interactive Storybook Reading

After seeing videotapes of storybook readings at the first workshop, many family members are then eager to videotape themselves as they read with their own children. For other families, the home videotaping may, at first, seem uncomfortable or threatening, but given the choice to participate, parents are likely to choose to tape themselves. Suggest that they check out a camera from your program or borrow one from a friend to tape the reading of one of the storybooks from a **Read, Play, and Learn!** module in addition to a much loved and favorite book. You could also offer to tape the parent and child during reading time at your center. You can then set up a second workshop and have families bring in their videotapes. Use a small-group activity format, in which participants break into small groups to share and review their tapes. Encourage the parents and caregivers to look for strengths first. Then, lead the participants in a self-identification process to name *next steps* for both themselves and their child. Help participants reflect on what they might do to encourage their child to "bump up" in skill or concept attainment. A handout, like the one shown in Figure 3, gives family members a convenient way to note their reactions to the videotape in a positive format. In addition to helping caregivers spell out strengths they see in themselves and in their child, the worksheet can continue to be used to add next steps for the child and specific strategies the parent wants to try.

As participants complete the second half of the "Stories and Strategies" worksheet, they are beginning to develop an individualized literacy plan for themselves and their child. Such a plan helps parents and caregivers clarify expectations for their child. It also supports family members as they recognize all they can do to encourage interactive storybook reading at home.

Introduce the "Cards on the Table" Game

Another activity to incorporate into a workshop with family members is "Cards on the Table," an interactive game that demands that participants work together to solve a word puzzle. Divide the participants into small groups. Give each group a set of cards with various words or phrases from a notable quotation about reading, literature, or literacy. Instruct the groups to arrange the cards until they arrive at a readable quote. Figure 4 displays some quotations that have been used and enjoyed by families participating in workshops at the Child Learning Center at the University of Colorado at Boulder.

Asking participants to make sense out of a mixed-up pile of words helps family members experience the struggle of learning to read. Participants may share feelings of frustration and failure recalled from their own school days. This activity can be used productively to reflect on the reading process itself and learn more about what is involved for children in "cracking the code." It may also dramatically demonstrate the frustration that can occur if even one word does not fit or make sense or if you do not know the language being used. (To enhance cultural sensitivity, consider using quotations translated from researchers' writing in other languages or familiar quotations from a different culture written in a parent's native language.) "Cards on the Table" should also evoke positive feelings experienced when working together, especially when a project comes to a successful completion.

Play "Let's Watch TV"

This activity is designed to heighten caregivers' awareness about what young children are exposed to when they spend hour after hour in front of a television. Ask participants about television viewing practices in their households; name with the group readily recognized commercials, popular cartoons, and commonly watched programs. With just a few examples, it is easy to kick off a productive discussion of how time can be spent in other ways. Explore with participants the ramifications of passive watching versus the interactive participation of young children during play or when reading.

Read, Play, and Learn!
Storybook Activities for Young Children

STORIES AND STRATEGIES: A FAMILY AND TEAM WORKSHOP

Worksheet for Viewing Videotapes of Interactive Storybook Reading

Family member name: *Susan*

Parent/caregiver strengths
- *Relaxed*
- *Repeated what Chris said*
- *Says what Chris is pointing to*
- *Pace matches child's*
- *Supportive*
- *Left off end of sentence for Chris to fill in*
- *Nice pace of turns*

Child strengths
- *Relates written words to spoken word*
- *Active and involved in reading process*
- *Points to words*
- *Names letters as he points*
- *Persists in trying to name letters; good concentration*
- *Good book-handling skills*
- *Pointed to pictures and commented*
- *Good memory*

Next steps for child
- *Relate his experiences to the book*
- *Expand labels to tell more of the story*

Strategies for parent/caregiver
- *Tell Chris, "It's your turn to tell the story"*
- *Keep using fill-in-the-blank technique and allow bigger spaces for him to fill in*
- *Relax about "not finishing"—be happy with any page*

From *Read, Play, and Learn!*® by Toni W. Linder © 1999 by Paul H. Brookes Publishing Co., Inc.

Figure 3. After families have videotaped themselves at home reading to their child, hold a workshop in which parents view each others' tapes in partner groups. Provide participants with a worksheet to complete for each tape they view. The example shown in this figure has been completed by a mother, Susan, who has just watched the tape of her own reading with her son Chris. Rather than focusing on problems in the interactive reading, the worksheet helps participants focus on caregiver and child strengths and identify what they want to work on in the future. (Adapted by permission for the *Read, Play, and Learn!*® curriculum from Moore et al. [1997]. Child Learning Center, University of Colorado at Boulder.)

Quotations for "Cards on the Table"

"Learning to read and write is critical to a child's success in school and later in life."

IRA and NAEYC, 1998, p. 30

"Children who are frequently read to will then 'read' their favorite books by themselves."

Sulzby and Teale, 1987, p. 5

"Reading is a complex developmental challenge that we know to be intertwined with many other developmental accomplishments."

Snow, Burns, and Griffin, 1998, p. 15

"Only 39% of parents read or look at a picture book with their children once a day."

Young, Davis, and Schoen, 1996, Appendix B-5

"Our challenge as educators is to make it possible for all children, regardless of ability, experience, or cultural heritage, to feel successful in their attempts to be literate."

McCord, 1995, p. 105

From *Read, Play, and Learn!*® by Toni W. Linder © 1999 by Paul H. Brookes Publishing Co., Inc.

Figure 4. "Cards on the Table" is a word puzzle game that can help simulate some of the frustrations felt by inexperienced readers. Using quotations like the ones shown in this figure, print single words or clusters of just a few words from the quote on a series of cards. Shuffle the cards and give each group a set of cards to reassemble into the quotation. (Examples here selected by the Child Learning Center, University of Colorado at Boulder. Sources are listed in the reference list at the end of this chapter.)

Spend time in this activity, too, talking with participants about how children love to watch their favorite videotapes over and over again. How is this viewing like reading and rereading a favorite book, and how is it different? Are videotapes used to create "down time" during an especially trying period of the day or when a child is tired? How do participants feel about these uses? Your discussion will soon center on how much is too much and what children should be watching. Although the decision about TV watching is ultimately the families' choice, such a discussion can lead to heightened awareness of benefits and consequences. Alternative activities that focus on literacy learning that can take the place of TV could be discussed and shared.

Hold a Book Share

Invite your librarian, an early childhood educator knowledgeable about children's literature, or a representative from the children's section of your favorite local bookstore to come talk to family members in a relaxed workshop format. You might suggest that everyone sit in a circle on the floor; place stacks of books in the center to be examined and passed around. Participants can pull out a book that looks interesting to them or appropriate for their child. Stop the passing to allow time for family members to select passages (funny or tender) to read aloud and enjoy the wealth of new discoveries. Participants can jot down titles and authors to refer to later when they go to the library or bookstore. A Book Share handout, like the one in Figure 5, gives everyone an easy way to note the books they want to try.

This workshop is also a good one to conduct with your team members or a group of early childhood care providers and educators. Sharing favorite stories gives everyone ideas for books that complement those used in the *Read, Play, and Learn!* modules; add these to the Literacy Center and other areas of your classroom.

Extend Your Connections with Family Members

In addition to your plans for a family involvement component and accompanying workshops, there are many other creative activities and ways to establish connections between home and school. The suggestions offered in this chapter are just a sampling of the many ways that parents can be connected to your program.

Book Share

Title:

Author:

Publisher:

Age range:

Special features:

This book is about . . .

It would be fun to use this book to . . .

From *Read, Play, and Learn!*® by Toni W. Linder © 1999 by Paul H. Brookes Publishing Co., Inc.

Figure 5. "Book Share" cards, copied and handed out during an informal workshop to talk about favorite storybooks, give participants an easy way to take notes about the books they would like to obtain from their local library or bookstore.

Set aside time during some of your team meetings to think about *What Do We Do Now?* List all of the ways you are communicating with, providing guidance to, and supporting family members and caregivers in their efforts to enhance their child's literacy learning at home. Next to this column, list *Possibilities,* the additional things you want to consider doing with family members and caregivers. Your third column should then be *Next Steps,* your ideas in terms of what you need to do next and what resources you have to bring to the tasks at hand. You now have an individualized action plan for extending your connections with family members. Review your plan regularly, and enjoy the excitement and positive results from this endeavor.

Plan to use a combination of communication methods so that distinct learning styles are respected. In addition to the many strategies provided in this chapter specifically pertaining to reading and writing skill development, the books that complement this transdisciplinary play-based curriculum, such as *Transdisciplinary Play-Based Intervention: Guidelines for Developing a Meaningful Curriculum for Young Children* (Linder, 1993), offer suggestions to use with parents in the areas of cognitive, social-emotional, communication and language, and sensorimotor skill development. The involvement of parents in their child's education is now recognized as an important factor in a child's success in school.

Certainly, parents can benefit from information we share about their child, child development, and the program. It is important to remember, however, that you and your team can benefit just as much from the information and skills parents and other family members have to offer you. Programs can be much richer and more consequential when the knowledge and expertise of professionals and families are integrated for the benefit of children.

CREATING HANDOUTS FOR FAMILIES

This section of the chapter describes how to create a set of handouts for families to use at home. Sample handouts are included, which you can photocopy and distribute to parents and caregivers as the topics become relevant to activities in your classroom. Handouts can be given to families during one-to-one or group meetings, handed out as children are picked up at the end of the day, or mailed home. You can bind them together as a single send-home handbook. You may also reproduce the samples with your own modifications to suit your particular program's circumstances. You and your team should discuss the most efficient methods for your program.

As stated previously, users of **Read, Play, and Learn!** are permitted to photocopy or reproduce these pages provided that proper credit to their source is included on every copy and no commercial gain is associated with their distribution. Your program cannot charge anyone for a copy of the handbook or for individual handouts.

Each new topic begins on its own page to facilitate your copying of the material. You will probably want to make one photocopy of the page and then add identifying information for your program before making the number of copies you will need.

REFERENCES

Individuals with Disabilities Education Act Amendments of 1997, PL 105-17, 20 U.S.C. §§ 1400 *et seq.*

International Reading Association & National Association for the Education of Young Children. (1998). *Learning to read and write: Developmentally appropriate practices for young children. A joint position statement of the International Reading Association (IRA) & National Association for the Education of young Children (NAEYC).* Newark, DE: Author.

Linder, T.W. (1993). *Transdisciplinary play-based intervention: Guidelines for developing a meaningful curriculum for young children.* Baltimore: Paul H. Brookes Publishing Co.

McCord, S. (1995). *The storybook journey: Pathways to literacy through story and play.* Upper Saddle River, NJ: Prentice-Hall.

Moore, S., McCord, S., & Boudreau, D. (November, 1997). *Language and literacy in the classroom: Transitions to kindergarten.* A presentation at the American Speech-Language-Hearing Association Convention, Boston, MA.

Morrow, L.M. (1985). Retelling stories: A strategy for improving children's comprehension, concept of story structure and oral language complexity. *Elementary School Journal, 85,* 647–661.

Morrow, L.M. (1987). The effects of one-to-one story reading on children's questions and comments. In S. Baldwin & J. Readance (Eds.), *Thirty-sixth yearbook of the National Reading Conference.* Rochester, NY: National Reading Conference.

Morrow, L.M. (1997). *Literacy development in the early years: helping children read and write.* Needham Heights, MA: Allyn & Bacon.

Roser, N., & Martinez, M. (1985). Roles adults play in preschool responses to literature. *Language Arts, 62,* 485–490.

Saint-Laurent, L., Giasson, J., & Couture, C. (1997, November/December). Parents + children + reading activities = Emergent literacy. *Teaching Exceptional Children,* 52–56.

Snow, C., Burns, S.M., & Griffin, P. (Eds.). (1998). *Preventing reading difficulties in young children.* Washington, DC: National Academy Press.

Sulzby, E., & Teale, W.H. (1987). *Young children's storybook reading: Longitudinal study of parent–child interaction and children's independent functioning.* Final report to the Spencer Foundation, University of Michigan, Ann Arbor.

Young, K.T., Davis, K., & Schoen, C. (1996). *The Commonwealth Fund Survey of Parents and Young Children.* New York: The Commonwealth Fund.

Wells, G. (1986). *The meaning makers: Children learning language and using language to learn.* Portsmouth, NH: Heinemann.

Provided to you by:

School/program name: _____

Teacher: _____

Telephone number: _____

Read, Play, and Learn!
Storybook Activities for Young Children

HELPING YOUR CHILD WITH A SPECIAL CURRICULUM

Your child's development and education are of great concern to you. Experts say that children will learn more and progress faster when *both* home and school are cooperating to make sure that your child has the most beneficial learning environment, a broad range of learning experiences, and meaningful personal interactions. While your child is in school with us, we will be sending home letters, handouts, and other materials to keep you informed about what we are doing during the day. We recognize that you know your child better than anyone. The information that you have about your child can help us to plan a better program. And so, we would like to begin an ongoing dialogue with you about your child's development and learning. Throughout the year, we will encourage you to share information with us about your child. We, in turn, will offer you information about your child and how you can support your child's development and learning at home—as part of your regular routine with your child—*without* sitting down to try to *teach* your child.

One of the areas that we know you care about is helping your child learn to read and write. Most parents think that this process begins with learning the letters of the alphabet. *That is not true!* Learning to read and write starts at birth. You naturally talk to and listen to your child, help your child learn new words, read to your child, and play with your child. What you may not realize is that all of these actions lay a foundation for reading and writing. The development of literacy is closely associated with your child's growth in language skills, cognitive (thinking and problem-solving) skills, fine motor abilities (using hands and controlling muscle movements), and sociability. In the classroom, we will be using storybooks and play in a curriculum called **Read, Play, and Learn!** to help your child develop in all of these areas.

Studies have shown that reading a storybook repeatedly helps children develop the language and thinking skills needed for learning to read and write. **Read, Play, and Learn!** is based on this important idea. At the beginning of each day, we will read a story, and we will read that same story for about 2 weeks before moving on to another one. We will involve all of the children in looking at the pictures in the book, naming things in the book, and discussing the story. Throughout the 2 weeks, the children will construct a setting related to the story, complete with structures, artwork, play equipment, and dramatic play (acting) props.

_____

continued

continued

Play activities in many centers in the classroom will further support learning. The children will be able to act out stories, make pictures and books, play with ideas presented in books, do experiments, cook, and construct and explore the unique setting created for each book. We will also have a reading time during which we will read and explore many other books related to the same concepts. At this time, we will have the children look at books together and have older peers, volunteers, and family members read to the children. We will be tailoring activities for your child to his or her appropriate developmental level. You are invited, as always, to join us for any of the classroom activities.

Our role is to provide the environment, structure, ideas, and materials needed to guide your child's learning and to inform you of what is happening in the classroom and how your child is progressing. We also know that what happens at home is as important to your child's development (if not more so) as what happens at school. Your child will have more fun and learn more if the family is also involved in our storybook adventures. By reading to your child the same books that we are reading at school, as well as many others, you will share in your child's school experiences, have a great deal to talk about with your child, and be able to observe your child's progress as new skills are acquired.

To help your child develop a foundation for success in school, we will be sharing ideas about how you can help us help your child learn. We will focus on one book at a time for about 2 weeks, and each time we start a new book we will send a letter home telling you the name of the book and a bit about the story. When you read this book at home, you will be helping your child gain more practice in the skills development we are working on during the day. Continue to read other books to your child, too; each and every reading provides valuable learning experiences and more familiarity with literacy. We will be giving you suggestions for the following:

1. What you can do at home to provide space and materials for learning
2. What you can do to help your child gain the developmental basis for reading and writing (without being a trained teacher!)
3. How to know what your child is ready for next

We will be sending home letters and newsletters, offering parent/caregiver conferences, scheduling workshops, and inviting you to our classroom so that you can join us in supporting your child's development. Although many of the materials we send home will emphasize how to make the most of books and print, we will also be offering suggestions throughout the year for other important areas of development. *Transdisciplinary* means that our teaching approach can focus on these many different elements of development at the same time. In this way, all of us working with your child in the classroom join you in helping your child grow in well-rounded ways.

We look forward to sharing the joy of watching your child learn! Please share your suggestions and questions with us. And come visit us when you can!

Provided to you by:

School/program name: _____
Teacher: _____
Telephone number: _____

Read, Play, and Learn!
Storybook Activities for Young Children

TEN GOALS FOR YOUR CHILD

We have many developmental goals for your child. Some of these goals are ones that you may have as well. The following are 10 goals related to literacy development and the *Read, Play, and Learn!* curriculum. With your help, we will do a better job of assisting your child in accomplishing these goals:

1. To develop a love of books and learning through doing
2. To develop an understanding of words and language
3. To develop an ability to communicate and express ideas in many ways
4. To develop an ability to produce, carry out, and evaluate ideas
5. To develop a desire to read and write
6. To develop an awareness of print in the surrounding environment
7. To develop an awareness of books and how they are used
8. To develop an ability to listen to, understand, and share stories and information
9. To develop knowledge of the functions, forms, and traditional rules of print
10. To develop the sensorimotor skills necessary for exploring, interacting, playing, reading, and writing

Provided to you by:

School/program name: _____
Teacher: _____
Telephone number: _____

Read, Play, and Learn!
Storybook Activities for Young Children

WHY IT IS IMPORTANT TO READ TO YOUR CHILD

First of all, reading together is fun! Even if you are just looking at pictures together, you are sharing an experience. Reading together provides a basis for talking together. You both, for a few minutes at least, share the same focus and interest. Reading together is a way of making your child feel closer to you as well as preparing your child for later experiences with books in school. Children who have not shared literacy experiences with family members come to school with a distinct disadvantage compared with those who have shared books with family members before reaching preschool or kindergarten. Sharing books enables your child to do the following:

1. Discover how books are used
2. Discover that print has meaning
3. Discover that print and speech are related but that reading sounds different from talking
4. Practice remembering and retelling stories in a sequence
5. Think about the details of stories
6. Begin to put a series of ideas in a meaningful order

Provided to you by:
School/program name: _____
Teacher: _____
Telephone number: _____

Read, Play, and Learn!
Storybook Activities for Young Children

HELPING YOUR CHILD MAKES A DIFFERENCE

Parents and other family members help their children learn in many informal ways. They show, suggest, tell, question, explain, respond, support, and encourage. You automatically did this when your child was learning to talk. You became excited with each new sound that your child made and each new understanding that your child displayed. You provided models for sounds, words, and sentences. You talked to your child when he or she tried to communicate with you (no matter how he or she may have communicated). The more your child listened, watched, experimented, and practiced *using* different kinds of words and sentences, the more his or her language developed. You can do the same informal things as your child learns to read.

All of us, even if we cannot read, use aspects of literacy in our daily lives. We recognize signs, symbols, numbers, or pictures that help us to understand our world. Those of us who read have the additional advantage of being able to use print to help us in our daily lives. All children come to preschool, child care, or school having been exposed to some form of literacy in their families (looking up telephone numbers, making shopping lists, noticing street signs, etc.). School merely provides the means for structuring and building on the learning that has taken place at home.

Children learn how to read and write in many ways. Important foundations for reading and writing develop, along with all areas of development, from *birth*. What you do with your child *between* birth and when he or she goes to school is as important as what happens after school begins. Learning about the alphabet, letter–sound relationships, and how to interpret print are only a small part of learning to read and write. Children learn about literacy through their interactions with you and their friends when they *use* reading and writing. The first words children identify are those related to recognizable symbols in their environment, such as the McDonald's golden arches. They first discover and remember words in a familiar context and later learn to use letter–sound cues to sound out words. When you *actively share* and *connect* reading and writing to real-life daily experiences, you encourage children to want to learn how to read and write, too.

continued

continued

One of the most important things you can do is to believe that reading and writing are important. Research has shown that parents who value reading and writing,

- Make the home a place where pictures and print are seen everywhere
- Show their children the value and use of print materials
- Interact with their children around print in daily activities

When you do these things, you are making a difference in how well your child will do in school.

Provided to you by:

School/program name: _____
Teacher: _____
Telephone number: _____

Read, Play, and Learn!
Storybook Activities for Young Children

HOW TO MAKE THE HOME A PLACE WHERE PICTURES AND PRINT ARE SEEN EVERYWHERE

To show your child that reading and writing are important, you need to have and use materials in the house that contain pictures and print. Your child needs to see you reading and writing. Although books are important, books are not enough. In each room of the house, and when in the community, you will find pictures and print. As you use these items, let your child watch you, and show him or her what you are doing. For example, explain to your child that you are making a list of items to buy at the grocery store, sorting coupons, paying a bill, or looking in the *TV Guide* to find out when the family's favorite program begins. Let your child examine the materials and play with those that are nonessential. In addition to the following items, feel free to think of others.

In the living room:

1. Newspapers
2. Mail (cards, letters, bills)
3. Advertisements (junk mail)
4. TV guide
5. Books
6. Magazines
7. Catalogs
8. Remote control

In the kitchen:

1. Telephone books
2. Cookbooks or recipes on cards or in boxes
3. Labels and writing on cans, boxes, and other food containers

continued

continued

4. Telephone notepads
5. Writing on appliances ("high," "low," "on," "off")
6. Messages to family members
7. School-related notes
8. Coupons
9. Grocery lists

In the bedroom:

1. Books
2. Labels and directions on toys and games
3. Labels on clothing
4. Writing on T-shirts
5. Pictures
6. Religious materials
7. School materials

In the bathroom:

1. Books
2. Magazines
3. Tub books and stick-on alphabet letters
4. Writing on vitamins, jars, toiletries, and boxes
5. Switches on lights, hair dryer, razors, and curling irons
6. Letters or words on faucets

In the community:

1. Road signs
2. Street signs
3. Billboards
4. Fast-food signs
5. Signs for chain stores and other commercial buildings
6. Numbers on buildings and in elevators
7. Names on buildings
8. Menus in restaurants
9. Exit signs
10. Restroom signs
11. Direction signs in buildings
12. Names on cars and vehicles

From *Read, Play, and Learn!*® by Toni W. Linder © 1999 by Paul H. Brookes Publishing Co., Inc.

Provided to you by:

School/program name: _____

Teacher: _____

Telephone number: _____

Read, Play, and Learn!
Storybook Activities for Young Children

HOW TO MODEL THE USES OF PRINT WITH YOUR CHILD

One of the easiest ways you can help your child learn about reading and writing is to show your child the various uses of reading and writing in everyday situations, such as those listed in "How to Make the Home a Place Where Pictures and Print Are Seen Everywhere." Another good way to help your child learn about reading and writing is for him or her to actually see how print is used. This will help to motivate your child to want to use print to communicate. Whenever you have the chance, you can do the following:

1. Show your child that you *like* to read.
2. Take advantage of every opportunity to point out what print says (in ads on television, at the movies, on the washer and dryer panels, at stores, when sorting your mail, on road signs, etc.).
3. Read directions out loud, following along with your finger as you read.
4. Explain why lists and messages are used. (If the child speaks some words, he or she can name his or her favorite foods to put on the grocery list.)
5. Explain how telephone books, cookbooks, and so forth are used to get information.
6. Show your child that personal objects can be labeled with his or her name.
7. Write letters or messages together to give or mail to family members or friends.

Provided to you by:

School/program name: _____

Teacher: _____

Telephone number: _____

Read, Play, and Learn!
Storybook Activities for Young Children

HELP YOUR CHILD APPRECIATE THE VALUE OF READING

ENCOURAGE YOUR CHILD TO EXPLORE MATERIALS WITH PRINT

Although exploration sometimes leads to a mess, the more exposure your child has to written material, the more he or she will learn about books. Your child needs to manipulate, examine the parts of, look at, and play with books and print materials. The following things are all good opportunities for your child:

1. Have children's books (appropriate for your child's development), old magazines or catalogs, and old telephone books available for your child to explore.
2. Offer your child a book to read while you read the newspaper or a book.
3. Take your child to the library frequently so that he or she can see the huge world of books. Remember, library books are free (if you take them back on time!), so your child can enjoy many different types of books, books with audiotapes, and books with videotapes. Checking out library books is a great habit for your child to establish.

INCLUDE READING AND WRITING PROPS IN DRAMATIC PLAY

Dramatic play (play with trucks, animals, dolls, kitchen sets, toy gas station, etc.) provides an opportunity for your child to practice acting out familiar sequences, to use new vocabulary, to organize his or her ideas, to construct, to develop social skills, and to solve problems. With just a little thought, you can add simple print to the dramatic situation in which your child is involved. For example, you could add a cookbook to the house area, street signs to the road, labels for the fast-food restaurant, or signs to the gas station. Add pencils and paper for your child to write lists, take orders, draw details, and so forth. In this way, your child can practice using these materials. It does not matter if your child cannot read the words or write letters. He or she is experimenting with how to use print. As your child's language, thinking, and fine motor skills develop, he or she will also refine his or her ability to read and write. You can point out what the words say or pretend to "read" the writing.

_____
continued

continued

Use your child's interests to introduce reading and writing into his or her play. For example, when reading *The Kissing Hand*, your child may show an interest in pretending to play "school," or when reading *Friends*, your child may want to set up a farm. You can provide the materials (paper and markers) for your child to draw, make signs, and make labels or name tags. Whenever possible, try to engage in the dramatic play *with* your child. You may then suggest ways to incorporate print. When pretending to go to the restaurant, as in *The Knight and the Dragon*, you can ask for a menu (or make one together), make a sign for the restaurant, ask for the bill, and pay for your dinner. All involve using print in meaningful ways. Keep in mind the following tips:

- Follow your child's actions, adding your ideas as opportunities present themselves.
- Try not to ask too many questions (especially questions that require only a one-word response or "yes" or "no"). Your child will have more fun and talk more if you let him or her lead the conversation.
- Emphasize taking turns. Imitate your child's actions, then add new actions of your own.
- Suggest ideas that require pretending to read or pretending to write.
- Have FUN!

READ TO YOUR CHILD OFTEN

Take advantage of every opportunity to read to your child. For example, a word on a sign ("That says EXIT. That's where we go out"), a phrase on a wall ("No Smoking"), and a sentence on a paper ("Please wait for your name to be called") all offer excellent opportunities. Every reading experience gives your child information about the world and about reading and writing. With this in mind, you should make every effort to do the following:

1. Read frequently to your child—anything in print. By hearing you read frequently, your child will begin to learn that written language is more formal than spoken language.
2. Read the same book repeatedly. Children love to hear the same book over and over. In this way, they become familiar with the words in the book, the sequence of the words, the questions and answers related to the book, and the pattern of your voice as you read the book. (The more experiences your child has with print, the more quickly he or she will come to understand that print has meaning.)
3. Repeating the same story helps your child learn that the meaning of the print is the same every time the story is read. After a time, he or she may begin to read (or pretend to read) to you.
4. Read many different books as well as your child's favorites.
5. Read information books (nonfiction) as well as storybooks. (Simple books on trucks, dinosaurs, animals, and so forth teach new words and concepts.)
6. Read, read, read!

Provided to you by:

School/program name: _____

Teacher: _____

Telephone number: _____

Read, Play, and Learn!
Storybook Activities for Young Children

TIPS FOR READING BOOKS WITH YOUR CHILD

BEFORE READING A BOOK

1. Examine the cover of the book. Point out the title and the pictures on the front. For children who already are listening to stories being read, point out the name of the author who wrote the book and the illustrator who did the drawings. This helps the child to recognize where a book begins.

2. Tell your child what the book is about, or if your child can talk, ask him or her what the book is about or what happens in the story.

3. Look at some of the pictures in the book before reading the book and talk about what might happen. This will help your child learn to predict and anticipate by looking at clues.

4. Relate the book to the child's previous experiences.

WHILE READING THE BOOK, USE INTERACTIVE STRATEGIES

1. Let your child turn the pages of the book. Do not worry if your young child cannot wait for you to read everything on the page before anxiously flipping the page. He or she is learning that you read a book from front to back.

2. Help build your child's vocabulary by labeling and talking about characters, objects, and events in the book. For instance, as you read *The Snowy Day*, point out the boy, snowsuit, stick, and so forth. Describe the colors in the pictures, the way the little boy feels, and what he is doing.

3. Comment on the pictures in the book by labeling, pointing out details, telling the child what is happening in the picture, and so forth. For example, in *The Three Billy Goats Gruff*, there is a small frog hiding in many of the pictures. You could say, "I see a little frog." Let your child comment, too ("Right here, under the bridge"). Such back-and-forth commenting encourages having a conversation.

4. Encourage your child to ask questions; you may need to ask or model a question yourself so that your child learns by example to inquire about things that relate to the book. "What's that?" and "Where's the bird?" are very simple questions that

continued

continued

can be reserved for children who are just learning to name objects. You can model higher level questions, such as "How did he get up the tree?" and "Why is he crying?" when reading *A Porcupine Named Fluffy*. Answering your child's questions will encourage him or her to ask more questions (as anyone who has ever answered the question "Why?" will attest!).

5. Give your child plenty of *wait time*. This means you need to wait several seconds before commenting again.

6. As your child learns to anticipate the next page or event in the story, talk about what might happen next or what might be on the following page. Predicting will help your child learn to sequence ideas and predict consequences. For example, when reading *The Little Old Lady Who Was Not Afraid of Anything*, you might say, "Ooh, she just got chased by a pair of pants and a shirt! I wonder what will happen next?"

7. Relate the animals, people, objects, or actions in the book to what your child already knows. When reading *Picking Apples & Pumpkins*, you might point out how the pumpkins that the children in the story are getting are like the one you bought at the store. Talk about what happened to your pumpkin as well as what the children will do with theirs.

8. As your child begins to repeat the words in the story, point to the print as you say the words. This helps your child understand that the words that you are saying are related to the print that is above your finger on the page. This is particularly useful when children know the words that are coming next ("I'll huff, and I'll puff, and I'll blow your house in!"). By pointing to the words as you read, your child is also learning that you read from left to right and from top to bottom.

9. When your child is repeating words from the story, use it as an opportunity to play or rhyme with the words by changing the beginning.

10. Let your child point to words as you read them. This supports your child's awareness of and ability to discriminate differences between sounds, which is an important skill when learning to read. (If your child does not point to each word as it is said, there may be print left over or not enough print for all of the words that you say.) Such exploration will lead to the child eventually being able to relate one oral word to one written word.

11. Let your child tell as much of the story without help as he or she is able. Do not worry if the words or events are inaccurate. You are giving your child practice in pretend "reading."

12. Interrupt the story frequently so that you and your child can talk.

AFTER READING THE BOOK

1. Look at the back of the book when you are finished. This helps the child recognize the "end" of the story or book.

continued

continued

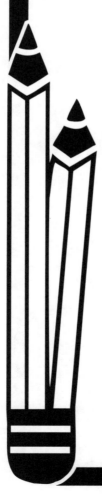

2. Ask whether your child liked the book, and share with him or her how you liked it ("I like the way the friends played together. What did you like?").

3. If your child can talk, encourage your child to tell the story in his or her own words and help by pointing to some of the pictures or asking questions, such as "What happened after . . . ?"

4. If your child can tell a story, let him or her retell or "reread" the book to you, a stuffed animal, a brother or sister, or a doll. Do not worry if the story is not the same as the one you read.

5. Record one of your child's favorite books as you read it into a tape recorder. He or she may enjoy listening to this tape and looking at the book when you are busy. If your child has difficulty going to sleep without your presence, the tape recording and a doll or a cuddly toy may help your child fall asleep.

Provided to you by:

School/program name: _____

Teacher: _____

Telephone number: _____

Read, Play, and Learn!
Storybook Activities for Young Children

SELECTING BOOKS FOR YOUR CHILD

The following tips will help you select the right type of books for your child depending on the five levels of readiness described below. For each level, there is also a corresponding list of what you can do to encourage your child's interest.

For children who are more interested in the book itself than what is inside it:

- Books that can be chewed, sucked, or crumpled (cloth and vinyl books)
- Books with simple, bright pictures against a contrasting background
- Books with nursery rhymes and pictures (singing and reciting helps the child pick up the patterns in words and sentences)

What you can do with your child at this level:

- Get your child's attention by showing excitement ("I see the baby!").
- Read your child's cues and respond to any interest or vocalization by acknowledging your child's interest and commenting.
- Give your child time to look at the pictures.
- Sing songs and rhymes.

For children who are just beginning to hold books:

- Books with thick, stiff pages (board, block, or small, thick-paged books)
- Books with pictures of things that are familiar to the child
- Old books, magazines, and catalogs (that you do not mind getting torn)

What you can do with your child at this level:

- All of the above
- Comment on the pictures using few words ("Yes, it's a doggie!"). If your child is unintelligible or just makes a noise, provide a label for the picture.
- Give your child plenty of wait time before continuing with the book.
- Your child may respond to "what" and "where" questions.
- Take turns with your child—commenting, pointing, labeling, questioning—make it a fun game!
- Allow your child to come and go, as he or she may have a brief attention span.

continued

continued

As your child becomes more interested in the pictures than in the book itself:

- Books and magazines
- Books with simple, clear pictures that portray action or a very simple story
- Books with familiar content
- Books that repeat lines or rhymes in a predictable, repeatable way
- Pop-up books

What you can do with your child at this level:

- All of the above
- Allow your child to initiate the reading process by opening the book, pointing, or commenting.
- Allow wait time for initiation as well as response.
- Introduce new songs and fingerplays.

As your child begins to follow the action in the story:

- Books in which the pictures illustrate what the text says
- Books with predictable, repetitive words
- Books with simple stories about topics of interest to the child

What you can do with your child at this level:

- Encourage your child to assume the lead role in commenting and questioning.
- Leave out a word at the end of a repetitive line so that the child can fill in the blank.
- Have a conversation with your child about what is happening in the book or how it is like something he or she knows.
- Encourage your child to ask questions by answering the questions he or she asks and modeling other forms of questions ("Why do you think . . . ?").
- Explain vocabulary, and help the child learn new words.

As your child begins to tell you the story:

- Books with more characters and more complex stories
- Books that introduce new settings, cultures, languages, and topics
- Books with poetry, songs, and rhymes

What you can do with your child at this level:

- All of the above
- Take turns with your child in "reading" the story (especially after several readings of a book).
- Have discussions about the story or the theme of the book.
- Read additional books related to the same theme to expand your child's understanding of a topic.
- Take turns reciting rhymes, songs, and fingerplays.
- Let your child "read" to siblings, dolls, and stuffed animals.

Provided to you by:

School/program name: _____
Teacher: _____
Telephone number: _____

Read, Play, and Learn!
Storybook Activities for Young Children

TALKING WITH YOUR CHILD

What you say to your child and how the two of you interact will vary, of course, depending on the age and developmental level of your child. Research has shown, however, that parents who are supportive of their child's learning tend to talk and listen to their child in the following specific ways:

1. Listen to your child and follow his or her interest in the conversation.
2. Talk with your child in a conversation. Avoid primarily asking questions.
3. Read your child's nonverbal cues (facial expressions, gestures, and sounds) as well as his or her verbal language to determine what your child is thinking and feeling.
4. Let your child start the conversation. Then support and add to the conversation with comments, questions, and new information.
5. Try to repeat what your child has said in the same or different words. This will help your child to understand what you heard. You may want to clarify or comment on his or her ideas.
6. Provide a correct language model for your child, and give your child feedback on his or her statements.
7. Provide experiences that will expand your child's knowledge and vocabulary (visit a pet store, go to the park, or cook together). Many opportunities for children are not expensive.

These are helpful hints to think about as your read with your child. This will make reading to your child more interactional and conversational. Have fun!

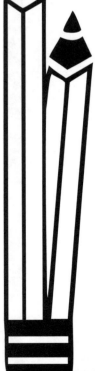

Provided to you by:

School/program name: _____
Teacher: _____
Telephone number: _____

Read, Play, and Learn!
Storybook Activities for Young Children

HELP YOUR CHILD LEARN TO WRITE

You can help your child learn to write at the same time that you are supporting his or her emerging reading. As with reading, what you do as a parent complements what the educators are doing at school. Your role is to allow your child to explore, experiment, and practice drawing and writing. You can encourage the development of writing skills in the following ways:

1. Provide a place for your child to write. A child-size table and chair are best so that the child knows that this is his or her special place to draw or write. If this is not possible, however, the child can sit on your lap, at a coffee table, or at any table with seating at a height that your child can comfortably write on paper.

2. Provide a variety of materials for your child. You may want to make a unique box for the child's writing tools so that he or she sees these materials as special. Let your child explore the possibilities of crayons, markers, pencils, and so forth on old newspapers, wrapping paper, index cards, old envelopes, or notepaper. (Having plenty of old paper materials available will discourage your child from marking on walls and furniture.)

3. Provide rubber stamps for your child so that he or she can make designs and letters without having to have enough finger and hand coordination to write. Letter and design stencils provide a guide for your child as fine motor control is developing. Magic slates allow the child to correct and practice over and over without using a lot of paper.

4. Have out tools and materials that are related to paper and pencil as they are also very stimulating to children. Pencil sharpeners, staplers, hole punches, and paste or glue provide excellent opportunities for developing fine motor skills and motivate your child to turn drawing and writing into more complex, creative projects.

5. Let your child use inexpensive magnetic letters, which he or she will probably enjoy moving around on the refrigerator. As your child learns about letters and sounds, the letters can be manipulated to make real words. Give your child paper and pencil to use while other family members are writing or doing homework.

continued

continued

6. Provide many examples of drawing and print from the environment (from cards, letters, newspapers, magazines, and so forth).

7. Draw and write along with your child. For example, when you are writing a grocery list, give your child a piece of paper and pencil, too.

8. As with reading, you can have a conversation with your child about his or her efforts. Comment, question, and respond to your child's efforts to talk about his or her work.

9. You can observe the following sequence evolve. Children often begin by scribbling and progress through interrelated phases of development and emerge as conventional writers:
   - More controlled arcs and circles
   - Horizontal and vertical lines
   - Lines and circles are arranged in patterns
   - Draws people and objects
   - Scribbling in linear patterns arranged horizontally like writing
   - Actual letters may be mixed into the scribbling
   - Scribbling becomes separate marks with the characteristics of letters, combinations of arcs, circles, lines, and angles
   - Experimenting with the direction, number, position, and length of lines in a letter, the spacing of letters, and so forth
   - Letters are organized both horizontally and vertically into words, spaces, and lines of print

10. Recognize the above efforts as drawing or writing, and "read" the writing with your child.

11. Help your child to see how others understand what has been written by questioning the meaning of the writing, asking for more information, or commenting on your child's writing. (*Rather than give negative feedback, ask for an explanation.*)

12. Point out how the form of writing differs in lists, letters, stories, and so forth.

13. When you read and write with your child, he or she will discover how the sounds of speech relate to the letters on the page. As your child learns to match sounds and letters, he or she will experiment with sounds being letters, syllables, and words and will "invent" spellings. You can help your child by pointing out print in the environment and noting the sound–spelling relationships. Correct spelling will come as the child learns the "rules" in school. Encourage all attempts at making words.

14. Most important, respond to your child's efforts with interest and enthusiasm!

Although in reality you are your child's first and best teacher, you do not need to try to teach specific skills. We will be teaching your child the rules related to writing and

continued

From ***Read, Play, and Learn!*** by Toni W. Linder © 1999 by Paul H. Brookes Publishing Co., Inc.

continued

spelling at school. You can be most helpful by providing opportunities and materials to allow your child to explore, question, and practice. You can also share, show, and support:

- SHARE with your child books, ideas, feelings, experiences, and play.
- SHOW your child the pleasure of reading and writing, how to read and discuss a book, and how the ideas in books relate to real life.
- SUPPORT your child's interests and efforts to **Read, Play, and Learn!**

APPENDIX

CONTENTS

Master Planning Sheets 206

Sample Art 208

Resources 220

Curricula 223

Play-Based Curriculum Planning Sheet: Storybook Activities

Date: _____

Theme (optional): _____

Book title (optional): _____

Play area	Monday	Tuesday	Wednesday	Thursday	Friday
Reading the Story					
Dramatic Play: Theme Area					
Literacy Center					
Science and Math Center					
Art Area					
Sensory Area					
Motor Area					

From *Read, Play, and Learn!*® by Toni W. Linder © 1999 by Paul H. Brookes Publishing Co., Inc.

TPBA | Play–Based | TPBI

TPBC | ™

Play-Based Curriculum Planning Sheet: Storybook Activities

Date: _____

Theme (optional): _____

Book title (optional): _____

Play area	Monday	Tuesday	Wednesday	Thursday	Friday
Floor Play					
Table Play					
Outdoor Play					
Snack					
Books and Music					
Software					

From *Read, Play, and Learn!*® by Toni W. Linder © 1999 by Paul H. Brookes Publishing Co., Inc.

TPBA Play-Based TPBI

TPBC TM

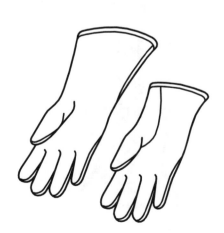

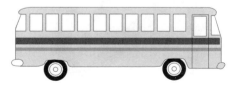

RESOURCES

The following is a list of resources that you may find useful when looking for ways to accommodate all of the children in your classroom.

AbleNet
2808 Fairview Ave.
Roseville, MN 55113
(800) 322-0956

ADAMLAB
55 East Long Lake Road
Suite 337
Troy, MI 48045
(248) 362-9603

Artic Technologies
John R. Road, Suite 108
Troy, MI 48083
(248) 588-7370

Aurora Systems, Inc.
D.J. Technical Sales
2647 Kinsway
Vancouver, B.C. V5R RH4
CANADA
(604) 436-2694
(800) 361-8255

Boston Educational Systems and Technology
63 Forest Street
Chestnut Hill, MA 02167
(617) 277-0179

Brøderbund Software, Inc.
100 Pine Street
Suite 1900
San Francisco, CA 94111
(800) 521-6263

Chapel Hill Training OutReach Project, Inc.
800 Eastown Drive, Suite 105
Chapel Hill, NC 27514
(919) 490-5577

Closing the Gap
Post Office Box 68
Henderson, MN 56044
(507) 248-3294

Compass Learning Customer Support
9920 Pacific Boulevard, Suite 500
San Diego, CA 92121
(800) 247-1380

Comput-Teach
16541 Redmond Way, Suite 137C
Redmond, WA 98052-4482
(425) 885-0517
(800) 448-3224

Creative Communicating
Post Office Box 3358
Park City, UT 84060
(435) 645-7737

Don Johnston, Inc.
26799 West Commerce Drive
Volo, IL 60073
(847) 526-2682
(800) 999-4660

Dunamis, Inc.
3423 Fowler Boulevard
Lawrenceville, GA 30044
(800) 828-2443

DynaVox Systems, Inc.
2100 Wharton Street, Suite 400
Pittsburgh, PA 15203
(412) 381-4883

Edmark Corporation
Post Office Box 97021
Redmond, WA 98073
(800) 691-2986

Educational Activities, Inc.
1937 Grand Avenue
Baldwin, NY 11510
(516) 223-4666
(800) 645-3739

Eloquence Technology, Inc.
24 Highgate Circle
Ithaca, NY 14850
(607) 266-7025

GW Micro, Inc.
725 Airport North Office Park
Fort Wayne, IN 46825
(260) 489-3671

Humanware, Inc.
175 Mason Circle
Concord, CA 94502
(916) 652-7253
(800) 722-3393

HyperActive Software
5226 West Nokomis Parkway
Minneapolis, MN 55417
(612) 724-1596

Innocomp
26210 Emery Road, Suite 302
Warrensville Heights, OH 44128
(216) 464-3636
(800) 382-8622

IntelliTools
1720 Corporate Circle
Petaluma, CA 94954
(800) 899-6687

Lakeshore Learning Materials
2695 East Dominguez Street
Carson, CA 90895
(800) 421-5354

Laureate Learning Systems, Inc.
110 East Spring Street
Winooski, VT 05404
(802) 655-4755
(800) 562-6801

LockFast, Inc.
4430 Mitchell Street
Las Vegas, NV 89031
(800) 626-0034

Mayer-Johnson Co.
Post Office Box 1579
Solana Beach, CA 92075
(800) 588-9548

Milliken Publishing Company
11643 Lilburn Drive
St. Louis, MO 63146
(314) 991-4220

MOBIOUS Corporation
405 North Henry Street
Alexandria, VA 22314
(703) 684-2911
(800) 426-2710

Prentke Romich Co. (PRC)
1022 Heyl Road
Wooster, OH 44691
(800) 262-1984

Productivity Works, Inc.
7 Belmont Circle
Trenton, NJ 08618
(609) 984-8044

Roger Wagner Publishing, Inc.
1050 Pioneer Way, Suite P
El Cajon, CA 92020
(800) 421-6526

SoftTouch/KidTECH
4300 Stine Road, Suite 401
Bakersfield, CA 93313
(805) 396-8676

Toys for Special Children (Stephen Kanor, Ph.D.)
385 Warburton Avenue
Hastings-on-Hudson, NY 10706
(800) 832-8697

UCLA Intervention Program for Children with
    Disabilities
1000 Veteran Avenue, Room 23-10
Los Angeles, CA 90095
(310) 825-4821

Zygo Industries, Inc.
Post Office Box 1008
Portland, OR 97207-1008
(800) 234-6006

CURRICULA

The following is a list of curricula, storybook activities, and other publications that are excellent for use in the early childhood classroom. Teachers will find, as we did, that these references are helpful when planning for their classrooms. Although a few of these may now be out of print, many other excellent resources are available to help you generate ideas.

Beall, P.C., & Nipp, S.H. (1981). *Wee sing and play.* Los Angeles: Price Stern Sloan.

Beall, P.C., & Nipp, S.H. (1994). *Wee sing children's songs and fingerplays.* Los Angeles: Price Stern Sloan.

Becker, J., Reid, K., Steinhaus, P., & Wieck, P. (1994). *Theme storming.* Beltsville, MD: Gryphon House.

Brashears, D. (1985). *Dribble drabble: Art experiences for young children.* Fort Collins, CO: DMC Publications.

Brown, M. (1980). *Finger rhymes.* New York: Puffin Books.

Brown, S.E. (1981). *Bubbles, rainbows, and worms: Science experiments for pre-school children.* Beltsville, MD: Gryphon House.

Brown, S.E. (1982). *One, two, buckle my shoe: Math activities for young children.* Beltsville, MD: Gryphon House.

Carlson, L. (1990). *Kids create! Art & craft experiences for 3-to-9-year-olds.* Charlotte, VT: Williamson Publishing Co.

Catron, C.E., & Allen, J. (1993). *Early childhood curriculum.* New York: Macmillan.

Charner, K. (Ed.). (1993). *The giant encyclopedia of theme activities for children 2 to 5: Over 600 favorite activities created by teachers for teachers.* Beltsville, MD: Gryphon House.

Cherry, C. (1971). *Creative movement for the developing child: A nursery school handbook for non-musicians.* Belmont, CA: Fearon Pitman Publishers.

Cleveland, A., Caton, B., & Adler, L. (1994). *Activities unlimited: Creative and exciting sensory motor activities.* Elgin, IL: Building Blocks.

Cole, J., & Calmenson, S. (1991). *The eentsy, weentsy spider: Fingerplays and action rhymes.* New York: Mulberry Books.

DeFranco, E.B. (1975). *Learning activities for preschool children: A home teaching handbook for parents and teachers.* Salt Lake City, UT: Olympus Publishing Company.

Durkin, L.L. (Ed.). (1997, January/February). *First Teacher, 18*(1).

Feldscher, S. (1979). *Help! The kid is bored.* New York: A & W Publishers, Inc.

Findlay, J., Miller, P., Pegram, A., Richey, L., Sanford, A., & Semrau, B. (1976). *A planning guide to the preschool curriculum: The child, the process, the day.* Winston-Salem, NC: Kaplan Press.

Flemming, B.M., & Hamilton, D.S. (1979). *Resources for creative teaching in early childhood education.* San Diego: Harcourt Brace & Co.

Foster, J., & Thompson, C. (1996). *Finger rhymes.* Oxford, England: Oxford University Press.

Goin, K., Ripp, E., & Soloman, K.N. (1989). *Bugs to bunnies: Hands-on animal science activities for young children.* New York: Chatterbox Press.

Hanson, M.J., & Harris, S.R. (1986). *Teaching young children with motor delays: A guide for parents and professionals.* Austin, TX: PRO-ED.

Herb, S., & Willoughby-Herb, S. (1994). *Using children's books in preschool settings.* New York: Neal-Schuman Publishers.

Isbell, R. (1995). *The complete learning center book.* Beltsville, MD: Gryphon House.

King-DeBaun, P. (1990). *Storytime: Stories, symbols, and emergent literacy activities for young, special needs children.* Solana Beach: Mayer-Johnson Company.

King-DeBaun, P. (1993). *Storytime: Just for fun! Stories, symbols, and emergent literacy activities for young children.* Park City, UT: Creative Communicating.

Kohl, M. (1994). *Preschool art: It's the process, not the product.* Beltsville, MD: Gryphon House.

Kohl, M.F. (1989). *Mudworks: Creative clay, dough, and modeling experiences.* Bellingham, WA: Bright Ring Publishing.

Kohl, M.F. (1994). *Scribble art: Independent creative art experiences for children.* Bellingham, WA: Bright Ring Publishing.

Larson, N., Henthorne, M., & Plum, B. (1994). *Transition magician.* St. Paul, MN: Redleaf Press.

McCord, S. (1995). *The storybook journey: Pathways to literacy through story and play.* Upper Saddle River, NJ: Prentice-Hall.

McElderry, J.S., & Escobedo, L.E. (1979). *Tools for learning: Activities for young children with special needs.* Denver, CO: Love Publishing Co.

Michel, M. (Ed.). (1996). *The mailbox: The idea magazine for teachers.* Greensboro, NC: The Education Center, Inc.

Milord, S. (1989). *The kids' nature book: 365 indoor/outdoor activities and experiences.* Charlotte, VT: Williamson Publishing.

National Gallery of Art. (1991). *An illustrated treasury of songs for children.* New York: Rizzoli International Publications, Inc.

Opitz, M.F. (1995). *Getting the most from predictable books: Strategies and activities for teaching with more than 75 favorite children's books.* New York: Scholastic Professional Books.

Petrash, C. (1992). *Earthways: Simple environmental activities for young children.* Beltsville, MD: Gryphon House.

Raines, S.C., & Canady, R.J. (1989). *Story stretchers: Activities to expand children's favorite books.* Beltsville, MD: Gryphon House.

Raines, S.C., & Canady, R.J. (1991). *More story stretchers: More activities to expand children's favorite books.* Beltsville, MD: Gryphon House.

Rasmussen, R.M., & Rasmussen, R.L. (1981). *The kid's encyclopedia of things to make and do.* St. Paul, MN: Redleaf Press.

Rockwell, R.E., Sherwood, E.A., & Williams, R.A. (1983). *Hug a tree and other things to do outdoors with young children.* Beltsville, MD: Gryphon House.

Scharlatt, E.L. (Ed.). (1979). *Kids, day in and day out: A parent's manual.* New York: Lonesome Sparrow Press, Inc.

Schillar, P., & Rossano, J. (1990). *The instant curriculum: 500 developmentally appropriate learning activities for busy teachers of young children.* Beltsville, MD: Gryphon House.

Schlosser, K.G., & Phillips, V.L. (1992). *Building literacy with interactive charts: A practical guide for creating 75 engaging charts from songs, poems, and fingerplays.* New York: Scholastic.

Schwede, O. (1977). *An early childhood activity program for handicapped children.* Glen Ridge, NJ: Exceptional Press.

Sherwood, E.A., Williams, R.A., & Rockwell, R.E. (1990). *More mudpies to magnets: Science for young children.* Beltsville, MD: Gryphon House.

Spewock, T. (1995). *A year of fun just for five's: Fun seasonal activities, songs, poems, and fingerplays—plus practical advice for parents.* Everett, WA: Warren Publishing House.

Taylor, B.J. (1991). *A child goes forth: A curriculum guide for preschool children.* New York: Macmillan.

The Mailbox. (1995, October/November). *The Mailbox: the idea magazine for teachers of preschool, Vol. 1.*

Tunick, B.P., & Cohen, R. (1993). *Snail trails and tadpole tails: Nature education for young children.* St. Paul, MN: Redleaf Press.

Wanamaker, N., Hearn, K., & Richarz, S. (1979). *More than graham crackers: Nutrition education & food preparation with young children.* Washington: National Association for the Education of Young Children.

Williams, R.A., Rockwell, R.E., & Sherwood, E.A. (1987). *Mudpies to magnets: A preschool science curriculum.* Beltsville, MD: Gryphon House.

Wilmes, L., & Wilmes, D. (1986). *Exploring art.* Elgin, IL: Building Blocks.

INDEX

Page numbers followed by *f* indicate figures; those followed by *t* indicate tables.

Abiyoyo (Seeger, P.), 58, 120, 138, 174
    for children with hearing impairments, 78, 85
    for children with visual impairments, 103, 107, 110, 111
    and diversity, 162
    in sensorimotor development, 67, 68, 69
Administrators, 13
Adult involvement, as component of curriculum, 22
Advisory boards, for community contact, 169
Alexander Graham Bell Association for the Deaf, 94
American Foundation for the Blind, 113
American Printing House for the Blind, 113
American Sign Language (ASL), 81–83
American Speech-Language-Hearing Association (ASHA), 95
Amplification systems, for children with hearing impairments, 76–77
Areas and centers, 8
    arrangement of, 34, 34*f*
      planning for, 40–42
    in curriculum, 6
    design of, 8–9
    print incorporated into, 121
    types of, 29–33
Art
    in cognitive development, 57–58, 58–59
    expression through, 24
    tactile adaptations in, for children with visual impairments, 107–108
Art Area, 32, 41
Articulation, in expressive communication skills development, 59, 61
ASHA, *see* American Speech-Language-Hearing Association
ASL, *see* American Sign Language
Assistive listening devices, for children with hearing impairments, 77
Audio books, *see* Recorded books and magazines
Audio recording, in Literacy Center, 31, 39
Audiological care, for children with visual impairments, 100
Auditory adaptations, for children with visual impairments, 105–106
Auditory input, enhancement of, 77

Balance, in sensorimotor development, 68–69
Bibliotherapy, 53
The Blind Children's Center, 114

The Blind Children's Fund, 114
Blindness, legal, 99
Book bags, 167–168
Book shares, 180–181, 181*f*
Books
    braille, 115, 116
    braille/print, 116
    concept, 154
    counting, 154–155
    in curriculum, sample of, 7–8
    fairy tales and folktales, 155–156
    fingerplays, 134, 155
    language-predictable, 145, 157
    nursery rhymes, songs, and poems, 131–132, 134, 154–155
    picture
      challenging, 158
      wordless, 154
    predictable patterned, 131–132, 136, 156
      innovations in, 144, 157
    recommended, 154–159
    recorded, 115
    selection of, handout for parents, 198–199
    for Stage 1 of literacy development, 127–130, 154–155
    for Stage 2 of literacy development, 131–132, 155–156
    for Stage 3 of literacy development, 156–157
    for Stage 4 of literacy development, 157
    for Stage 5 of literacy development, 157–158
    for Stage 6 of literacy development, 158
    storybooks
      beginning, 156
      easy, 158
      as holistic strategy, 23
      at home, 176–177, 177–178, 179*f*
      in literacy development, 131–132
    stretching, 158
    tactile, 106–107
Bourgeois, P., *see Franklin Has a Sleepover*
Braille, 106
    books in
      by the National Braille Press, 115
      by the National Library Service for the Blind and Physically Handicapped, 115
      by SEEDLINGS, 116
    encouragement of, 98
    writing, 108
Bunting, E., *see Night Tree*

Cards on the Table, interactive game for parents, 178, 180*f*
Caregivers, *see* Family involvement
Centers and areas, 6, 8
  arrangement of, 34, 34*f*
    planning for, 40–42
  design of, 8–9
  print incorporated into, 121
  types of, 29–33
Children
  communication among, 45
  communication between parents and, 46
  interactions with, 44–45, 120–121
    handouts to parents about, 188–189, 193–197,
      200–203
  in language comprehension, 63
Children with hearing impairments
  communication with, 82–83
  environmental adaptation for, 79–80
  experiential skill-building, 79–80
  listening instruction for, 78–79
  literature and resources for, 90–95
  specialists for, 81–82
Children with visual impairments
  ABC rule for, 100
  environmental adaptations for, 103–106
  experiential skill-building in, 97–98, 101–102
  levels of learning and, 109–111
  parental involvement with, 109
  resources for, 113–116
  routines and, importance of, 103
  specialists for, 108–109
  videotapes about, 116
Children with physical challenges
  environmental adaptations for, 70–72
  and Reading the Story, 53
Chronological age
  curriculum and, 5
  and developmental age, 124
Clark, B., *see Franklin Has a Sleepover*
Class projects, family involvement in, 167–168, 168–169
Classification skills
  in cognitive development, 58
  at different levels of learning, 56
  learned through experiments, 24
Classroom design and layout, 29–34
  for children with hearing impairments, 79–80
Closed circuit television, for children with visual impair-
    ments, 104
Cochlear implants, 77
Cognitive development, 49, 56–59
  functional learning level in, 56, 57–58
  sensorimotor learning level in, 56, 57
  symbolic learning level in, 56, 58–59
Cognitive skills, *see* Cognitive development
Communication
  among children, 45
  between children and parents, 46
  in children with hearing impairments, 82–83
  with families, 45–46, 162–170, 182
Communication and language development, 49–50
  expressive communication skills in, 59–63

receptive communication skills in, 59, 63–64, 127,
  130
Communicative challenges, children with, environmental
  adaptations for, 70–72
Comparison skills, learned through experiments, 24
Computers, 32
  for children who are physically challenged, 71
  for communication with families, 165
  games for, for differentiated fine motor movements, 70
Concept books, 154
Cortical visual impairment (CVI), 99, 100
  visual adaptations for, 104
Council of Families with Visual Impairment, 114
Counting books, 154–155
Cultural differences
  and child rearing, 45
  incorporation into curriculum, informing family about,
    162
  and play, 18
Curriculum for *Read, Play, and Learn!*, 5–6
  benefits of, 10–11
  books in, sample of, 7–8
  components of, 7–9
  field-tests of, 14
  goals of, 6–7
    handout for, 186
  informing families about, 162–163, 174
    handout for, 184–185
  interactions in, 43–46
  transdisciplinary play-based foundations of, 14
  where and when to use, 9–10
CVI, *see* Cortical visual impairment

Dance, assertion of ideas through, 25
DB-Link, 114
Deaf culture, 82–83
Deaf parents, and reading strategies, 84–85
dePaola, T., *see The Knight and the Dragon*
Developmental age, and chronological age, 5, 124
Developmental domains, 49–50, 56–72
  cognitive development, 49, 56–59
  communication and language development, 49–50,
    59–64
  sensorimotor development, 49–50, 66–72
  social-emotional development, 49–50, 65–66
Dictated language experience (DLE), in literacy develop-
    ment, 135–136, 141
Directionality, in literacy development, 135
Discovery learning, 31
Discussion groups, parent-led, 168
DLE, *see* Dictated language experience
Dramatic Play: Theme Area
  adapted to levels of learning, 53–56
  area for, 30–31
  planning for, 40
  special needs children and, involvement in, 55–56
Dramatization
  by children, 24
  and expressive communication skill development,
    60–61

Drawing
in expressive communication skills development, 59,
62–63
see also Art

Early Childhood and Literacy Development Committee of
the International Reading Association, 23
Early childhood educators, curriculum and, 13
Early education, holistic model for, 26
Early literacy development
components of, 22–23
differences in, in classroom, 124–125
family and, 21–22
Early phonemic stage, of spelling development, 139–140
Emergent literacy, 119–120, 151
family's awareness of, 170, 174
Emotional development, 65–66
Environment, literacy-rich, 22, 120–122, 175–176
handouts for families, 190–192
Environmental adaptations
for children with hearing impairments, 79–80
for children with physical challenges, 70–72
for children with visual impairments, 103–106
Environmental print, 134–135
Equilibration, 18
Esotropia, 99
Experiential skill-building
for children with hearing impairments, 79–80
for children with visual impairments, 101–102
Experimentation
in cognitive development, 58
through dramatic play, levels of learning and, 54
through play, 24
through science projects, 24
Exploration, in cognitive development, 57
Exploratory learning level, 9, 49, *see also* Sensorimotor
learning level
Exposure, literacy, importance of, 22
Expression, 11, 17
in cognitive development, 58
through art, visual, and tactile projects, 24
Expressive communication skills, 49–50, 59–63
articulation in, 61
in first stage of literacy, 127, 130
functional level of learning in, 60
phonology in, 61
sensorimotor level of learning in, 59–60
symbolic level of learning in, 60–61

Family involvement, 8, 12, 21–22, 45–46, 161–183
with children with visual impairments, 109
and communication with children, 46
development of, 162–170, 181–182
handouts to encourage, 187–203
interactive games for, 178, 180f
through interactive storybook reading, 176–177,
177–178, 179f
workshops for, 170–182
Family Resource Room, 169

Field tests, of curriculum, 14
Field trips, family involvement in, 168
Fingerplays, 134, 155
Fingerspelling, 91, 92, 93
First Flight (McPhail, D.), 30, 32, 36, 63, 122
for children with hearing impairments, 80, 81, 85
in sensorimotor development, 68
in supportive literacy environment, 120, 121
Flexibility, in curriculum, 14, 42
Floor Play area, 33, 41–42
FM system, for children with hearing impairments, 77
Format, of modules, 8–9
Franklin Has a Sleepover (Bourgeois, P., and Clark, B.), 8, 123
Friends (Heine, H.), 25, 36, 53, 65, 194
and oral-language development, 118
for children with visual impairments, 107, 111
Functional learning level, 9, 49
children with hearing impairments at, 86
children with visual impairments at, 109–110
in cognitive development, 56, 57–58
in Dramatic Play: Theme Area, 54–55
in drawing and writing, 62
in expressive communication skills, 60
in Reading the Story, 52
and second stage of literacy development, 131

Gallaudet University
National Information Center on Deafness, 95
Sign Language Materials Catalog, 95
Glaucoma, 99
Graphophonics, in literacy development
Stage 3, 135, 142
Stage 4, 143

Hadley School for the Blind, 114
Hallinan, P.K., *see A Rainbow of Friends*
Handouts for families, 163–164, 182
Help Your Child Appreciate the Value of Reading,
193–194
Help Your Child Learn to Write, 201–203
Helping Your Child Makes a Difference, 188–189
Helping Your Child with a Special Curriculum, 184–185
How to Make the Home a Place Where Pictures and Print
Are Seen Everywhere, 190–191
How to Model the Uses of Print with Your Child, 192
Selecting Books for Your Child, 198–199
Talking with Your Child, 200
Ten Goals for Your Child, 186
Tips for Reading Books with Your Child, 195–197
Why it Is Important to Read to Your Child, 187
Hearing aids, 79
for children with hearing impairments, 76–77
stories for children involving, 90–93
Hearing loss
in children with visual impairments, 100
indications of, 76
and residual hearing, capitalizing on, 76–77
temporary, 78
types of, 75–76

Heine, H., *see Friends*
Hemanopsia, 99
Holistic model for early education, 26
Home environment, 21–22, 123, 175–176
  handout for families about, 190–191
Home visits, 163
House area, in Dramatic Play: Theme Area, 30–31
Hutchings, A., *see Picking Apples & Pumpkins*
Hutchings, R., *see Picking Apples & Pumpkins*
Hypertonicity, 67
Hypotonicity, 67

Ideas, assertion of, 25
IEPs, *see* Individualized education programs
IFSPs, *see* Individualized family service plans
Individualized education programs (IEPs), 14
  meetings, 166
Individualized family service plans (IFSPs), 14
  meetings, 166
Inner control, in literacy development, 143–146
Interactions
  with children, 44–45, 120–121
    handouts to parents about, 188–189, 193–197,
    200–203
    in language comprehension, 63
  within families, 176
  between team members, 43–46
Interactive charts
  in literacy development, 144
  in Reading the Story, 30
Interactive reading, by families, 176–177, 177–178, 179f
  handout for, 195–197
Intervention, aided by curriculum, 13
Isolated skill development, 23

John Tracy Clinic, 95
Journals, for communication with families, 164

Kansas School for the Deaf, 94
Keats, E.J., *see The Snowy Day*
Key words, in modules, 52
The Kissing Hand (Penn, A.), 31, 34, 53, 56, 123, 131, 132,
  167, 194
  for children with hearing impairments, 81, 85, 86
  in sensorimotor development, 69
The Knight and the Dragon (dePaola, T.), 25, 63, 123, 132,
  168, 194
  for children with hearing impairments, 84, 86, 87
  in supportive literacy environment, 121

Language
  aural, in literacy development
    Stage 2, 132
    Stage 3, 136–137
  expressive communication skills in, 49–50, 59–63, 127, 130
  hearing loss and, 78

oral
  development of, 19–20, 125–126
  and literacy, 117–118
  in literacy development
    Stage 1, 130
    Stage 2, 132
    Stage 3, 136–138
    Stage 4, 145
    Stage 5, 147–148
    Stage 6, 149–150
  receptive communication skills in, 49–50, 59, 63–64, 127,
    130
  universal, 90
  written, *see* Writing
Language comprehension, 63–64, *see also* Receptive communication skills
Language play, 126, 131
Language-predictable books, 145, 157
Lea Symbol Test, 98
Learning
  play as natural form of, 10–11
  see also Levels of learning
Lester, H., *see A Porcupine Named Fluffy*
Levels of learning, 9, 49, 50–56
  and children with visual impairments, 109–111
  in curriculum for children with hearing impairments,
    85–87
  Dramatic Play: Theme Area adapted to, 53–56
  functional, *see* Functional learning level
  mix of, 55–56
  Reading the Story adapted to, 51–53
  sensorimotor, *see* Sensorimotor learning level
  symbolic, *see* Symbolic learning level
Lightbox, 32, 104
Lighthouse Visual Acuity Pictures, 98
Linder, T.W., *see Transdisciplinary Play-Based Assessment: A
  Functional Approach to Working with Young Children,
  Revised Edition; Transdisciplinary Play-Based Intervention: Guidelines for Developing a Meaningful Curriculum
  for Young Children*
Listening devices, assistive, 77
Listening games, 78–79
Listening skills, in children with visual impairments,
  101–106
Literacy, 19–22
  concepts of print in, 123–124
  curriculum, elements of, 20
  emergent, 19–21, 119–120
    parent awareness of, 170, 174
  experiences, 123
  exposure to, importance of, 22
  home environment and, 21–22, 123, 175–176
    handout for, 190–191
  materials for, importance of variety in, 122
  mixed levels in classroom, 124–125
  oral language and, 117–118
  in preschool and kindergarten, 19, 21–22
  stages of, 125–151
    materials for, 154–159
  strategies for children with hearing impairments, 83–85

Literacy—*continued*
        supportive environment for, 120–122
Literacy Center, 31–32, 40
Literacy development
  for children with visual impairments
    experiential skill-building and, 101–102
    videotapes about, 116
  family involvement in, importance of, 21–22
    handout for, 188–189
  level of, determination of, 124–125, 151
  play in, 17
  stages of, 125–127, 127*t*
    materials for, 154–159
    Stage 1, 127–131, 154–155
    Stage 2, 131–134, 155–156
    Stage 3, 134–143, 156–157
    Stage 4, 143–146, 157
    Stage 5, 147–149, 157–158
    Stage 6, 149–150, 158
  value of, 10
Literacy mode, 102–103
Literacy-rich environment, 22, 120–122
  at home, 175–176
    handout for, 190–191
The Little Old Lady Who Was Not Afraid of Anything (Williams,
    L.), 30, 132, 168, 196
  for children with hearing impairments, 78, 81
  for children with visual impairments, 105
  at fourth stage of literacy development, 144
  in sensorimotor development, 67
Lowell, S., *see The Three Little Javelinas*
Low vision, 99

Magazines, recorded, 115
Magnification devices, for children with visual impair-
    ments, 104
Manipulation, in cognitive development, 57
Manually coded English, 83
Materials, list of, in module, 8
Math, *see Science and Math Center*
McPhail, D., *see First Flight*
Measurement, learned through experiments, 24
Mediation, in literacy development
  Stage 1, 131
  Stage 2, 133–134
  Stage 3, 141–143
  Stage 4, 146
  Stage 5, 148–149
  Stage 6, 149–150
Middle-ear infections, 78
Modules, 5, 7–9
  books in
    Collection 1, 7
    Collection 2, 7–8
  field-testing of, 14
  format of, 8–9
  implementation of, 38–43
  sample letters in, 12
Motor Area, 32, 41

Motor movements
  fine
    in cognitive development, 57
    in sensorimotor development, 70
  gross, in sensorimotor development, 69–70
Motor planning, in sensorimotor development, 68–69
Movement, assertion of ideas through, 25
Muscle tone, in sensorimotor development, 67–68
  for fine motor movements, 70
Myopia, 99

National Association for Visually Handicapped, 115
National Association of Parents of the Visually Impaired, 115
National Braille Press, 115
National Federation of the Blind, 115
National Information Center on Deafness, 95
National Library Service for the Blind and Physically Handi-
    capped, 115
National Technical Institute for the Deaf, 95
Natural literacy model, 22
Newsletter, for families, 164–165
Night Tree (Bunting, E.), 34, 58, 122, 131
  in literacy development, Stage 4, 145
  in sensorimotor development, 69, 70
Numeration, learned through experiments, 24
Nursery rhymes, in literacy development, 131–132, 134,
    154–155

O&M specialist, *see* Orientation and mobility specialist, for
    children with visual impairments
One-to-one correspondence
  in cognitive development, 57–58
  at different levels of learning, 56
  learned through experiments, 24
Optic nerve hypoplasia, 99
Oral communication, *see* Expressive communication skills;
    Language, oral
Orientation and mobility (O&M) specialist, for children
    with visual impairments, 108
Otitis media, 78
  monitoring, 100
Outdoor Play, 33, 37, 42

Parent conferences, 163, 165–166
Parent consultants, 169–170
Parents, *see* Family involvement
Partial sight, 99
Patterned books, *see* Predictable patterned books
Penn, A., *see The Kissing Hand*
Pfister, M., *see The Rainbow Fish*
Phonemic awareness, 20, 21
  through interactions, 120
  in language development, 61
  in literacy development, 126, 136–137
  play in, 22
Phonemic stage
  early, of spelling development, 139–140

Phonics approach, 20–21
Phonological awareness
    in expressive communication skill development, 61
    in reading and writing development, 126
    in third stage of literacy development, 136–137
Piagetian concept of equilibration, 18
Picking Apples & Pumpkins (Hutchings, A. and R.), 24, 52, 63,
        69, 81, 107, 121, 122, 132, 144, 168, 196
Picture acuity charts, 98
Picture books, 154, 158
Pincer grasp, in sensorimotor development, 70
Planning, 38–43
Planning sheets
    in module, 8
    in selection of activities, 39
Play, 18–19
    cultural variations and, 18
    experimentation through, 24
    and literacy curriculum
        components of, 22–23
        strategies in, 23–25
    as mode of learning, 10–11
    observation of, 14
A Porcupine Named Fluffy (Lester, H.), 24, 36, 58, 61, 65,
        135, 136, 166, 196
    for children with hearing impairments, 79, 81
    for children with visual impairments, 106
    in sensorimotor development, 67, 68, 69, 70
    in supportive literacy environment, 121
Positive feedback, for benefit of families, 164
Predictable patterned books, 131–132, 136, 156
    innovations in, 144, 157
Prephonemic stage, of spelling development, 139
Print
    in areas and centers, 121
    concepts about, 123–124
    environmental, 134–135
    around the home, handouts about, 190–191, 192
    in literacy development
        Stage 2, 132–133
        Stage 3, 134–135
    variety of, 122
Print-braille books, by SEEDLINGS, 116
Problem solving
    at different levels of learning, 56
    and expressive communication skill development,
        61
Projects, family involvement in, 167–168, 168–169
Props
    in areas and centers, 34–36
    in Dramatic Play: Theme Area, 30–31
    literacy, 34–36
        in curriculum, 22
    story, 34–36

The Rainbow Fish (Pfister, M.), 8, 25, 52, 122
    for children with hearing impairments, 85, 87
    for children with visual impairments, 101, 107
    in sensorimotor development, 68, 69, 70
A Rainbow of Friends (P.K. Hallinan), 162, 166

Reading
    books and resource materials for, 154–159
    by children with hearing impairments, 83–85
    by children with visual impairments, 106–108
    children's observation of, 121–122
    developmental continuum of, 125
    home environment and, handouts for parents about,
        184–203
    independent, in literacy development, 147–150
    initiation of searching behaviors in, 142–143
    interactive strategies for
        handout for parents, 195–197
        by parents, 176–177, 177–178, 179f
    in language comprehension, 64
    play in, 22–25
    storybooks, *see* Storybook reading
    versus television, 180
    see also Literacy; Literacy development
Reading specialists, 13
Reading the Story
    adapted to levels of learning, 51–53
    area for, 30
    daily involvement of children in, 23–24
    planning for, 40
Receptive communication skills, 49–50, 59, 63–64
    in first stage of literacy, 127, 130
    reading in, 64
Recorded books and magazines, by National Library Service
        for the Blind and Physically Handicapped, 115
Reenactments, 53–54, *see also* Dramatic Play: Theme Area
Related-services personnel, 13
Residual hearing, 76–77
Resources
    for children with hearing impairments, 90–95
    for children with visual impairments, 113–116
    for stages in literacy development, 154–159
Retinopathy of prematurity (ROP), 99
Role-playing, in literacy development, 134–136
ROP, *see* Retinopathy of prematurity

Sample letters
    in modules, 12
    to parents, 46
    in program preparation, 43
Schedule, 36–38
    setting, 43
Science and Math Center, 32, 40–41
Science projects, experimentation through, 24
Scotoma, 99
Script
    as beginning point, 53–54
    preparation of, 39
    for reenactments, 30–31
Searching behaviors, initiation of, 142–143
SEE-2, *see* Signing Exact English
SEEDLINGS, 115–116
Seeger, P., *see* Abiyoyo
Self-expression, 11, 17
Sensorimotor developmental domain, 49–50, 66–72
    for children with physical challenges, 70–72

fine motor movements in, 70
gross motor movements in, 69–70
muscle tone in, 67–68
stability, weight bearing, balance, and motor planning,
    68–69
Sensorimotor learning level, 9, 49
    children with hearing impairments at, 85–86
    children with visual impairments at, 109
    in cognitive development, 56, 57
    in Dramatic Play: Theme Area, 54
    and drawing and writing, 62
    in expressive communication skills, 59–60
    in Reading the Story, 51–52
    versus sensorimotor developmental domain, 49
Sensory Area, 32, 41
Sequential thinking
    at different levels of learning, 56
    learned through experiments, 24
Shared reading, in literacy development, 136
Sign language, 91, 93
    American Sign Language (ASL), 81–83
    Signing Exact English (SEE-2), 83
Signing Exact English (SEE-2), 83
Snack
    area for, 33
    planning for, 42
    preparation of, 37
Snellen chart, 98
The Snowy Day (Keats, E.J.), 24, 32, 56, 60, 138, 167, 195
    for children with hearing impairments, 79
    in sensorimotor development, 69
Social-emotional development, 49–50, 65–66
Software, 32
Somebody and the Three Blairs (Tolhurst, M.), 30, 34, 55, 63,
    122, 123, 134
    for children with hearing impairments, 80
    for children with visual impairments, 102
    at fourth stage of literacy development, 144
    in sensorimotor development, 68
Song, assertion of ideas through, 25
Sound production, in language development, 61
Sound–symbol relationships, in literacy development
    Stage 3, 135
    Stage 4, 143
Speechreading, 79, 92
Spelling development, stages of, 139–141
Stevens, J., *see The Three Billy Goats Gruff*
Storage space, 36
Storyboards, for reading the story, 30
Storybook reading
    as holistic strategy, 23
    at home, 176–177, 177–178, 179*f*
    in literacy development, stage 2, 131–132
Strabismus, 99
Supported writing, in literacy development, 141
Surveys, of families, 170, 171*f*–173*f*
Symbolic learning level, 9, 49
    children with hearing impairments at, 86
    children with visual impairments at, 110–111
    in cognitive development, 56, 58–59
    in Dramatic Play: Theme Area, 55

    and drawing and writing, 62–63
    in expressive communication skills, 60–61
    in literacy development
        Stage 3, 135
        Stage 5, 148
    in Reading the Story, 52–53

Table Play, 33
    planning for, 42
Tactile adaptations, for children with visual impairments,
    106–108
Tactile books, for children with visual impairments,
    106–107
Tactile projects, expression through, 24
Teacher assistants, 13
Teachers, 11–12, 13
Team members
    and communication with families, 45–46
    composition of, 15, 43–44
    and interactions with children, 44–45
Television
    closed circuit, for children with visual impairments,
        104
    family's awareness of, 178–180
The Three Billy Goats Gruff (Stevens, J.), 30, 63, 123, 131,
    135, 141, 163, 195
    for children with hearing impairments, 80, 81, 86
    for children with visual impairments, 110
    and oral-language development, 118
    in sensorimotor development, 67
The Three Little Javelinas (Lowell, S.), 58, 167
    for children with hearing impairments, 78
    in sensorimotor development, 69
    in supportive literacy environment, 121
Theme-based approach, benefits of, 5
Therapists, 13
Therapy
    bibliotherapy, 53
    in curriculum, 13
Tolhurst, M., *see Somebody and the Three Blairs*
Toys and materials, 34–36
TPBA, *see* Transdisciplinary play-based assessment
TPBC, *see* Transdisciplinary play-based curriculum
TPBI, *see* Transdisciplinary play-based intervention
Transdisciplinary Play-Based Assessment: A Functional Approach
    to Working with Young Children, Revised Edition (Linder,
    T.), 14, 50, 61
Transdisciplinary play-based assessment (TPBA), 14
Transdisciplinary play-based curriculum (TPBC), 6–7,
    14
Transdisciplinary play-based intervention (TPBI), 14
Transdisciplinary Play-Based Intervention: Guidelines for Develop-
    ing a Meaningful Curriculum for Young Children (Linder,
    T.), 14, 50, 61, 67, 182
Transdisciplinary team, 15
Tripod grasp, in sensorimotor development, 70
Tunnel vision, 99

Universal language, 90

Variety, of print materials, importance of, 122
Videotapes
    for parents
        of classes, 168
        to teach interactive reading skills, 176, 177–179,
            179f
    for parents of children with hearing impairments, 95
    on visual impairment and literacy, 116
Visual adaptations, for children with visual impairments,
    104–105
Visual field, 98–99
Visual impairments
    causes and types of, 99–100
    videotapes about, 116
    visual performance and, 98–99
Visual projects, expression through, 24
Visual Storyreading Program, 94
Visually Impaired Preschool Services, 116
Vocabulary
    lists, 8
    in literacy development
        Stage 1, 130
        Stage 5, 147

Whole language approach, 20–21
Williams, L., *see The Little Old Lady Who Was Not Afraid of
    Anything*
WOLF vocal output communication device, 71

Woodcock-Johnson Psychoeducational Battery-Revised, 22
Woodworking Center, 33
Wordness, in literacy development
    Stage 3, 135, 139
    Stage 4, 143
Workshops, for families, 168, 170–182
    agenda for, 174, 175f
    surveys in, 170, 171f–173f, 174, 175f
World Wide Web, to purchase storybooks, 7
Writing, 19–20, 21, 59
    braille, 108
    children with visual impairments, 108
    children's observation of, 121–122
    at different levels of learning, 56, 62–63
    incorporation into areas and centers, 63
    in literacy development
        Stage 1, 130
        Stage 2, 132–133
        Stage 3, 138–139, 141
        Stage 4, 145–146
        Stage 5, 148
        Stage 6, 149–150
    parental involvement in, handout for, 201–203
    play in, 22–25
    supported, 141

Zone of proximal development, 44
Zones, areas and centers in, 43

ORDER FORM

READ, PLAY, AND LEARN!® STORYBOOK ACTIVITIES FOR YOUNG CHILDREN
The Transdisciplinary Play-Based Curriculum from Toni Linder

Storybook Activities also sold individually! US$18.95 each

Please send me the following:

___ Teacher's Guide / Stock Number: 4005 / US$45.00

___ Teacher's Guide and Collections 1 & 2 / Stock Number: 4773 / US$229.00

___ Module Collection 1 / Stock Number: 4013 / US$99.00
Includes Storybook Activities for:
The Kissing Hand / Stock Number: 403X ISBN 1-55766-403-X
Somebody and the Three Blairs / Stock Number: 4048 ISBN 1-55766-404-8
Picking Apples & Pumpkins / Stock Number: 4056 ISBN 1-55766-405-6
The Little Old Lady Who Was Not Afraid of Anything
   Stock Number: 4064 ISBN 1-55766-406-4
The Knight and the Dragon / Stock Number: 4072 ISBN 1-55766-407-2
Abiyoyo / Stock Number: 4080 ISBN 1-55766-408-0
Night Tree / Stock Number: 4099 ISBN 1-55766-409-9
Snowy Day / Stock Number: 4102 ISBN 1-55766-410-2

___ Module Collection 2 / Stock Number: 4021 / US$99.00
Includes Storybook Activities for:
A Porcupine Named Fluffy / Stock Number: 4110 ISBN 1-55766-411-0
First Flight / Stock Number: 4129 ISBN 1-55766-412-9
Friends / Stock Number: 4137 ISBN 1-55766-413-7
The Three Billy Goats Gruff / Stock Number: 4145 ISBN 1-55766-414-5
The Three Little Javelinas / Stock Number: 4153 ISBN 1-55766-415-3
A Rainbow of Friends / Stock Number: 4161 ISBN 1-55766-416-1
Franklin Has a Sleepover / Stock Number: 417X ISBN 1-55766-417-X
The Rainbow Fish / Stock Number: 4188 ISBN 1-55766-418-8

Storybooks themselves are not included with the booklets.
Visit www.readplaylearn.com to learn more.

ADDITIONAL TRANSDISCIPLINARY PLAY-BASED RESOURCES

Transdisciplinary Play-Based Assessment uses a play-based process with accompanying Observation Guidelines to assess a child's abilities and learning styles. Intervention guidelines in the companion volume, *Transdisciplinary Play-Based Intervention*, help individualize instruction to match each child's developmental level and personal characteristics. Forms to use with TPBA and TPBI are sold separately. Two training videotapes, developed by Toni Linder, are also available.

___ Transdisciplinary Play-Based Assessment, Revised Edition / Stock Number: 1626 / US$44.00

___ Transdisciplinary Play-Based Intervention / Stock Number: 1308 / US$49.95

___ Transdisciplinary Play-Based Assessment and Intervention: Child Program Summary Forms / Stock Number: 1634 / US$27.00
   (pkg. of 5 tablets)

___ And You Thought They Were Just Playing / VHS videotape / 65 min. / Stock Number: 2223 / US$175.00

___ Observing Kassandra / VHS videotape / 50 min. / Stock Number: 2665 / US$169.00

___ Check enclosed (payable to Brookes Publishing Co.)
___ Purchase order attached (bill my institution) *Add 2% to product total for P.O. handling fee.
___ Please charge my credit card: ○ American Express   ○ MasterCard   ○ Visa

Credit Card #: _____ Exp. Date: _____

Signature (required with credit card use): _____

Name: _____ Daytime Phone: _____

Street Address: _____ ❑ residential ❑ commercial
Complete street address required.

City/State/ZIP: _____ Country: _____

E-mail Address: _____
❑ Yes! I want to receive email about new titles and special offers! My e-mail address will not be shared with any other party.

Shipping & Handling

For subtotal of	Add*	For CAN
$0.00 - $49.99	$5.00	$7.00
$50.00 - $69.99	10%	$7.00
$70.00 - $399.99	10%	10%
$400.00 and over	8%	8%

Calculate percentage on product subtotal.

Shipping rates are for UPS Ground Delivery within continental U.S.A. For other shipping options and rates, call 1-800-638-3775 (in the U.S.A. and CAN) and 1-410-337-9580 (worldwide).

Convenient ways to order:
CALL toll-free 1-800-638-3775 M–F, 8 A.M. to 5 P.M. ET;
FAX 410-337-8539;
MAIL order form to: Brookes Publishing Co.,
P.O. Box 10624, Baltimore, MD 21285-0624;
ON-LINE www.brookespublishing.com

Money-back guarantee! Ordering with Brookes is risk-free! If you are not completely satisfied, you may return books within 30 days for a full credit of the purchase price (unless otherwise indicated). Refunds will be issued for prepaid orders. Items must be returned in resalable condition. Policies and prices subject to change without notice. All prices in U.S. dollars. Prices may be higher outside the U.S.A.

Subtotal $ _____
5% sales tax, Maryland only $ _____
7% business tax (GST), CAN only $ _____
2% P.O. of subtotal $ _____
Shipping (see chart) $ _____
Total (in U.S. dollars) $ _____

Your list code is BA18